PRAISE FOR
I WASN'T READY TO SAY

"As one who deals with unexpected death, I am so pleased to find a truly valuable reference for those souls who are blindsided by such misery. I would characterize this work as thoughtful, thorough, and intensely meaningful. The personal passages, which share feelings and experiences . . . are superb. They turn a scholarly treatise into one that will touch those in suffering greatly and help them understand the wide range of emotions that they will experience. Up until now, Rabbi Kushner's reference, *When Bad Things Happen to Good People,* has been my mainstay in such circumstances; I will add this book to my recommended list to loved ones and friends."

E. Charles Douville, MD,
Cardiothoracic Surgeon,
Providence Portland Hospital

"Noel and Blair's *I Wasn't Ready to Say Goodbye* ranks right up there with *When Bad Things Happen to Good People* to help people deal with the sudden loss of a loved one. Particularly helpful is the degree of permissiveness to grieve in one's own unique way without regarding it as pathological in a supportive and nonjudgmental way. It is informative and practical, yet personal and warm. It is both practical and instructive, taking a developmental approach to grieve with the understanding that one doesn't simply "get over it," but deals at various stages down the road. I particularly like the sections devoted to children and to special occasions and challenges as these are frequently overlooked in these kinds of books. I highly recommend it."

Edward S. Beck, EdD,
Harrisburg, PA,
Mental Help.net

"I Wasn't Ready to Say Goodbye is a book that is easily related to by anyone struggling to cope with the sudden death of a loved one. I highly recommend this book, not only to the bereaved, but to friends and counselors as well. If you want to

experience what the pain of grief is like, to better understand what the bereaved are going through, read this book."

Helen Fitzgerald, author of The Grieving Child, The Mourning Handbook, The Grieving Teen

"This book does an excellent job of addressing a topic that most people choose not to address until they are directly confronted. Grief has a tendency to creep up in the odd hours of the day and the night and can be overwhelming to those experiencing loss. To have a title, a book that you can reach out and grab at any hour offers comfort. I wish this title had been available sooner as it often was a book that comforted and calmed me most during my own deep dark hours of despair. Written from knowledge and from a place of understanding and guidance is sure to make this book a winner and a timeless treasure for anyone who has known a deep loss. This book is excellent and necessary."

Bernadette Moyers, author of Angel Stacey

"The authors have captured a means of discussing and exploring a very painful life passage in real life, down to earth language and experience. Many thanks to Pam and Brook for having strength to get through their sudden loss of a loved one, wisdom to understanding the Way, and the generosity in sharing their discoveries to further our healing."

Charlotte A. Tomaino, PhD, Neuropsychologist

"Finally, you have found a friend who can not only explain what has just occurred, but can take you by the hand and lead you to a place of healing and personal growth. Whether you are dealing with the loss of a family member, a close personal associate or a friend, this guide can help you survive and cope, but even more importantly . . . heal."

The Rebecca Review

"This book, by women who have done their homework on grief, offers a companion for others still recuperating. Further, it introduces us to so many others, both famous and ordinary, who can hold a hand and comfort a soul through grief's wilderness. Outstanding references of where to seek other help."

George C. Kandle, Pastoral Psychotherapist

"A well written book about a very difficult subject. *I Wasn't Ready to Say Goodbye* will be useful for those going through these difficult times."

Bradley Evans, MD,
Cardiologist, Providence Portland Hospital

"As an emergency department nurse with fifteen-plus years experience in that area, I have had first hand experience with sudden death. I have always felt that not enough has been written to address the problems and difficulties that face those that have experienced sudden death/loss, and how it differs from a loss that can be anticipated. This book carefully pointed out the many ways we may grieve, but also gently addressed that point at which the grieving process was no longer healthy and that professional counseling was needed. The overall feeling from this book was of gentleness, guidance, and a sense of spirituality. The reader is given choices, resources, and suggestions to enable them to plan and implement their own grief process. I am planning an in-service education program for the emergency dept. staff (MDs and RNs) on sudden death and grief reduction and will share your book. The list of resources is very comprehensive and it is evident that much time and energy was spent to provide the reader with a very complete guide."

Kathleen Reilly; RN MS CEN

"*I Wasn't Ready to Say Goodbye* is the best non-religious book I have read on grieving from an unexpected death. The authors have direct experience with the subject and share their own deep traumas . . . they also sought out stories different from their own so that you would have specific examples that come closer to your own situation. I found the book to be "right on" in describing the issues that my family and I have dealt with."

Donald Mitchell, Amazon Top 10 Reviewer

"I Wasn't Ready to Say Goodbye," by Noel & Blair is just beautiful! It is easy to read, yet covers everything a grieving person could possibly be thinking of or be going through. It is sensitive, yet realistic. (Sometimes those two don't go together well, but in this book they do.) The book is empowering and healing, but in baby steps."
Your Life Magazine

"The death of a loved one is always an emotionally difficult experience. When it comes suddenly and unexpectedly it is even more difficult. In *I Wasn't Ready to Say Goodbye* the authors take you through the grieving process as well as learning how to deal with such a tragic loss. For those dealing with the loss of a loved one, or for those who want to help someone who is, this is a highly recommended read."
Midwest Book Review

"What really makes this book a great resource is their hands on approach to dealing with grief. They share research on why we feel the way we do after a loss, but they go on to give us specific actions to take at a time when we NEED someone to guide us to the next step. The authors write in a friendly but knowledgeable style. They don't talk down to us, but also don't talk over our heads with lofty theories and philosophies. I felt as if they were looking me in the eye and saying "THIS is what you can do to help yourself!" During a time of grief this is exactly what we need."
Seeds of Knowledge

"I've seen many books that deal with grief, but none that do it so comprehensively and accessibly! The authors write with that rare combination of personal passion and professional detachment which allows the grieving to find a pathway to health, in their own way, in their own time. I recommend this wonderful resource for those that have lost a loved one through death or divorce, and to the professionals who endeavor to help them."

Mary Kalifon, Cedars-Sinai Los Angeles, and author of **My Dad Lost His Job**

"There aren't many 'firsts' these days. Most books being published are like so many others. This book, *I Wasn't Ready to Say Goodbye* is a first and it is valuable beyond my ability to describe it. Suffice it to say that it is truly excellent. It understands. It supports. It comforts. It sheds light. It holds your hand. It is there for you, in a time of unbearable anguish and need, like no other book ever written on the subject."

Art Klein, author of Dad and Son

Reader Reviews
"After I lost my son in a tragic accident, this book reinstilled my hope and helped me cope with my heart wrenching grief over a parent's worst nightmare—that of losing a child."

M. Pierce, GA

"I bought this book three years ago when my mom died suddenly. It was such a big help to me to get through the stages of grief. It explained everything that I was feeling and going through at the time. It was a tremendous comfort to me and had a big healing effect. I have since bought it for a few of my friends who have lost their parents, and they have in turn bought it for others."

Iris C.

"This book is currently helping my mom deal with her feelings after the death of my dad a few months back. She picks it up almost every morning before she starts her day. It helps her to understand her feelings and realize that she is 'normal' in her grief. I highly recommend it."

A. Geiger

"This book provided the support and answers I needed at my time of grief. I shared this book with the rest of my family who also found it extremely helpful and easy to read. You will find that you can pick it up and read from any chapter in any order. The explanations are very helpful and the information can be comforting. I would highly recommend this book to anyone grieving the loss of a loved one."

D. Canton, MI

"The examples and special cases of losses by others written and shared in the book help one place themselves in the midst of others' losses and compare and differentiate the circumstances. Sometimes learning about another's more difficult time within your own loss helps get things into perspective. I keep reading and rereading this wonderful book. Each time I review a certain area I find that something else jumps out in regards to "where I am" in my walk with grief that day."

J. Conforti

I Wasn't Ready to Say Goodbye is such a wonderful, wonderful book! To see my thoughts, actions, and feelings of everything that comes along during the grief of a loved one, particularly one lost by a sudden death. I was even comforted by carrying it with me for over a year. Just having it near me helped so that I could read it anytime. I recently loaned it to my best friend who just lost her younger sister to suicide and I actually feel very naked without my copy!

My favorite aunt was murdered by my uncle and then he committed suicide. Trying to deal with it was so hard because I felt there was no one in the world who understood my pain, my fears, my irrational thoughts, "griefbursts," guilt, and that overwhelming feeling of being lost. This book helped me to find my way, to know that everything I was feeling and thinking was completely normal, and just to see it all in print is such a relief. This book teaches you the grief process from just about every point of view possible (parent, child, sibling, friend, etc.), gives you tips on how to cope and memorialize the ones you've lost, advice on where to seek professional help when needed, and the writers tell their own stories of loss and everything they experienced. *I Wasn't Ready to Say Goodbye* mentions the taboos surrounding sudden deaths such as suicide or homicide and lets you know that it's okay to talk about it and that you need to talk about it."

Wyatt, St. Louis, MO

I Wasn't Ready to Say Goodbye offers much practical advice for getting through the immediate days, months, and years following the sudden death of a loved one. For many who experience the unexpected death of a loved one, the shock is so great that the survivors don't even know how to get through the time between the death and the funeral. I know that I fell into this category, and was knocking myself out to try to be "normal" when in fact nothing at all in my family was normal or the same. This book does a great job of explaining practical, small steps to recover from a great loss.

The authors offer the premise that the grief process is a bit different for survivors of a sudden death, when compared to an "expected" death, such as a death from a lingering illness. I did feel that the authors had felt my pain of having a loved one snatched away in a matter of minutes, and talked about the added confusion and anger this sort of death gives the survivors. I found the compassionate tone of the authors and the pragmatic exercises to be extremely helpful."

L. Kelly, CO

"I purchased this book when my step father died suddenly three years ago to help me understand my loss. I now have turned to it again as I'm faced with the sudden death of my seventeen-year-old son to suicide. I highly recommend this book as a starting point for anyone that has lost a loved one or friend suddenly! Thank you Brook and Pamela for your hope."

J. Daniellson, MN

"A friend gave me this book shortly after my younger brother died suddenly at the age of twenty-four. It was a lifesaver—something I could relate to and that could guide me through my grief, even down to details that authors less acquainted with the unique aspects of sudden death grief might not understand. I read it at the beginning and then reread it after several months, when I picked up more helpful advice that I hadn't been ready to notice the first time around. I strongly recommend it to anyone who has the misfortune to find him- or herself coping with the sudden death of a loved one."

Jessica, Princeton, NJ

"I had almost given up in the search for a book which even mentioned sibling grief when I noticed this book in a bookstore. The subtitle in the sibling section "overlooked in the grieving process" caught my eye and for the first time since my sister died more than a year before, I felt less alone. I also found the resource section helpful and have hooked up with a grief support group."

Kit, TX

"I purchased this book at the recommendation of my therapist, along with the companion workbook. She told me that it was like having a "mini support group" that I could access whenever I need it. She was right. Thank you Pam and Brook for caring enough to take your own difficult tragedies and find a way to help others. I have grown so much as a result of working through this book."

Janet, O., TX

"I found this book shortly after my thirty-one-year-old brother, Chad, became the victim of a homicide. What a relief to read that I was not alone in my feelings, that I wasn't going crazy! This book helped me deal with emotions that I had never dealt with before and get through some rough times. I passed it on to my Mother and it is helping her."

Julie L., FL

"This book was a gift and I almost read it from cover to cover the first reading. It covers a lot of important scenarios that I related to. It helped me understand that my bizarre behavior and thoughts were not bizarre after all. It also forewarned me about firsts and gave good suggestions on how to deal with them effectively. Overall, I recommend this book highly."

Judi H., NH

"When I first came across this book, I was hurting so very badly. Mike, my very dearest friend and the man I was in love with had been killed in an accident. I didn't have a chance to say goodbye to him. I hurt so bad that I walked in a blind maze. I really didn't want to live on. What I remember the most about this book . . . wasn't just the story of the loss that was encountered by the authors but their wisdom in helping others see ways to go on with their lives and not be full of such engulfing sadness. I will always be grateful that this book found me and helped reach such a deeply hurting area in my life."

Natalie, AZ

"The authors have done an excellent job of covering a topic that has not received the attention it deserves. As a grief counselor I frequently interact with mourners who are struggling to adjust to the sudden death of a loved one. I use this book in my sessions and many of my clients read it as part of their grief work. The book is written in plain language and comes across as conversational."

J.D. Ferrara, FL

"My seventeen-year-old son, Roman, died in the prime of life and I didn't have a chance to say goodbye. I found the book to be more than a reference, or quick handling of the matter, I identified with similar emotions, the kick in stomach when you are already emptied of air, and the loss of "clean" closure. This book offered perspectives and "normal" responses and actions for each stage of loss. It identifies and provides descriptions for your recognition and insight. I wanted to read every word, I felt we were joined, in a lot of ways, in our losses and I wanted the insight. The book is organized for easy handling and easy reading. You benefit from the experiences of the writers as they each experienced losses in their lives, and due to their losses, I find myself more apt to believe what they are writing about. If you have experienced loss, you need a book that gives you information and is readable at the same time. This book is it."

C. Slabach, WI

I WASN'T
READY
TO SAY
Goodbye

Also by Brook Noel and Pamela D. Blair, PhD

You're Not Alone: Resources and Support for Those Who Are Grieving

Living with Grief: A Guide to the First Year of Grieving

I Wasn't Ready to Say Goodbye Workbook: A Companion Workbook for Surviving, Coping, and Healing After the Sudden Loss of a Loved One

Also by Brook Noel

The Change Your Life Challenge: Step-by-Step Solutions for Finding Balance, Creating Contentment, Getting Organized, and Building the Life You Want

Grief Steps: 10 Steps to Rebuild After the Loss of a Loved One

Grief Steps Workbook: 10 Steps to Regroup, Rebuild, and Renew after Any Life Loss

The Single Parent Resource: An A-Z Manual for the Challenges of Single Parenting

❖

Surviving Holidays, Birthdays, and Special Occasions in the Grief Journey

❖

Understanding the Emotional and Physical Effects of Grief

Also by Pamela D. Blair, PhD

The Next Fifty Years: A Guide for Women at Mid-Life and Beyond

I WASN'T READY TO SAY

Goodbye

surviving, coping,
and healing after
the sudden death
of a loved one

UPDATED EDITION

BROOK NOEL and PAMELA D. BLAIR, PhD

 sourcebooks

Published by Sourcebooks, Inc.
P.O. Box 4410, Naperville, Illinois 60567-4410
(630) 961-3900
Fax: (630) 961-2168
sourcebooks.com

Originally published in 2000 by Champion Press, Ltd.

Library of Congress Cataloging-in-Publication Data
Noel, Brook.
  I wasn't ready to say goodbye : surviving, coping, and healing after the sudden death of a loved one / Brook Noel and Pamela D. Blair.—Updated ed.
    p. cm.
  1. Bereavement—Psychological aspects. 2. Death—Psychological aspects. I. Blair, Pamela D. II. Title.
BF575.G7N653 2008
155.9'37—dc22
                          2007050486

Printed and bound in the United States of America.

DR   60 59 58 57 56 55 54 53

For George, who taught me how to let go,
and for Steve who taught me how to love again.
—*Pamela D Blair*

For 'Samson', who taught me that friendship goes beyond
human dimensions, and for Caleb who taught me that
love and kinship go beyond earthly dimensions.
—*Brook Noel*

Acknowledgments

Pamela D. Blair ...

Thanks so much to Dr. Charlotte Tomaino, Kathy Murphy, and to everyone in the TBI group. To Gary Leistico, Patricia Ellen, Alyce Branum, Carl and Wilma Machover, and Delores Paddie and Keri for their inspiration. To my children, Aimee, Ian, and Rachel, for their contributions. To my husband, Steve: with all my heart I thank you for believing in me. My sister, Marilyn Houston, for her constant support and input to this book. A great big thank you and hug to my clients who inspired me, and to all those close to me who helped me through a very trying time. Brook Noel, fellow writer and spiritual journeyer, I thank you for your vision, talent, and perseverance in seeing this work from its inception to its completion.

And finally, to all those seen and unseen who have been instrumental in this book.

Brook Noel ...

The first edition of this book was a rather lonely process from concept through publication. I am grateful to have found a compassionate, caring, talented, and thoughtful team in Sourcebooks this second time around. You are all wonderful. A special thanks to Dominique, Barb, Peter, and Todd for their dedication and time to make this journey a reality. To my editor, Shana, thank you for your patience, respect, kind words, and wisdom throughout this process. You are everything I hoped an editor would be.

To Sara Pattow, thank you for being an anchor in my life. As was true in 1997 and now in 2007 your friendship will always be cherished as one of my life's richest treasures. To Mary Ann Klotz, thank you for standing by me and walking me through my darkest nights. To all of Caleb's friends—especially Rob, Steve, and Jeremy—thank you for standing by and becoming a part of our family. To Pamela D. Blair—I feel fortunate to have found you and am thankful for your guidance, help, input, support, and partnership throughout the walk of grief and the evolutions of this book.

To my family: Andy, thank you for standing by me through the good times and the bad and providing a steady hand when my world was crumbling. To Sammy ... a decade ago when I worked on the first edition you were my little angel reminding me daily of life's beauties. You have become even more of angel with the years and remain my greatest joy in life. And for my Mother, thank you for your support and love through my trials and triumphs. You are the absolute best. I love you with all my heart and soul.

Do not stand
at my grave and weep
I am not there,
I do not sleep.

I am a thousand
winds that blow.
I am the diamond
glints on snow.

I am the sunlight
On the ripened grain.
I am the gentle
Autumn's rain.

When you awaken
in the morning hush,
I am the swift uplifting rush
of quiet birds in
circled flight.
I am the soft stars
that shine at night.

Do not stand
at my grave and cry.
I am not there.
I did not die.

—*Hopi Prayer*

Contents

**48   CHAPTER FOUR: MYTHS AND MISUNDERSTANDINGS
OF THE GRIEVING PROCESS**

Part Two: The World Is Upside Down: Collecting Our Scattered Pieces

Part Three: Sharing Our Stories

Introduction

Each year about eight million Americans suffer the death of a close family member. The list of high-visibility terrorism, war, human suffering, and sudden loss is long and will continue to grow. The survivors of these losses include families and individuals we don't see in the media. Mourners are suffering behind closed doors, in our neighborhoods, in our own homes, in hospital waiting rooms. They are pacing ICU hallways, watching as life support is discontinued, sitting numb in hard chairs. They are impatiently waiting in hotel rooms for a body to be found. They are torn apart by an unexpected phone call. They are grappling with a sudden death, a sudden ending, a sudden tragedy. None of them was ready to say goodbye.

From our very first breath we enter and trust the cycles of life. As infants we trust our parents to tend to our needs. As children we trust the good in those around us. We are taught that if we are good to others, they will in turn be good to us. Soon we become adolescents who are taught cause and effect. We are taught that if we eat nutritionally and take care of our bodies they will serve us well for years. And we grow into adulthood, where we continue to trust these basic cycles. We trust that the sun will rise each morning and set each evening; that our children will outlive us; that there will be many days to cherish those we love.

Then, in a split second, with the news of a loved one's sudden death, the world changes forever. The orderly world of predictable cycles ends. We are thrown into an abyss with few tools at hand. No time for preparation. No time to gather what we will need for our journey. No time for unfinished business or goodbyes.

Physically we may be composed of cells and genes and skin and bones, but emotionally we are composed of thoughts and feelings and memories and pieces of the people we have touched, and of those who have touched us. The death of the person we love creates a gaping wound. We have somehow changed. Our cyclical structure has been eternally disrupted and we find ourselves wandering through the broken pieces of yesterday's foundation.

Grief brings that moment when you look into the mirror and no longer recognize the eyes staring back at you. Though the sun still rises and sets as it always has, everything looks just a bit different, a bit distorted. Grief casts far-reaching shadows around us.

When we wrote the first edition of *I Wasn't Ready to Say Goodbye* (published in 2000, Champion Press, Ltd.) the vocabulary for expressing grief was very limited. Generally society encouraged us to "move on," "get back to normal," or suppress our grief. A year later, the United States faced the inconceivable attack that took the lives of thousands. Political leaders addressed the nation, encouraging Americans to try and "get back to normal."

But in the wake of a sudden death, "normal" ceases to exist. Our grief needs to be expressed and our lives rebuilt. While these leaders' words were well-intended, we were a society that for the most part did not understand sudden loss or grief. Since 2001, much has changed, yet much has stayed the same. While we are more aware and better prepared to support one another, when sudden loss knocks on our personal door or the door of someone we are close to, we realize all the guidelines and preparations in the world will never be enough. We cannot understand the true scope of grief until we walk through it.

According to Kearl's guide to the *Sociology of Death: Death's Personal Impacts*, the grief associated with bereavement is one of the most profound of all human emotions—and one of the most lethal. Each year, approximately eight million Americans suffer the death of a close family member, disrupting life patterns for up to three years. According to the National Academy of Science, of the approximately 800,000 Americans widowed each year, up to 160,000 are thought to suffer pathological grief. As of July 2007, over 4,000 members of coalition forces had sacrificed their lives, bringing the reality of war and its casualties to the forefront of our daily lives. Each year suicide takes the lives of over 32,000 United States citizens, and accidents account for over 110,000 deaths. The list of how we die goes on and continues to grow. As a culture, we struggle to handle and help those around us who are grieving.

No one teaches us what to do when the foundation we believe in crumbles and we are left in the midst of ruin, while society anxiously awaits our quick and tidy rebuilding and return to "normal." Society has little time for our pain, while we can see nothing outside of it. For example, about 85 percent of wives outlive their husbands. In *Time Wars,* Jeremy Rifkin notes how in 1927 Emily Post reported that a widow's formal mourning period was three years. Twenty-three years later, Rifkin found this period had declined to six months. By 1972, Amy Vanderbilt advised the bereaved to "pursue, or try to pursue, a usual social course within a week or so after a funeral." We impose time limits and expectations for how long one must suffer. While over ninety-percent of American companies grant official time off for bereavement, most have established three days as the formal bereavement period for a death within your immediate family.

You cannot explain the impact of tragic death to someone who has not experienced it firsthand. You cannot understand the challenges until you have faced them. You cannot explain the questioning, the disorientation, the helplessness that arises when facing the world without your loved one.

Ask any survivor of sudden death if they thought they could cope with that loss of a child or spouse or sibling or friend and they will tell you, "No." Many will say they would have gone crazy in the face of such tragedy. The majority of survivors would never expect themselves able to confront and work through the grief journey. Yet these same people are the ones who face the adversity and climb out of the abyss, who find trust again, who rebuild.

This book includes our stories as well as those of mourners we have come to know over the past decade; stories of people who are rebuilding through the courage and sharing of each other's words. It is through these stories we recognize ourselves. It is through these stories we step out of isolation and into a community where others are walking the maze of recovery with us.

In this updated edition, we bring you new stories, wisdom, and information we wish we would have had access to during our journey. We bring you the work of those who have gone before you in the dark labyrinth of life's night. We bring you the words of those who have hit walls, stumbled in the maze, skinned their knees, and risen up to emerge in a new place. For as much as this book is about death, it is also about beginning. After losing someone we love, we begin again. We learn how to take courageous baby steps, how to walk and talk, how to dream different dreams, how to trust again, and how to create life anew while honoring the past. We are forever changed. We see life differently. More than anyone else, we understand the value of each minute, we understand the importance of saying what needs to be said today, we understand what is truly important.

We weren't ready to say goodbye, and there have been thousands of others and will be thousands more who will pick up this book also unready to say goodbye. This book is meant to serve as a touchstone of sanity for navigating the unknown emotional terrain of sudden death—a terrain full of walls, shrouded in fog. We offer you the words of analyst and philosopher Carl Jung, who wrote, "When you are up against a wall, put down roots like a tree, until clarity comes from deeper sources to see over that wall and grow."

Brook Noel
Pamela D. Blair, PhD
September 11, 2007

PART ONE
An Unfamiliar World:
The Journey into Grief

When sudden loss enters our reality, we awaken in an unfamiliar world. In this first section, we explore this unwelcome place and offer ideas to help navigate through the darkness. If you have purchased or been given this book in the immediate days or weeks after the death of your loved one, please read *Chapter Two: Notes for the first few weeks,* as your energy allows. Come back to the rest of this book as you are ready.

Chapter Three provides important insight to the emotional and physical aspects of grief. In this unfamiliar place we notice we are forgetful, distracted, and exhausted, and we wonder if we are "going crazy." This chapter can help you understand the many ways we react to loss.

In Chapter Four we explore the many myths and misunderstandings that surround the grieving process. Over the years we have received countless letters from readers who found this myth-busting section to be one that offers peace amidst chaos.

You will also find our stories in this section. We share them with you because we believe that people who have shared sudden loss firsthand can offer a level of understanding, compassion, and hope to one another. We share our stories in hope that in your darkest hours you can read them for reassurance knowing that life does go on and that this unfamiliar world can be survived.

Chapter One
The Starting Point: Notes from the Authors

"What we call the beginning is often the end.
To make an end is to make a beginning.
The end is where we start from."
—*T.S. Eliot*

Pam's Story

I believe no matter how much pain we're in, there is something inside of us stronger than the pain. That something allows survivors of the worst tragedies to want to live and tell their stories. You can see it in the eyes of someone who has managed to hang on to their dignity in the midst of adversity. It's a kind of stubbornness. You can call it God, the soul, or the human spirit. It is found only when we have been oppressed, or broken, or abandoned, and we remain the one who holds onto what's left. It is this inner something that has allowed me to go on in the face of tremendous loss.

I remember all the vivid, surrealistic details of that morning. The smell of fresh ground coffee brewing lingered in the air as I came to consciousness. I was trying to squeeze one or two more minutes out of my warm bed and feather pillow when the phone rang. Grabbing at the intrusive noise, I put the receiver to my ear and heard nothing but the sound of someone trying to catch her breath. I thought it might be one of those weird "breather" calls until I heard LeAnne say, "Pam, George is in a coma . . . *(long pause)* . . . he had a hemorrhage or something." I felt the molecules in the air begin to thicken as I tried to take a breath so I could talk to George's younger sister. "LeAnne, where are you? What do you mean? I just saw George yesterday afternoon. He looked fine!"

Crying and gasping for air, she replied in a thin voice, "You and Ian have to come here—to the hospital. I think it's important that you bring Ian here now." I tried to remain rational as I remembered that Ian, my twelve-year-old son with George, was getting ready to bolt down the stairs on his way to school. I still needed to pack his lunch box. I thought, *Why is LeAnne bothering me with this? I'm sure it's just nothing. After all, George is young and healthy (and handsome). Comas don't happen to people like him. They don't happen to people I know.*

"LeAnne, why don't we wait and see. He'll probably come to. And besides, Ian is just about to leave for school and he has a test today. Why don't you call back in a few minutes after you have more information and I'll bring him down to the hospital later. It's probably not as bad as ..." She interrupted my rambling with a bold, deliberate, almost cold intonation in her voice. "*Now.* You have to come now. It's really bad. There's a lot of blood in his brain and he probably won't live."

Blood in his brain. I sat down hard. What was I hearing? Was I hearing that George, the man I had loved as my husband and the father of my child, and who had become a dear friend and loving co-parent after our divorce, was about to leave the earth? Come on. People exaggerate. LeAnne is exaggerating. After all, George means as much to her as he does to me, and his son Ian, and his once stepdaughter, Aimee.

"Okay, LeAnne, I'll take the day off from work and I'll bring Ian to the hospital. Where are you?"

She replied in an almost inaudible voice, "The emergency room. I'll meet you here."

My limbs were numb, the blood was gone from my face and neck, and I wasn't sure I could make my mouth work. Steve, my husband of seven years, had left for his office in the city, and I was alone. I would have to tell Ian myself. I would have to tell Ian that the dad who loved to be with him on weekends, who lived for his son's little league games and karate matches, was probably brain dead. I would have to tell my daughter, Aimee. Part of me thought that if I could just see George and tell him loudly how much his son needed him, he wouldn't slip away into death's darkness. That's it. I would scream at him and bring him back to us.

Somehow I made my legs work. One numb foot in front of the other. At the bottom of the stairs I called, "Ian, meet me in my bedroom. I have something to tell you." I kept telling myself, *You will remain calm . . . think logically . . . don't upset the boy too much, just keep calm.*

How do you describe this strange limbo moment where life slows down and everything around you falls away into unimportance? It felt like there was no house with its comfortable furniture around me, no more smell of coffee, no cat rubbing my legs for attention, no appointments on the calendar—all that existed for now were the two small, round, brown eyes of my little boy resting on mine.

I told Ian what little I knew. There, sitting on the edge of my now neatly made bed, he melted into tears. Deep sobs and a lot of "How did this happen? What happened to him?" over and over again. His voice was cracking, rising and falling, the way twelve-year-old boy's voices sometimes do. I comforted him. I knew that was my only role, comforter to my son with no one to comfort me.

I called my daughter, Aimee, George's stepdaughter, nine months pregnant with her first child. She agreed to join us. We made our way to the hospital, not talking. Ian looked out the car window and I could tell he wondered why everyone driving past us looked so normal, so unaffected by our plight. Didn't they know what was going on? How could they go about their business knowing George was dying *or dead?* Why are they behaving as if nothing happened? I felt as if I were moving through someone else's movie. Everything felt surreal, in slow motion.

No human being is without feelings. From a baby's first cry to a dying person's last look at friends and family, our primary response to the world around us is colored by emotion. Whether that world seems to us friendly or frightening, beautiful or ugly, pleasant or disagreeable, affects the way we approach others, and indeed influences everything we do. I do not believe that such feelings arise in us solely due to environmental conditions, or to genetic factors, however important these both may be. Members of the same family, placed in the same kinds of situations, react in very different ways. Our emotions are a conscious response to our experience, but they are self-generated and reveal something important about our character.

It felt like I had no emotions and no character that day. I was skin and bones and brain and blood vessels making attempts at movement. Lips in slow motion on a frozen face with unfamiliar arms and legs, a mind repeating over and over, *this is crazy, this is crazy.* George's mother and sister waited with Ian, Aimee, and me in the emergency room. We all looked the same as we did last week, only now we were more robot-like, sitting and standing and walking and pacing around a room with hard plastic chairs and a TV set hanging from the ceiling. I couldn't look at George's mom with her soft round face and gray hair. A gentle lady of sixty-two with kind blue eyes—the same kind blue eyes that George had. If I looked at her I would have seen the pain. The pain of a woman who was told she would probably never have children and to whom George was a miracle, a gift from God—her first-born.

To me, the emotions are "real" in the sense that I can perceive them objectively as a luminous atmosphere surrounding every living being. Every time we feel an emotion, there is a discharge of energy in the emotional field, whether slight or strong, and this produces a characteristic vibration and a color—the "footprint" of that particular emotion. I could "see" the emotion in the room.

George was brain dead. The doctor said he had suffered a massive cerebral aneurysm. He was dead and he looked like he was sleeping—the machines kept his lungs rising and falling, his heart beating, his face a rosy healthy glow. I encouraged Ian to hold his hand, to say goodbye. He was brave. He did. He cried and said, "Goodbye, Daddy, I love you." Aimee took her private moment with him also. George had, only the week before, stopped by to visit her in her new apartment, to place his hand on her baby-full belly, to say congratulations.

George's wife said I could have some time alone with him. Because I believe that people in comas can "hear," I told him "thank you for our son and for the love you showed Aimee. Thank you for the time we had together." I think he heard me, if not with his ears, with his soul. I asked him to please be an angel in our son's life—to watch over him. The hospital staff began disconnecting the machines as the family encircled the hospital bed, holding hands, and praying.

I tell my story because I believe in the power of story to heal. As a therapist and workshop leader, I find it rewarding to help others tell their story. The stories I hear about loss are as diverse as fingerprints—each one slightly different from

6

the next. And yet, when we gather like we did at a recent workshop I conducted, the attendees share and the connection to each other is immediate and profound. Regardless of where we are in the process of loss, we become supportive as we relate and recognize each other's pain. A sense of community and acceptance is vital to our spiritual and emotional healing.

In her book, *The Fruitful Darkness,* Buddhist anthropologist and depth psychologist Joan Halifax reflects on our collective as well as personal stories when she writes, "stories are our protectors, like our immune system, defending against attacks of debilitating alienation . . . They are the connective tissue between culture and nature, self and other, life and death, that sew the worlds together, and in telling, the soul quickens and comes alive."

In his classic book, *Reaching Out,* Henri Nouwen writes that though our own story "can be hard to tell, full of disappointments and frustrations, deviations and stagnations . . . it is the only story we have and there will be no hope for the future when the past remains unconfessed, unreceived, and misunderstood."

Hopefully, the stories and information in this book will help you feel less alone as you struggle to find the path that will lead you across rivers of grief and through forests of sadness. We hope in some small way that we can be your support network and a touchstone for sanity during a very difficult time.

Brook's Story

It was a day in October that changed my perception of life, and my perception of death, forever. It was the day I lost my brother, who was not only a brother, but in many ways a father, a friend, and a lifeline.

The day was unseasonably warm for a Wisconsin October. It was the fourth of the month and the thermometer showed a temperature near seventy degrees. With weather like that, no Wisconsinite would stay indoors. My husband, daughter, and I decided to take a trip to Manitowoc, a town about an hour north of our then-home-base in the Milwaukee suburbs. Manitowoc housed a Maritime Museum that we had yet to visit. The main feature was a submarine, complete with tour. That afternoon we walked the streets, looked in the shops, took the tour, and bought our two-and-a-half-year-old daughter a blue hat, which read *U.S.S. Cobia.* Our daughter posed with the hat, her smile radiating happiness.

We left Manitowoc around five that evening to return home. A dear friend of mine had traveled into town and we had planned to meet at six for dinner. I glanced at my watch as we continued the drive, knowing I would be a few minutes late. We had planned that she would leave a message with her restaurant choice and I would meet her.

We arrived home a bit after six. My neighbors, Kevin and Mary Ann, were outside barbecuing. I stopped over briefly to say hello and let Samantha show off her new hat. I apologized for my quick departure and ducked into the house to check messages and find out where Sara had chosen for dinner.

The red digital display showed four messages. I hit play. The first was from my mother. Five simple words, "Brook—call me right away." The second was from Sara, with the name of the restaurant. The third was my mother again, this time her voice thick with a tone I couldn't discern. "Brook you *must* call me right away. There has been a terrible accident." I immediately pushed stop on the machine and dialed my mother's number.

Both my brother and mother continued to live in the town where I was raised. It's a small resort town called Manitowish Waters, about five hours north of my then-Milwaukee home. Life is simple there. You work; you ski; you enjoy the woods, the lakes; you watch the Packers and enjoy the seasons as they unfold. Outsiders make great attempts to vacation there. Often the north woods has been dubbed "God's Country," and life is full and fun there.

My mother answered on the first ring. I can still hear our voices to this day and picture myself standing beneath the archway of our guest bedroom. "Mom, it's me. What's up?" I asked inquisitively, never prepared for the two-word response that would vibrate over the phone.

"Caleb's dead."

Immediately my knees gave out and I shouted "No," before falling to the floor, the questions, the disbelief, lingering around me. I asked how, but did not hear the reply. I crawled into the guest bed with the cordless phone pushed to my ear and curled my body into a tight ball. My daughter had walked up from behind and was patting me gently on the back. "It's all right Mama," said the innocent two-year-old voice. "It's all right Mama." Andy, my husband, came to take Samantha from the room and I simply mouthed the two words my mother had spoken: *Caleb's dead.*

Still on the line, my mother was talking and crying and I couldn't unscramble the words. I remember only one sentence, "Brook, is Andy there? You need to hang up the phone and call me back. Have Andy call me back." I set down the phone still writhing on the bed, wanting desperately to escape the unwelcome reality that had suddenly become claustrophobic. Rising, I walked into the living room. I looked briefly at my daughter and Andy, before running from the house. The points thereafter are somewhat vague and gathered from what I've been told of my response.

I entered into my neighbor's kitchen and fell into her arms as I told her the news. She quickly took me outside and huddled me close. She held me on the wooden steps as I stared at the cement and she whispered, "You are in shock. Try and breathe. Don't talk." I remember my hands and body trembling violently. "Look at my hands," I whispered, "What happened to my hands?" I watched them jump from left to right, operating independently of my mind. Her words soothed me from some otherworld. "You are in shock. Try and breathe."

MaryAnn's husband, Kevin, went to my house and took Samantha back to have dinner with their family. With Samantha out of the house, MaryAnn escorted me back home to Andy where the two of them called my mother.

The details unfurled. Caleb and his faithful chocolate lab, Samson, had been duck hunting on a marsh with three friends. They had rowed a boat out about twenty minutes to the site that was thought to have the best potential. While waiting for the official opening time, Caleb was eyeing some geese flying overhead. At that moment he was stung by a yellow jacket just over his eyebrow. Within minutes, Caleb would go unconscious. His friends performed CPR as they frantically rowed back to shore. Unable to fit in the boat, his faithful dog swam across the marsh, unwilling to leave his master. His friends broke into his truck, using his cellular phone to call the paramedics. The local paramedics arrived and were then intercepted by a special team sent from the hospital twenty-five miles away.

Despite the efforts of friends, paramedics, and doctors, Caleb never came to nor responded to Epinephrine or any other drug. My mother was told he had suffered a fatal, profound, anaphylactic shock reaction to the sting of a bee. Caleb had been stung by bees before and never had anything more than a mild reaction. We, nor he, even knew of this bee allergy.

My brother was a strong and vital young man. He owned a successful printing shop, which he built from the ground up. He was a National Barefoot Water-ski Champion who was in great physical health and a prime athlete. He was about 200 pounds, and in one day, we had to come to understand that a bee, no bigger than an inch, had taken the life from this handsome twenty-seven-year-old man. It is something that I think we all are still trying to comprehend. It is something that I don't think we ever fully will, but we each must find our own way to cope and go on successfully—that is the best tribute we can give to this great man who touched our lives.

When Caleb died, I looked for someone to hold my hand and to understand what I was feeling. I wasn't ready for a support group; all I wanted to do was to curl up in my bed, hide from the world, and have something or someone convince me it would, someday, be all right again. I scanned bookstores looking for something I could relate to but found very little coverage on sudden death. The other books didn't understand the unique challenges of facing a death in this way. Eventually, I gave up the search for that book.

As time has passed, I have learned more about what I have endured and what I have to endure to move on with my life. I have spoken with others—some in the recent aftermath of loss and some who lost someone tragically years ago—many of whom are looking for guidance similar to what I had searched for. With these people in mind, I decided to create the book I wish would have been there for me. I met my coauthor, Pam, while working on a book entitled *The Single Parent Resource*. There was an immediate closeness between the two of us, even though we lived two thousand miles apart. When I decided to write this book, I felt compelled to call her and see if she would consider writing the book with me. Fate must have nudged me to call, since at that point, I didn't know she had experienced sudden loss in her life as well.

We cannot offer you any quick fixes. We cannot give you a tidy outline that will divide grief recovery into a neat and precise process or stages. We cannot tell you that six months from now the world will be back in alignment. We have seen too much to offer such hollow promises. What we can promise is that in these pages we will do our best to offer you a hand to hold and words to guide you through this unfamiliar maze.

Sudden Loss Comes Again
Brook's Story . . . February 2005
It was a Sunday morning much like any other. The Wisconsin weather was cold and brittle while I was warm and cozy in my home with my daughter and husband. The ringing of the phone interrupted our family moment. Most would say the ring sounded like it always had, but I heard it echo through the hallway—issuing a warning to the answerer. My father, age sixty-one, had entered a hospital while traveling abroad in Trinidad. In an all-too-short three-week span he was diagnosed

and died from advanced colon cancer, unable to reach a condition that was stable enough for me to bring him back to the United States.

Although well-versed by now in grief, the road before me was still unfamiliar.

I found myself grieving not only my dad, but my brother—even harder than I had the first time.

As I waded through this maze with grief both new and old, I kept a list of the lessons I learned along the way and will hold with me always. I share these with you in hopes they offer comfort in your journey.

I learned that sometimes "not knowing" is the only thing to know.

I learned that sometimes it's okay to forget everything and just sleep for ten or twenty hours.

I learned I have a lot more to learn about myself.

I learned that the answers we often look for outside of ourselves, can only be found within.

I learned that I can blame anything and everything until I run out of breath—but I become empowered when I quit asking, "why me?" and start asking, "what will I do with this?"

I learned that there is nothing as precious as right now—even when "now" doesn't seem precious.

I learned that I cannot make up for today by living or working "harder" or "doing more" or "being healthier" or "spending more time" tomorrow.

I learned that I can never know what the day may bring, but it is up to me at its close, to know what the day brought.

I re-learned the value of a moment.

Chapter Two
Notes for the First Few Weeks

"And people answered the phone for me.
And people cooked for me.
And people understood for me.
My dearest friends cared for me
when I didn't care."
—*Wendy Feiereisen*

At this moment, in the direct aftermath of losing someone tragically, there is so little anyone can say. We cannot find the words to offer you peace—though we wish it were a gift we could give you. We promise you now that we will give you everything we can to help you make your way through this. We will help you wind a path through the haze, the confusion, and the pain that is gripping at your core.

For the first few weeks, do not concern yourself with what you will do, where you will go, or what lies in the future. For now, we ask that you simply follow the guidelines in this chapter. There will be time to cope, to understand, to process—later. Right now, you simply need to take care of *you*.

Treat Yourself as if You Were in Intensive Care

You are in the process of going through one of the most traumatic experiences a person can endure. The challenges you have already faced, both physically and mentally, will leave you vulnerable, exhausted, and weak. It is imperative that you focus directly on yourself and on any dependents. Find ways to get your needs met first in these few weeks.

In the first week or so you will probably feel stunned and overwhelmed. You may also feel numb or hysterical. Your emotional system shuts down, providing temporary insulation from the full impact of your loss. You will go through the motions; it will look like you're coping well sometimes.

In her book, *The Worst Loss,* Barbara D. Rosof writes, "In shock you may be unable to move or speak coherently; people report that they cannot think. Shock responses may also be active and intense; you may have screamed, or run from the room, or physically attacked the bringer of the news. All of these behaviors are means of shutting down, or distancing yourself from a reality that you do not yet have a way to deal with. As you look back, your behavior may seem bizarre and totally out of character for you. Remember that your entire world had been knocked out from under you. You were in free fall, and your first task was to find any way to stop the fall."

When the funeral is over and your relatives and friends have gone home, the shock begins to wear off. It is important not to make any decisions that will have a lasting impact on your life (for example, sell the house, give away the person's belongings, etc.) while you are in shock.

Expect to Be Distracted

During the first few weeks, your mind will be filled with racing thoughts and unfamiliar emotions. Many people report having difficulty with simple tasks. Losing one's keys, forgetting where you are while driving, and sluggish reaction time are all commonly reported problems. With everything you are mentally and physically trying to process, it's normal to be distracted. Take special caution. Try to avoid driving and other activities where these symptoms may cause injury.

Have Someone Near You

If possible, choose a close friend to keep near you through the first week or two. Let this person help you make decisions, hear your fears or concerns, and be the shoulder for you to lean on. Give them a copy of this book. Later, as you move through the grieving process, it will be very helpful to have someone who has "been there" and understands thoroughly what you are talking about.

Accept the Help of Friends

Our energy is so depleted in the first few weeks after loss, it's hard to even ask for help. We have included a handout at the end of this chapter that can be photocopied freely and given to your inner circle of friends and relatives. You may be reluctant to do this, but please do. Even if we don't think we need people right now, we do indeed. Brook shares her story of friendship . . .

"When I lost my brother, my friend Sara was my anchor. I never asked her to come over that evening but as soon as she heard, she came (even though I told her there was nothing she could do). She simply sat next to me. Then she went upstairs and packed my bag for the upcoming week. She hugged me when I needed it and sat in the other room when I needed to be alone. To this day, her warm presence brings tears to my eyes. It was an extension of love and caring like few I have known."

If, like Brook, you are too grief-ridden to ask for help, simply show friends this book and let them read these few pages so they have an idea of what you need and how to support you. Friends want to help, but they rarely know how. The cycle of your grief will be more bearable when you hold the hand of a friend. Reach out.

The following two entries summarize beautifully what those who face grief need from the people around them.

"I'll cry with you,"
she whispered
"until we run out of tears.
Even if it's forever.
We'll do it together."
There it was . . . a simple
promise of connection.
The loving alliance of
grief and hope that
blesses both our breaking

14

apart and our coming
together again.
Molly Fumia, *Safe Passage*

Needed: A strong, deep person wise enough to allow me to grieve in
the depth of who I am, and strong enough to hear my pain without
turning away.

I need someone who believes that the sun will rise again, but who
does not fear my darkness. Someone who can point out the rocks in my
way without making me a child by carrying me. Someone who can stand
in thunder and watch the lightning and believe in a rainbow.

Fr. Joe Mahoney, *Concerns of Police Survivors Newsletter*

(This is excerpted from a beautiful book on grief titled *Forever
Remembered: Cherished messages of hope, love and comfort from courageous
people who have lost a loved one.* Compendium Publishing.)

Caring for Your Children

If you have small children, contact friends and relatives to help you care for them.
Consider having someone stay with you for the specific task of caring for your children, since some children may be further traumatized by separation. In Chapter
Nine we cover the specifics of children and grief. While it is human nature to want
to help and care for others, we must understand at this trying time we will barely
have enough energy to care for ourselves. Even if we want to help those around
us, we won't have the resources. It's in our best interest to allow this time for our
own grief.

Someone to Take Calls and Check Email

If the person who has died is of your immediate family, you will be receiving many
phone calls, visitors, and cards. Have a friend come by to take messages, check
emails, answer the door, and answer the phone. Most callers do not expect to speak
directly with the family but simply wish to express their condolences. Have someone keep a notepad handy to record the names and messages of callers.

Be forewarned, occasionally you may receive a strange call or a strange card. Brook once took a message from a caller who offered condolences for the loss of her brother and then in a second breath requested a current picture of her daughter. Pam remembers a caller who said, "I'm sure George's death was easier for you, because you were divorced after all." These thoughts and comments are inappropriate and can be very hurtful, though the caller does not intend them to be. In our society, we just don't know how to handle grief and loss. People cope with grief differently—many people don't know how to cope at all. When you think of it, our world is geared toward *gaining* and *acquiring;* we have few lessons on how to handle *loss.* Occasionally people will ask a strange question or perhaps write a note in a card that seems a bit "out of place." Realize that this is not done to hurt you; these are just people who are inept at handling loss and the thought of loss.

Seek Assistance with Final Arrangements

In addition to getting help to answer the phone and email, seek out your most trusted friend to help with any final arrangements that are your responsibility. You may be the person who needs to organize the funeral service or you may have insurance agencies to contact or an estate to settle. While you can and should be involved in these areas at some level, it is important to find someone who can do most of the calling for you, make trips to the funeral home, find out information and then let you make the final choices. In the direct aftermath of loss your judgment may also be impaired, and a trusted friend can act as a guide in decision making. In the Appendix of this book, you will find some worksheets that will guide you and your support person through these processes.

Don't Worry about Contacting People

In the first few days you will make initial calls to immediate family and friends. Beyond that, try to limit the number of calls you are personally responsible for. At this time, you are unlikely to have the energy or the will to make these calls. In the Appendix we have included a worksheet that you can give to a trusted friend. This worksheet will guide them through needed calls and arrangements. Additionally, you may want to obtain the deceased's address book and let your trusted friend make those contacts.

Let Your Body Lead You

Grief affects us all differently. Some of us may become very active and busy, while others may become lethargic or practically comatose. Let your body lead you. If you feel tired—sleep. If you feel like crying—cry. If you are hungry—eat. Don't feel you need to act one way or another. There are no "shoulds" right now, simply follow the lead of your body.

One caution: With the shock of losing someone tragically, it is not uncommon for people to turn to medication. This can be as minor as a sleep aid or as major as consuming large amounts of alcohol. Try to resist these urges. This will not make the grief easier. In some cases a doctor may choose to prescribe medication to help you cope. Be aware that medicating your grief will only postpone it.

Religious Traditions

If you were married or your loved one adopted a religion you are unfamiliar with, you may encounter traditions that are uncomfortable for you. The religious requirements around death and burial may cause confusion and unrest in the family and among friends.

For example, Marjory comes from a family where a wake lasts for days and cremation is preferred. Since Marjory was the custodial parent, she took her son to Sunday school on a regular basis. When her young son died unexpectedly, her ex-husband, a religious Jew, was adamantly against the plans she was making. Religious Jews are required to bury their dead within twenty-four hours and believe that cremation is a most undignified method of disposing a body. Also, after the immediate burial, Jews "sit shiva" for seven days with the nearest of kin.

It is so important at a tragic time like this to be caring and understanding of the traditions of both the deceased and the families involved. To honor the deceased, the living must find ways to compromise. In Marjory's case, because most of her family had been uninvolved in her son's life and her ex-husband's family had been so close to her, she decided on burial for her son instead of cremation. Her ex-husband in turn agreed to participate in the Christian-oriented wake Marjory had planned.

If you are unclear about what is best for you, your family, or your loved one, seek counsel with a clergyperson, family mediator, or therapist. Keep in mind that people's needs will be different. When Brook's brother died, she and her mother chose a small informal viewing for close friends. Many of Caleb's friends chose not to attend. They preferred to remember Caleb as they had seen him last. Others found the viewing helpful. There is no right or wrong way to grieve, it is simply important to be open and respectful of individual needs.

For more information on funeral traditions for different faiths, go to everplans.com.

Wills and Arrangements

While those who die a lingering death often have wills and have told the living what they would like as far as funerals, burial, etc., one who dies a sudden death has frequently not indicated to friends and family how they would like to be treated in death. This presents an extra burden to loved ones, since they are required to go ahead with arrangements under assumptions of what their loved one may have wanted. With our emotional and physical levels depleted, these decisions become even harder. You may find it helpful to discuss your options with a group of close friends who knew the deceased. When Brook and her mother were trying to figure out what type of service to hold, they talked to each other first, and then asked Caleb's friends for input and ideas. With the help of others, they decided a celebration in his honor would be the way he would choose to be remembered. Since the decision had been a group effort, everyone felt comfortable.

Cultural Differences

There isn't room in this book to go into the specific cultural differences in handling death and grief. All we can do here is make you aware that these differences bear consideration. The U.S. is considered the world's melting pot, and there are many beliefs about the meaning and purpose of life and what happens after death in all corners of the world. Our specific culture informs the meaning of death for each person and also the emotional response to the death of a loved one. Some believe the pain of the loss can be eased by believing that people (or their souls) live on in a hereafter. Some have the belief that they will be born again to a better life. The spirit of a deceased loved one directly influences the living in some cultures where bereaved family members feel comforted by the knowledge their loved one is watching over them.

Each culture has its rituals and customs that help the bereaved grieve. Rituals offer culturally supported ways to express grief and opportunities for community members to support the bereaved. Sudden death can create enormous chaos and confusion. Cultural rituals offer a sense of predictability for the bereaved and for the community. The following cultural customs and rituals should be carefully considered:

- Ceremonies that should be performed at the moments before and after death
- How the body is handled after death—how the body should be cleansed and dressed, who should be permitted to handle the body, and whether the body should be buried or cremated
- Whether grief will be expressed quietly and privately or loudly and publicly, such as with public crying, keening, or wailing
- Different grief expectations for men versus women or for children versus adults
- The ceremonies and rituals that should be performed and who should participate, such as children, community members, friends, etc.
- How the family is expected to grieve—what they are expected to wear and how they are expected to behave
- New roles that surviving family members are expected to take on—whether a widow is expected to remarry, or the oldest son is expected to become the family leader

If the expected rituals and customs aren't carried out, this can interfere with the necessary grieving process and can lead to feelings of unresolved loss. Familiar rituals and customs offers a sense of stability and security. To find out more about the customs and mourning practice of someone from another culture, talk to someone who shares a similar cultural background, look for books at the library, or search the Internet.

Going Back to Work

Depending on your circumstances and company policies, you may find that a week or two is all you can get off from work and in some cases only three days. While grief experts recommend around twenty days of bereavement leave for close family members, four days is the average bereavement leave allotted for the death of a spouse or child, and three days is the average for the loss of a parent, grandparent, domestic partner, sibling, grandchild, or foster child. Before returning, explore any other options you have. If you have savings or any other sources that can help you secure a four-to six-week break, consider using it. If that is impossible, take some time to discuss with your boss or supervisor what you are going through.

We strongly suggest setting up a meeting or lunch with your employer before returning to the work environment. Ask if any part-time options or shorter days could be arranged for a few weeks. If not, ask for their support and understanding. Let your supervisor know that you are low on energy and very emotional. Ask for his or her patience and tolerance. Let him or her know you will not use grief as an excuse to avoid working, but you will need a little leeway as you figure out how to function while grieving. Many supervisors will probably be accommodating when they understand what you're going through. Let your co-workers know that you could use some extra support as well. (You may want to use the handout we offer on page 23). Many times people are unsure if they should treat you "the same as always," or if they should be careful about discussing certain things. Only you know how you want to be treated. Don't keep it to yourself. If you tell others what you need at this time, many will be willing to stand by you and support you if given the chance.

Some companies offer bereavement leave. Make sure to check with the Human Resources Department (if your company has one) to see what is available to you. There is also information that can be valuable to companies and employees. The AARP—Widowed Person's Service publishes a brochure entitled, *When an Employee Loses a Loved One*. Bereavement Publishing provides a "Grief in the Workplace" program to help corporate America understand the needs of grieving employees. See the resource section for information and addresses.

Grief Sessions

In Brook's grief support groups, she recommends "Grief Sessions," which are set times to honor your feelings. In our busy days, we tend to immerse ourselves in activities (sometimes mindful, sometimes mindless) so we don't experience our grief. But we can't get through what we do not feel.

Some people find success in spending an hour taking a walk and getting in touch with their grief. Some people can sit outside with a journal and express their feelings. Just as our grief is unique, so will our grief sessions be. In the immediate months following our loss, this space for grieving will be extremely beneficial for processing our complex emotions.

These days will be long and challenging. There may seem no resolution for any of the pain that plagues you. That's all right. It's all right to feel hopeless, as if life has lost its focus or purpose. These are natural and normal feelings. Trust that life will go on, and that in time, you will reestablish your place within it. For now, simply take care of yourself. In a few weeks, return to this book or refer to it as needed. Trust that there will be light again and know this book will be here for you in a month or so when you're feeling stronger and better able to cope with your journey through grief.

A Guide for Those Helping Others with Grief
(photocopy and give to close friends and loved ones)

Don't try to find the magic words or formula to help me eliminate the pain. Nothing can erase or minimize the painful tragedy your friend or loved one is facing. Your primary role at this time is simply to "be there." Don't worry about what to say or do, just be a presence that the person can lean on when needed.

Don't try to minimize or make me feel better. When we care about someone, we hate to see them in pain. Often we'll say things like, "I know how you feel," or "perhaps, it was for the best," in order to miminize their hurt. While this can work in some instances, it never works with grief.

Help me with responsibilities. Even though a life has stopped, life doesn't. One of the best ways to help is to run errands, prepare food, take care of the kids, do laundry, and help with the simplest of maintenance.

Don't expect me to reach out to you. Many people say, "call me if there is anything I can do." At this stage, the person who is grieving will be overwhelmed at the simple thought of picking up a phone. If you are close to this person, simply stop over and begin to help. People need this but don't think to ask. There are many people who will be with you during the good times—but few that are there in life's darkest hour.

Talk me through decisions. While working through the grief process, many bereaved people report difficulty with decision making. Be a sounding board for your friend or loved one and help them think through decisions.

Don't be afraid to say the name of the deceased to me or around me. Those who have lost someone usually speak of them often, and believe it or not, need to hear the deceased's name and stories. In fact, many grievers welcome this.

Excerpted from I Wasn't Ready to Say Goodbye: A Guide for Surviving, Coping, and Healing after the Sudden Death of a Loved One *by Brook Noel and Pamela D. Blair, PhD (Sourcebooks, 2008)*

Don't tell me that time will heal all wounds. Your friend or loved one will change because of what has happened. Everyone grieves differently. Some will be "fine" and then experience their true grief a year later, others grieve immediately. There are no timetables, no rules—be patient.

Remind me to take care of myself. Eating, resting, and self-care are all difficult tasks when beseiged by the taxing emotions of grief. You can help by keeping the house stocked with healthy foods that are already prepared or easy to prepare. Help with the laundry. Take over some errands so the bereaved can rest. However, do not push the bereaved to do things they may not be ready for. Many grievers say, "I wish they would just follow my lead." While it may be upsetting to see the bereaved withdrawing from people and activities—it is normal. They will rejoin as they are ready.

Avoid judging me. Don't tell the person how to react or handle their emotions or situation. Simply let him/her know that you support their decisions and will help in any way possible.

Share a meal with me. Since meal times can be especially lonely, invite the bereaved over regularly to share a meal or take a meal to their home. Consider inviting the bereaved out on important dates like the one-month Anniversary of the death, the deceased's birthday, etc.

Help me make a list of everything that needs to be done. This could include everything from bill paying to plant watering. Prioritize these by importance. Help the bereaved complete as many tasks as possible. If there are many responsibilities, find one or more additional friends to support you.

Make a personal commitment to help me get through this. After a death, many friendships change or disintegrate. People don't know how to relate to the one who is grieving, or they get tired of being around someone who is sad. Vow to see your friend or loved one through this, to be their anchor in their darkest hour.

Excerpted from I Wasn't Ready to Say Goodbye: A Guide for Surviving, Coping, and Healing after the Sudden Death of a Loved One *by Brook Noel and Pamela D. Blair, PhD (Sourcebooks, 2008)*

Chapter Three
Understanding the Emotional
and Physical Effects of Grief

"Shock has rearranged our insides. The disorientation comes from
not yet recognizing the new arrangement. Grief is a molting where
we shed the parts of us that are no longer applicable to the new parts.
It isn't a time to understand anything."
—*Stephanie Ericsson,* Companion Through Darkness

The unexpected loss of someone close to us can quickly turn our world into an unfamiliar place. Coping with what used to be routine becomes exhausting. The simplest task may seem daunting. Grief affects us not only emotionally, but also physically. When we can understand how grief affects us, we are better equipped to deal with its grip. While we wish we never had to learn or understand these emotions, being aware of them may offer us comfort.

A common experience of people dealing with tragic loss is the feeling of going crazy. The emotions are so strong and intense, those grieving often think they are the only ones to feel that way or that their reactions are wrong. In the pages to come, we have addressed many of these emotions. You're not crazy and you're not alone. By understanding these emotions, we take the first step toward realization and thus our first step on the pathway of healing.

In her book, *A Journey Through Grief: Gentle, Specific Help to Get You Through The Most Difficult Stages of Grief,* Alla Reneé Bozarth, PhD, writes, "While you are grieving, your emotional life may be unpredictable and unstable. You may feel that there are gaps in your remembered experience . . . You may alternate between depression and euphoria, between wailing rage and passive resignation . . . If you've experienced loss and are hurting, it's reasonable that your responses will be unreasonable."

In this chapter, we will explore many of the ways grief affects us. Some grievers report feeling many of these pains early on, while others report experiencing them later and still some report few of these experiences. Your relationship to the loved one will make your individual dance with grief different.

Exhaustion

Perhaps the most commonly reported symptom of grief is utter exhaustion and confusion. In her book *Surviving Grief,* Dr. Catherine M. Sanders explains "we become so weak that we actually feel like we have the flu. Because of our lack of experience with energy depletion, this weakness frightens and perplexes us. Before the loss, it happened only when we were sick."

Little things we used to do without thinking, like mailing a letter, can easily become an all-day task. Getting a gallon of milk can seem monumental. The thought of getting dressed, driving a car, getting money, paying a cashier, carrying the gallon, driving home—just these thoughts alone can leave a griever hungry for sleep.

Brook sought the help of a psychotherapist in working through grief. The psychotherapist had a valuable viewpoint on exhaustion.

"Her first words to me were simple and powerful. 'Brook,' she said, 'What has happened here has the same effect on you as if you had gone through major surgery. Consider yourself in intensive care and treat yourself as if you are in intensive care.' Her point hit home. Although emotionally I had experienced a 'triple bypass,' I expected myself to return to jogging the day after. My body was carrying its own messages of what it needed—and that was rest and extra care."

There are many remedies for exhaustion. People may prescribe vitamin combinations, exercise, eating well, staying busy, and more. The suggestion of the psychotherapist is perhaps the most important: *You are in recovery. Give yourself some time to grieve and let the emotions work through you.* If you jump to stay busy now, to sidetrack part of the grieving process, it will only resurface down the road. It's all right to be exhausted and to rest. Take time to heal. If, however, you have any suicidal thoughts, are not eating, become dehydrated, or are suffering any additional serious symptoms, seek professional help immediately.

Days of Distraction

Most people function fairly well in their daily lives. We know how to get things done, stay organized, and accomplish what we set out to do. After experiencing a sudden death, it's like we lose the most basic of skills. Those things that we once did with ease become difficult and challenging. Brook found distraction to be a major hurdle during her first few months of grieving.

> "I remember shortly after Caleb's death, I needed to weigh two envelopes to take to the post office. I have a postage scale in my home office and I always use that to avoid holding up the line at our one-clerk, small-town post office. Well, that day I could not find the scale.
>
> I walked through my office, through my living room. I even checked the kitchen, bedroom, and bathroom. Nothing. Off and on throughout the day, I would repeat my search. For three hours, I scanned the house for that scale. Finally, in frustration, I threw my hands up and decided just to have the items weighed at the post office.
>
> When I returned, I walked into my office and there on my desk was the scale. It had been sitting there the entire time, covered by nothing. It was in an area I had stared directly at for hours, yet I had not seen it. This is the type of distraction that often accompanies grief.
>
> I noticed on these days I didn't always feel down or sad, but when I was trying to cope with grief and didn't have an outlet, situations like

this would occur. Many of these "days of distraction" happened a couple of months after Caleb's death. They became an alarm for me. During these days, I would quit trying to do so much and instead relax and work through my grief.

I had a similar challenge one day while trying to pay a bill. For an hour I couldn't find my checkbook. When I finally found my checkbook, I had lost the bill that I wanted to pay. The cat-and-mouse search continued a few more times and before I knew it, an entire day had passed while simply attempting to mail out a single payment. When this first happened, I would push myself and try to keep going. By the end of the day I was often near tears from frustration."

These moments of distraction are signals from your body that you *must* slow down. No matter how small the task, it is too much for you right now. Be careful not to overburden yourself. Lower your expectations. Know that your ability to function will return—it takes time—it takes recovery.

Denying Our New Reality

We are not usually conscious of our denial; it happens below the level of our awareness. Denial is sometimes characterized by immersing one's self in fantasies such as, "He's just away on a trip," or "She'll be walking in the door any minute," or "He can't be dead, we have plans to go away this summer and he wouldn't let me down that way."

Denial is a natural, instinctive, protective response that actually gives us time to grasp reality. Barbara D. Rosof tells us that "as shock fades, and your mind and body reclaim their control, you start to take in the news. But it still may be too much; you may move in and out of denial. Lasting for hours or sometimes days, denial is another way of retreating from a reality too painful to bear . . . As irrational as it may seem to others, denial serves a necessary purpose. It is a psychological emergency measure, a temporary forestalling. You are not yet ready to confront your loss head-on."

For some, the passage through the denial phase will be accelerated by reading the obituary, seeing pictures in the newspaper, reading the death certificate, or viewing the headstone. Caregivers should not prevent their loved ones from seeing these things or saying "he's dead" over and over.

Denial can be helpful for short periods of relief; however, you must move through it into the painful reality of the loss and begin to feel the feelings. If you find yourself stuck in the denial stage, you may need professional help to move on.

How Does Grief Differ from Depression?

Depression is more than a feeling of grief after losing someone or something you love. Clinical depression is a whole-body disorder. It can take over the way you think and feel. Symptoms of depression include:

- A sad, anxious, or "empty" mood that is almost constantly negative;
- Loss of interest in what you used to enjoy;
- Low energy, fatigue, feeling "slowed down;"
- Changes in sleep patterns;
- Loss of appetite, weight loss, or weight gain;
- Trouble concentrating, remembering, or making decisions;
- Feeling hopeless or gloomy;
- Feeling guilty, worthless, or helpless;
- Thoughts of death or suicide or a suicide attempt; and
- Recurring aches and pains that don't respond to treatment.

If you recently experienced a death or other loss, these feelings may be part of a normal grief reaction. But if these feelings persist with no lifting mood, ask for help. *Source: National Institutes of Health: National Mental Health Information Center*

Anger . . . a Normal Response

Who wouldn't be angry when someone they loved so dearly is suddenly taken from them? Anger is natural in this situation and it is actually a healthy part of the grieving process. Yet anger takes different forms, some of them healthy and some of them unhealthy.

Let's examine the types of anger that are natural, though unhealthy. Some of us will express anger when we are not getting the support we need from friends, family, or work. While intensely wrapped in our grief, we usually don't think to ask for support. Instead we lash out at those close to us with hostility, irritability, and anger. If we can recognize this anger for what it is, we can use it in a healthy way. This is a clue that we are not receiving the support we need. We need to ask for more or seek out other support networks.

Displaced anger is simply misdirected anger. We want someone to take responsibility for what has happened. We need someone to blame and to be held accountable. We may scream or yell at those who cared for the person at the hospital. We may become angry with those who were with the person when he died. Displaced anger is completely natural and will lessen as you learn to accept what has happened.

Anger can also surface when we recall past moments or turmoil, pain, or unresolved anger within our relationship with the person we have lost. Suddenly we are forced to realize we will never share another physical interaction with this person. When that happens, memories flood through. Within these memories there are bound to be recollections of feisty exchanges, arguments, and past hurts. Wishing we had more time with the loved one, we may overcriticize ourselves for any time there was conflict in the past. It is unrealistic, however, to expect perfection in any relationship. Immersing ourselves in the "should haves" and "could haves" of the past will only prevent us from dealing effectively with anger in the present.

Anger also occurs when we suppress our feelings. Anger is not the most accepted emotion in today's culture. In fact, many people don't even recognize anger as part of the grieving process. Depending on our support network and situation, we may be encouraged not to show our anger. When this happens, the anger still exists and needs to be released, so it is released inward. This can cause a variety of problems. We may become sick, depressed, have chronic pain, or begin having nightmares. Begin to look at healthy alternatives for releasing this anger.

Anger is an especially common response to tragic deaths. Since we could do nothing to stop or prevent the loss and are left only to interpret it, we may become frustrated and develop feelings of helplessness. Bouts of crying are the most common release for this anger. It's easy to not release this anger and to turn it inward. If you suspect you may be doing so, talk to a friend or counselor to help release these feelings.

Appropriate anger is the point that we all hope to get to eventually. In this phase we can take our anger, in whatever form, and vent it. There are many ways to release anger appropriately. Here are a few . . .

- beat a pillow
- create a sacred space where you can go and not be heard or seen to let the anger out of your system
- use journaling to record and release your angry feelings
- take a walk out into an unpopulated area and scream until you are exhausted
- rant with a friend, therapist, or counselor
- see the Appendix for other ideas

Sarah, a young client of Pam's, once said, "I am very angry at my fiancé. It feels like I'm angry all the time. I mean, he was killed one month before we were to get married and it wasn't his fault. So, why am I angry at *him?*"

The death of someone we care about and who made promises to be there and love us forever, turns us upside down and inside out. It affects our equilibrium. We think and feel things we never imagined we were capable of.

In addition, women are especially uncomfortable with anger because we have been acculturated to be "nice" and to seek solutions other than confrontation. In her book, *The Dance of Anger,* Harriet Lerner, PhD writes, "Women, however, have long been discouraged from the awareness and forthright expression of anger. Sugar and spice are the ingredients from which we are made. We are the nurturers, the soothers, the peacemakers and the steadiers of rocked boats." Men, on the other hand, are generally quicker to experience anger but have a harder time with sadness.

Feel your anger, acknowledge it, and know that it is a normal part of the grieving process. If you don't express your anger, holding it in will cause you to become depressed. Anger turned inside out is depression. You might also seek a trained professional who will help you diffuse your anger by encouraging you to express it safely. Find a safe way to express this normal emotion and you will begin to feel less "crazy" and more at peace.

Warning Signs

As you work through your grief, it's important to monitor yourself and your stages. The following list can help you discern healthy grief from distorted grief. If you feel you may be suffering unhealthy grief, seek the help of a support group, clergyperson, or therapist.

- **Extreme Avoidant Behavior**—If you are avoiding friends and family for a prolonged period of time (over three weeks), you will want to talk to a professional. People need other people to work through grief.
- **Lack of Self-Care**—In order to have the energy and emotional capacity to work through grief, one must first take care of his or her basic needs. If you are having problems meeting basic needs, this is a warning sign to seek help.
- **Prolonged Denial**—If months have passed and you are still in denial, you will most likely need a support group to help you move through this stage.
- **Self-Destructive Thoughts**—These thoughts are not unusual during grief, but we can expect them to pass quickly. If they are persistent or obsessive, it is best to consult a professional for guidance in working through them.
- **Displaced Anger**—With few emotional outlets available to us, it is common for anger to be displaced. However, this can become problematic if your anger is hurting you in personal or professional areas, or hurting others— seek help immediately.
- **Prolonged Depression or Anxiety**—Like denial, prolonged and immobilizing depression or anxiety are signs to seek help.
- **Self-Medication**—If you are using substances in excess to self-medicate your pain (i.e., food, alcohol or drugs), seek the help of an organization that specializes in such disorders or the help of a professional.

The stages and procedures we have outlined in this chapter serve only as guidelines. We will each experience and manage grief differently. Take that which is useful to you and let the rest go. Perhaps most importantly, know that with time and some conscious effort on your part, life will get easier and more manageable.

Grief Knows No Schedule

In today's world we have grown accustomed to scheduling so much of life. Most of us own at least one organizer or appointment book. Yet grief is one thing that will never fit in an appointment-square. You may find there are times when you are in the midst of a normal, pleasant activity and suddenly a wash of grief comes over you. Know that this is common and that grief can surface at any time, without notice. Both of us experienced the common "ambush" of grief.

> "I remember watching a television comedy with my husband. I had been laughing throughout the show and it had been a while since I shed tears over Caleb's death. Then there was an ad to solicit funds for needy children—the theme song was *Amazing Grace.*
>
> The day before we cremated Caleb, we held a small viewing for his closest friends and family. We had given the pastor no instruction and the pastor sang that song. I had been driven to tears then, and I was driven to tears again as I watched the ad on television. A year and a half later, I was walking on Bourbon Street in New Orleans when I heard a street performer singing *Amazing Grace.* I had tears in my eyes then as well."
>
> Pam had a similar experience …
>
> "George was a Beatles fan. Many months after he died, while in a fast food restaurant and mid-bite of my hamburger, the piped-in music started with John Lennon's *Imagine* and a nail went into my heart."

There is so little of life we control. Grief's timing is among the uncontrollable. Expect experiences similar to these frequently over the first three to six months. The frequency is often based on how close you were to the deceased. Over the course of a year, they will lessen, but they may still happen from time to time.

Physical Symptoms

When grief covers us with its dark wings, it often resembles serious illness. We are emotionally and physically depleted and susceptible to a variety of symptoms. While these symptoms are often part of the grieving process, they may also indicate a more serious condition. It is advisable to consult a medical professional to have symptoms evaluated.

While it is important to be aware of these symptoms, they are not a sign of going crazy. If the symptoms are grief induced, they should pass or lessen by working through our grief. If you find any symptom to be overwhelming or unbearable, contact a medical professional. Commonly reported symptoms include:

chest discomfort	dizziness
sleep difficulties	dry mouth
poor appetite or overeating	crying
shakiness or trembling	exhaustion or weakness
numbness	shortness of breath
disorientation	listlessness
migraines or headache	heart palpitations

I feel like I'm falling apart, not just emotionally, but physically. Sometimes I feel like I'm going to die next. What's going on? What can I do?

There are many dimensions of the physical and emotional self to consider as you wind through the pathway of grief. Psychological, spiritual, nutritional, and social dimensions all play an important role as you struggle to find balance.

A loved one has died, suddenly, and it is a shock to the entire system because your thoughts and perceptions affect every cell and hormone in your body. One of the most neglected areas of health is the emotional component and its effect on physical well-being.

If you are unaware of the toll this shock can have on your body, you are not likely to take care of yourself when you need to most. Some people overindulge with nicotine, drugs, alcohol, sleep, or food.

If you are to prevent the ill effects of the loss from harming your physical body, you must pay close attention to the messages you are giving yourself. Are you giving yourself "die" messages because you wish it had been you who died instead of your loved one? Are you giving yourself "I don't deserve to live" messages because you believe there was something more you could have done to save them?

Your emotions are powerful. In her newsletter, *Health Wisdom for Women,* Dr. Christiane Northrup writes, "The brain and immune system communicate in two ways: By means of hormones that the brain regulates; and through protein molecules, called neuropeptides (or neurotransmitters) and receptors, which send messages back and forth. These same molecules are not only in your brain, but also in your stomach, your muscles, your glands, your bone marrow, your skin and all of your other organs and tissues. Since the network expands to every organ in the body, it means that every thought you think and emotion you feel is communicated to every cell in your body."

Willpower alone may not be enough to prevent self-destructive behavior. Many times we need a support group or therapist to assist in the process. Before going "over the edge," seek help. The resources chapter of this book contains many ideas that can assist you in finding a professional group or organization to act as a support network.

Emotional Ambushes

Deep pain and sadness, as if the death had just occurred, can surface at odd moments. Just when you think you're coping fine, along comes the dreaded ambush! Up from "nowhere" the rage resurfaces, the disbelief, the flashback, the horror, the insane feeling, the whatever. Just when you told yourself and your friends, "I'm finally beginning to feel better."

Emotional ambushes are particularly evident around special occasions such as birthdays, anniversaries, and holidays, or any time you are expected to participate in a celebration of some kind.

You may know exactly what kind of place or event triggers you (i.e. a particular store in the mall, the sound of children playing, the smell of pizza, a song, a football game), and you can chose to avoid those situations. However, sometimes the unexpected occurs—the tears begin to flow and the outrage returns. Pam had this type of experience.

"I remember going to the supermarket and seeing my loved one's favorite Campbells soup on the shelf. I dissolved into tears and the mascara ran in streams onto to my white blouse. You might try wearing sunglasses in public. I did and it helped disguise the red, puffy eyes and the raccoon look. I also carried tissues and told strangers that I was dealing with a lousy allergy attack. And sometimes I told the truth."

If practical, stop what you're doing and honor it. Have the feeling, weep the tears, beat the pillows; phone someone or everyone in your support group. Allow the full force of the pain to wash through you—it will pass.

A word of caution—if the "ambush" occurs while you are driving a car or other vehicle, pull over where it is safe. Driving with tears in your eyes and rage in your heart can be hazardous.

Grief and Dreams

Some people have dreams of the deceased and others do not. Each of us has a unique subconscious mind that copes with life and trauma differently. You probably know people who remember their dreams and others who rarely remember a thing. Similarly, how grief affects us in our dream world varies. If you don't have dreams of the deceased, don't worry.

If You Don't Dream

In *Intuition* magazine, Marlene King wrote an article entitled, "The Surrogate Dreamers: One couple's gift to a grieving friend." Marlene invited over a couple she knew for a causal Saturday night barbecue. The next night, Stephen, the forty-four-year-old husband in the couple, died of heart failure while dancing with his wife. Over the next week, Marlene helped her friend with details surrounding the tragic death. Marlene writes, "It was during this period that Janice told me she hoped to connect with Stephen through her dreams, but no dreams had come. Knowing that emotions often block us physically, I reassured her that her dreams would return, when she was less emotionally fragile."

A few days after this conversation, Marlene dreamt of Stephen. She saw him dressed in a tuxedo. She felt this odd, since Stephen usually dressed casually. She goes on to say, "I reported the dream to Janice . . . the absolute silence and lack of response on the other end of the phone made me question whether I was right to tell her about the dream. Unknown to me, she had elected to have Stephen cremated the day before, and had chosen to dress him in the same clothing he wore in my dream. For a while after that, it was as though my husband and I became Janice's 'surrogate dreamers.' Our love for her seemed to open us up to the dream communication that was temporarily unavailable to Janice due to her shattered emotional state."

If you find that you are not having dreams, know that this is normal. Our emotions can be so turbulent during these times that we are cut off from our dream source. Listen to others close to you. Listen to family and friends. What dreams are they having? If they don't bring it up, ask if you like. These dreams can carry messages for you as well.

If You Do Dream

A Dream Journal

Consider keeping a dream journal. Many people believe that dreams following closely after death are the deceased making contact. These dreams may be ones that you want to cherish and hold. If you remember your dreams, spend ten minutes each morning jotting down thoughts and impressions in your dream journal. If you only remember pieces of your dream, jot those down. Often just a few notes will spur other recollections.

Dreams of your deceased loved one can open up new avenues to healing, but you may not be aware you are having dreams or they may be hard to remember. One way to keep the dream upon waking is to keep still—don't move a muscle—don't get up to go to the bathroom or turn on the light. Start with any dream fragment that comes to your conscious mind and try to piece the entire dream back together. Or simply write down the dream fragment and the rest may come back later in the day. In her book, *Nature's Prozac,* Judith Sachs offers the following thoughts on remembering dreams, "Before you go to sleep at night, put a pad and pen on your bedside table. Tell yourself you are going to remember your dreams (this suggestion may take a few nights to penetrate.) As you relax in bed, give yourself permission to explore all the areas of your mind that you don't pay enough attention to during the day. We tend to be in REM sleep just before waking, so it's best to set your radio alarm to a soft music station rather than to the news or hard rock. This way you can wake slowly and take stock of what's going on in your mind."

Troublesome Dreams

Some grievers report nightmares or troublesome dreams. These dreams may involve a direct conflict between the dreamer and the deceased. Other times the dreamer may envision the deceased dying or in pain.

With sudden death we often have very little information. Dreams are where our subconscious mind works things through. If you awake from an unpleasant dream, realize it is your subconscious mind prompting you. Recall as much as you can. Try to fill in the blanks. Examine the dream the best you can. If you find it hard to face these dreams or have problems being objective, ask a trusted friend or psychotherapist to review them with you. Keeping a dream journal can also help you make sense of troublesome dreams.

Another way to handle disturbing dreams is to try to "reprogram" them. Think through your upsetting dream. Try to find the point within the dream where things become upsetting. Choose a different ending that would make you more comfortable. Visualize the dream playing out this way in your mind several times, especially before going to sleep. This can help change or diminish the dream's impact.

If nightmares are a problem, over-the-counter or prescription medications could be the cause. According to medical researcher Judith Sachs, if you are taking sleeping medications such as barbiturates or benzodiazepines (for anti-anxiety), these medications can give you nightmares. Additionally, some people have reported anti-depressants as causing vivid and shocking dreams. Also, getting off drugs can give you nightmares. So make sure you withdraw under a doctor's supervision and mention any side effects.

Communication Dreams

If you are a person who does dream, keep in mind that these dreams can be quite varied. Some may be peaceful and others may be disturbing. As you move through the process of grief, your subconscious mind will respond in varied and surprising ways. Brook had an intriguing dream shortly after her brother's death . . .

"I had my first dream three weeks after Caleb's death, which I was told was surprisingly soon, and I have had many since. I think that since I try so hard to be the foundation for others, I work through a lot of my grief and feelings in my sleep.

Three weeks after Caleb's death, my book on single parenting was due. In an attempt to meet the deadline I took three days to curl up in a hotel and get some solid writing done. I usually stay up until one or two when I'm on my writing escapades. Yet on this night, I had an overwhelming feeling to lie down and read some of my notes. I plopped onto the bed, my feet propped up on the pillows and my head near the bottom. I still had my contact lenses in, and being only 9 p.m. I knew I'd get at least five more hours of work in before calling it a night.

The next thing I knew it was 6:45 a.m. I was in the exact same place on the bed and I had dreamt of my brother.

We were in our childhood home in northern Wisconsin. Our rooms, as in reality when we were kids, were directly across from one another. I was in my room, as I had been during the week I had stayed up north after Caleb's death. In the dream I was fully aware that my brother was dead, and I was grieving it with my entire soul.

Suddenly there was the familiar thud of footsteps down the hallway. Caleb's, no doubt. At first, I peered out my door a bit nervously. I could see Caleb standing in his room. Every detail of his face, body, and clothing were clear to me. Caleb was wearing the clothes he had been cremated in. He was rustling through his room's contents with a frustrated expression. Then he saw me. 'Brook, where are all my clothes?' he asked, peering into his duffel bag.

I stood rigid. I knew he was dead, yet I knew he was there. 'Caleb, you're dead.' I said simply.

He looked up and said he knew that, but that he had to take care of a few things. First, however, he wanted to change his clothes.

'Where are you going?' I asked.

'I'm just going to see a few people,' he said grabbing something off his desk, though I couldn't tell what it was.

'Caleb,' I said gently, 'I don't think that's a good idea. Everyone thinks you're dead. And, well, you might scare some people.'

'Really?' He asked, with his head tilted in an inquisitive look.

'Caleb, don't leave without hugging me,' I said, tears filling my eyes. My brother took me in his strong arms. 'You cannot go,' I repeated; 'Everyone thinks that you are dead. Please don't go—I'll never see you again.'

He tilted my head up toward his and wiped a wisp of hair away from my face. Staring straight into my eyes with his little smirk he said,

'You poor little children.' In that moment I knew he was saying he lived on, though I never understood in what way.

Feeling somewhat foggy, I got up and slowly moved around the room. I had this feeling of incredible closeness with Caleb—so close I was tingling. Over the course of my writing weekend I had brought one large box that I wanted to go through during my breaks. Inside were photos, papers, and other miscellaneous things from Caleb's desk drawers. I wanted to sort through and divide up the photos for his friends and find any estate paperwork. At that point, I had yet to open the container.

I walked over and opened the box. I reached in and pulled out a picture of Caleb. I reached in again and pulled out a card. On the inside of the card was a quote in Caleb's handwriting. The quote was taken from Jonathan Livingston Seagull:

'If our friendship depends on things like space and time,
then we have already destroyed our brotherhood.
But overcome space and all you have is here;
Overcome time and all you have is now.
And in the middle of here and now
Don't you think we might see each other once or twice . . .'

To this day, when I recount this dream, people ask me what I think it meant. Many want to know if I feel I had actual contact with my brother or if that was Caleb trying to speak to me. All I can say is that for a night when we should have been the furthest apart—separated by death and the unknown—I had never felt closer to him."

Important Things to Remember on the Pathway

- Remember, if someone says something like, "It's time now to get on with your life," you have the right to say, "In my time and God's time, not in your time."
- If you want to wear black you can. You can also wear any other color you want during the time you are grieving.
- If you need isolation for a while that is okay. You will be with people when you are ready.
- Find a safe time and place to "go crazy" if you want to. Go yell in the woods, throw rocks at trees, swear at the TV or wear the deceased's clothes to bed.
- Be kind to yourself. Perfection is not necessary; there is no arriving, only going. There is no need to judge where you are in your journey. It is enough that you are traveling.
- Make a commitment to your future. Commitment enables you to bypass all your fears, mental escapes and justifications, so that you can face whatever you are experiencing in the moment.
- Get out of your own way. The main block to healing from loss is the thought that we shouldn't be where we are, that we should already be further along in our growth than we perceive ourselves to be. Let these expectations go.
- Affirm yourself. Who you were and who you will be are insignificant compared to who you are.
- Fear is not always a bad thing. If you allow yourself to experience fear fully, without trying to push it away, an inner shift takes place that initiates transformation.

There is no experience that exists in this life that does not have the power to lead you to greater knowledge and growth. Major loss can only become a vehicle for creating a renewed life when we stop thinking of it as punishment and start to see it as process. This process begins with the death of a relationship and proceeds through a period of grief and mourning, in which the death is recognized and accepted, and ends with a rebirth.

Feeling the Presence of the Deceased

Feeling the presence of the deceased is similar to the "phantom limb" syndrome some report after losing a limb. Many grievers feel like they have lost a part of themselves. Some spouses feel the deceased's presence in bed. Hearing footsteps, smelling that person's scent, hearing a voice or seeing a fleeting image of the deceased is common during the grief process. Often this occurs as we try to rationalize and understand what is happening. Is someone sending us a message? Are we being told something? Are we "losing" it?

In her book, *Surviving Grief,* Dr. Catherine M. Sanders writes about the flicker phenomenon, "a perception seen at the outside edges of our visual field as a flickering shadow. Immediately, thoughts of the deceased come to mind, but when we look directly at that area, nothing is there."

These sightings or feelings may well be the deceased trying to comfort us, trying to get through somehow. When we try to rationalize and make sense of these experiences, we rob them of their magic. Just as we don't understand why these unexpected deaths occur, we must try not to overanalyze these moments—simply let them offer comfort.

When You Don't Feel the Presence of the Deceased

Some survivors become distressed because they don't feel the presence of the deceased the way someone else does. Try not to judge yourself as unloved or unimportant to your loved one because you do not feel them "communicating" with you. Try not to be hard on yourself because you can't "tune in."

Some people may have a hard time believing that feeling the presence of the deceased is possible. If this is the case, look for simple signs that may indicate your loved one's presence. For instance, after George died, Pam heard his favorite song in an elevator and felt he was there with her. When her dad died, she saw a falcon (he used to train them) circling above her on a nature walk and instantly felt connected with him.

Communicating with Your Loved One (and If You Haven't)

It can give some grievers an extraordinary amount of comfort to "communicate" with their loved one in some way. In Pam's practice she encourages clients to say what was unsaid before their loved one died so unexpectedly. For instance, one widow from the 9/11 attacks who was asleep when her husband left for work and didn't kiss him goodbye that day wrote her husband a love letter and kissed her signature at the bottom. She then read the letter aloud, first in Pam's office, then to her grief group, and then she put the letter in the ground next to his headstone.

At one of her sessions she told me, "There are some days when I talk to him as I'm driving to work. I ask him to watch over the children and to be there for me when it's my time. Sometimes I think I hear him responding, other times it feels like I'm not making any connection. But it helps me to talk to him and I don't care if people think I'm crazy."

One of Brook's clients Beth felt different from other mourners because she did not talk to her mother who had died suddenly. All of her sisters reported regularly communicating with or talking to their mother. As Beth explored her emotions, she discovered she was nervous about reaching out to her mother. *What if she doesn't approve of the choices I have made? What if she can see my whole life now, and doesn't like some of the things I have done?* Brook encouraged Beth to open up little by little. Our own self-doubt can hamper our ability to communicate with our loved one. True love between people is unconditional, loving our strengths and weaknesses, even when they do not understand or agree with them.

The World Becomes Dreamlike

Many people who have lost someone suddenly find the world becomes a surreal place. It's almost as if we are floating without seeing or comprehending. Everything becomes a blur as the concept of time disappears. Days are measured by: one day after he died, two days after he died…all standard concepts fade away. Some have described it as slogging through molasses, a slow-motion movie, a feeling like they are not in their body. Perhaps this is nature's way of slowing us down to heal.

Helen Fitzgerald, author of *The Mourning Handbook,* writes, "During this initial period of grief you will feel a numbness and a disassociation with the world around you. People who are going through this often tell me that they feel as if they are watching a play in which they are but spectators. Others feel that what has happened is only a bad dream from which they will wake up to find everything back to normal." Know that this is part of the body coping with tragic loss. Our bodies and minds know better than to dump us back into reality after such an intense blow. Therefore we are nudged slowly, step-by-step, back into day-to-day life. Much of the world will remain out of focus, allowing us to gather our bearings one step at a time.

A Time to Withdraw

Many people will experience a state of numbness while moving through grief. The world may take on a dreamlike quality or seem to go on separate from them. Often experiences or people that once evoked joy and happiness evoke nothing at all. Activities once enjoyed seem foreign.

Some people spend a relatively short time in this numb state, as short as a few days, while others find it lingers. This is part of how our bodies help to protect us from the overwhelming emotions caused by our loved one's death. We become numb and filter through information as we are able, instead of all at once. The feelings will come back, but it will take time.

Hand-in-hand with exhaustion, performing our day-to-day activities, even if they are ones we used to enjoy, may seem overwhelming. Most people are unable to maintain a variety of activities immediately after this shock. Minimize the expectations on yourself to avoid adding to your stress. Contact event or group coordinators to let them know that you will be taking some time off, indefinitely. For example, if you are part of your child's home and school program, a softball coach, or part of a regular bowling league—take a break. At this point you need only focus on working through these hard times.

This advice runs contrary to what many will say. Many people will urge you to "stay involved," "take on more," "try something new," or "get back in the swing of things." Yet this advice doesn't make sense. If you don't have the energy or focus to take care of yourself, why should you be taking on additional responsibilities? Sure, they may take your mind off of your grief for a short period—but you still have to do your grieving. There simply is no bypass.

Hurtful Self-talk

Be aware of the following hurtful self-talk that can block the grieving process—keeping you stuck. The following statements are examples of commonly held misconceptions that may run through our minds.

My loved one is with God for a reason, so I shouldn't feel bad.
Grief is a mental illness.

It is wrong to feel anger at the deceased and it shouldn't be expressed.

If I acknowledge the loss, I'm afraid I will die too.

I should have died first.

If I allow my grief to surface, I'll go crazy.

If I grieve, people will think I'm weak.

If I appear sad too often, it will bring my family down.

If I cry in church, my fellow congregants will think I've lost faith.

If my children see me grieving, it will make them feel worse.

The deceased wouldn't want me to grieve.

I should grin and bear it and put it behind me.

If I stop grieving people will expect me to be happy again.

When you find yourself running on the treadmill of hurtful self-talk, it is important to come up with a positive statement for balance. Write down your destructive or hurtful thought and then write down a more positive, realistic thought. For example, "The deceased wouldn't want me to grieve," is an unhelpful statement. You could write, "The deceased would understand and respect the full spectrum of my emotions." Whenever a negative thought enters your mind, replace it with a positive, more realistic statement.

Impulsive Living

While some grievers withdraw, others will compulsively pursue activities. The thought process often goes like this, "Life is short. I'd better do everything now that I always wanted to do . . . spend all the money, sell the house and move to Hawaii, write that book, divorce my wife, etc." Others will take unnecessary risks.

It's imperative to carefully monitor your behavior during the first year. Do not make impulsive decisions. Do not sell your house, change locations, divorce a partner, etc. Wait until the fog has lifted and you can clearly see the options available to you.

Instant Replays and Obsessive Thoughts

At some point in our grief work, we are likely to find ourselves recounting the days with our loved one in our minds. We may also play out different scenarios of the death, trying to understand what has happened. For some, the review completely preoccupies the mind, and despite our wishes, we can think of nothing else.

As is the case with post traumatic stress disorder, you may find yourself living and reliving the experiences you had with your loved one during the days, hours, or minutes just before the death occurred. "If only I had not taken that road . . . If only I had said 'don't go . . .' If only I had been there I might have prevented the accident . . ." and on and on.

With the first news of loss, our mind acts as a filter. It immediately sifts through the facts and details offering only the barest to keep us informed. Too much detail would be more than we could bear. So our mind filters and filters until our bodies and hearts can cope with a little more. At some point, when the body has recovered somewhat, the mind lets larger blocks of information in. At this point, by human instinct, we look for resolution. We struggle to make sense of what has happened and that is where the instant replay begins. We explore every option—even the outlandish. These explorations are what allow us to slowly internalize the fact that life, as we once knew it, has changed.

This is a pivotal point in the grieving process. At this point, or close to it, we are finally acknowledging the reality of the death.

The "If Only" Mind Game

"If only" is the game of guilt that plagues many survivors. In cases of unexpected death, the "if only" questions surface intensely. The situation is so "out of control" that our human nature fights and searches for a way to control the uncontrollable. As we yearn to make sense of the senseless, often the only route of control we find is to blame ourselves.

"I should have known" or "If only I had talked to him for two minutes longer" or "I shouldn't have left her bedside" are sentiments that those who grieve may say to themselves. Realize this guilt is a way of trying to gain control over the uncontrollable, and then work to let it go. Each time it enters, remember that this is our longing for control, but don't give in to the guilt. You cannot change what has happened and odds are you couldn't have changed it beforehand. No one knows these things are going to happen—no one has that much control or foresight. Brook found that she ran on the "I should've known" treadmill.

"I have talked with many of the people surviving the loss of a loved one and in every situation the one who is grieving can somehow tie blame to themselves. Even with my brother's case, where it was such a freak accident, we could all find ways that we "should have known" or "should have been able to prevent it." Yet as each of us told our stories of prevention, others could see there were simply too many holes. None of us could have stopped what occurred."

Pam's client Barbara, whose only son, Brian, died in Iraq while with the U.S. Army, talked very candidly about her guilt:

"Brian wanted desperately to serve his country especially after the 9/11 attacks. I knew violence of any kind wasn't in his nature so I didn't understand his sudden change in values. He insisted that not only would this be a way to serve his country, but would also be a way to get some valuable training that he could use in his civilian life. I don't know too many mothers who would actively push their sons to go to war and I certainly wasn't one of them. But I wish I had been more adamant about his not going. What can you do though? Take away their car keys and their iPod? He was a grown man, making a grown man's decision. And he was my little boy. I should have figured out how to stop him."

Barbara has since realized that there really was no way to convince her son otherwise. She remains proud of him and has lessened her feelings of guilt. She recently told Pam, "We all make decisions that impact our lives. Despite my objections, Brian did what he felt in his heart was right and honorable and I will respect him as long as I live."

Don't run yourself around this wheel of pain. If you find that you cannot stop trying to tie the blame to yourself, relay your story to a professional counselor, therapist, or pastor. *While we grieve, we are not objective.* These professionals can help us to see how unrealistic and unfounded these thoughts are.

Fear

Throughout our grief work, fear can be debilitating. Some people experience fear in a small number of areas, while others are overwhelmed by it. It is perfectly natural to be fearful. We have experienced the most unexpected tragedy. Common fears include: fearing any situation that remotely resembles how the loved one died, fearing that others we love will be harmed, fearing we will be unable to go on, fearing we will die ourselves, and fearing the simplest activities will lead to tragedy.

Fear serves several purposes. In the initial stages of grief, it gives us something to focus on besides the death that has taken place. It also offers potential control. If we fear that riding in a car could kill us and we choose not to ride in a car, we create the illusion of control. As explained earlier, with tragic death it's common to seek any control we can find. Most of the time, fear will run its course naturally. If you find that you have any fear that is, or is becoming, debilitating, or that manifests itself as panic attacks, talk to a professional.

As you think about this chapter, remember that grief will be a unique experience for each one of us. If you experience symptoms that aren't listed here, or fewer symptoms, that is okay and normal. What is important to remember is that you need to work through these feelings. Sometimes you will require another person's help. Monitor yourself on the path through grief. You know, in your heart of hearts, whether you are walking down the path or stuck at the beginning or middle. There are many things we must face in life alone, but grief need not be one of them.

Chapter Four
Myths and Misunderstandings
of the Grieving Process

"Grief doesn't have to be a passive thing that happens to you.
Grieving is first and foremost something you do to heal your
wounds after experiencing a terrible loss in your life."
—*Bob Deitz*, Life after Loss

Grieving is like a foreign land to most of us, a land where we find ourselves speaking and hearing an inner language we cannot comprehend. Because it can help to have a guide in a foreign land, this chapter will describe the common myths and misunderstandings to help you navigate the territory within.

It is the rare school or family environment that teaches what to expect either emotionally or pragmatically when life collapses in tragedy, especially with the advent of sudden and unexpected death. A sudden loss can put one into a whirlwind of emotions and visceral responses, twisting and turning us until we are set down in a place that feels as foreign as another planet. Like a tornado, there is no time for preparations. We have little or no warning.

We don't expect life to be so tenuous, so fragile. However, once our lives are touched by the experience of tragic loss, we never look at life in quite the same way. We become acutely aware of the delicate nature of the human organism, and life becomes precious in a way it never was before.

You can consciously shift from feeling that "grief is something that happens to you" to "grieving is something you do to heal." Remember when life feels out of control, and it's bound to during this time, that you *do* have control over *how* you will grieve. This can be very empowering.

In this chapter we will cover many of the common grieving myths that people hold today. You may have encountered these false beliefs already. By understanding these myths, we are more prepared to challenge them when they occur.

Myth #1
Death is death, sudden or long-term, and we all grieve the same way.
Of course there will be some commonalities in the grieving process. Truth is, depending on our life experiences, age, sex, resiliency, number of previous losses, health, cultural expectations, and relationship to the deceased, we will each "do grief" in our own unique way. No two of us are exactly alike in our histories and in our relationship to the deceased.

The myth is that those of us who have lost someone with no warning should grieve and recoup in the same way, at the same pace, as someone who experiences loss as the result of long-term illness or injury. How easy it would be if all of us grieved the same and we could just print a rulebook, but that isn't the case. It's not important to explain to others that your grief will be different, it's simply important that *you* understand your unique pathway through grief.

Myth #2
By keeping busy I can lessen or eliminate my grief.
In an attempt to avoid the pain, grievers may choose to keep busy. We may find ourselves cleaning the house, dusting bookshelves, cleaning closets, rushing to get back to the office, and engaging in other time-consuming tasks. However, you will find this "busyness" is simply a sidetrack that will only work for a short time.

There is no way around grief. Keeping busy may temporarily alter your mood (as do alcohol, drugs, or overeating), but you will eventually need to face the reality that someone you cared for deeply is *gone.*

Myth #3

I must be going crazy or "losing it."

Sudden death creates trauma for the survivors on many levels. Trauma victims may not behave as people would expect. Many people report feeling numb and indifferent. Those around you may expect you to be more openly distraught, and you may hear comments like, "My, you sure are taking this well," or "I expected to find you in a more disturbed state." You may find yourself walking around in a fog with an inability to make decisions. You may behave in a matter-of-fact way and you may appear to be functioning at a rather high level. Blank stares are common as the mind tries to grapple with the unimaginable. You may not weep, cry, or wail for some time. These behaviors may puzzle onlookers and family members, yet they have been reported by the majority of those facing sudden death. These emotions are *normal and temporary.*

In some native cultures it is perfectly acceptable to "go crazy." Yet, in our modern culture, we medicate people to protect them (and their families) from their feelings. Why are we so afraid of feelings? Doctors have been known to prescribe medications, especially for women, to get them through the hard time, to get them over the difficult period. What they are doing in essence is delaying the normal grieving process. Going crazy (within limits) is perfectly acceptable and a healthy part of the grief process. As we let out painful emotions, we encourage the process of healing.

Myth #4

I will need to make sure I don't grieve for too long—one year should be enough.

Sometimes societal and religious beliefs impose rules for grief, such as time limits, what we should wear, how we should behave, when and where we should talk about the death, and to whom. With sudden death, as with any death, we must find our own way through to embrace life again. Readjustment after sudden death often takes two years or more, and in some ways we never "get over" the loss completely.

Our expression of grief needs to come out of our need to make meaning or sense from what feels like meaningless tragedy, and no time limit can be set on that.

Myth #5
If I express my anger at God or the circumstances of the death, I am a bad person and will "pay" for it.
Anger is an extremely uncomfortable emotion for some of us, but it is one of the most important ones to express. If you become angry with God, don't judge yourself too harshly. As Earl Grollman writes, "It's okay to scream at God. He can take it." The Psalms are full of raging at God about injustices. We believe God can handle anything we throw his way. However, if you find your anger is becoming out of control (i.e., breaking valuables, threatening or preparing to kill someone, or wanting to burn down the church or hospital, or if you have suicidal thoughts), immediately seek appropriate professional help and guidance.

Myth #6
My friends tell me it is time to let go. Since others have acclimated to life again, I should too.
According to *The Encyclopedia of Death and Dying*, until the twentieth century, maintaining a bond with the deceased had been considered a normal part of the bereavement process in Western society. In contrast, in the twentieth century, the view prevailed that successful mourning required the bereaved to emotionally detach themselves from the deceased. The work of Sigmund Freud contributed significantly to this view, largely as a result of the paper "Mourning and Melancholia," which he wrote in 1917. Grief, as Freud saw it, freed the mourner from his or her attachments to the deceased so that when the work of mourning was completed, mourners were free to move ahead and become involved in new relationships. When one looks at Freud's writing regarding personal losses in his life, one learns that Freud understood that grief was not a process that resulted in cutting old attachments. Nonetheless, his theory took on a life of its own, and the mourners were advised to put the past behind them. This practice still continues into the twenty-first century.

Unfortunately, misunderstood psychology can cause some people to impose a false grief schedule onto you. However, you can choose to hold onto the memories of love received, of lessons learned, and of gifts imparted. You can continue to love the deceased in a special place in your heart. As opposed to what your family and friends may be telling you, the desire to hold onto an important part of your history will not keep you stuck. One example is Brook's mother. She will always say she is the mother of two children—but one of her children is deceased. *A death does not erase the person nor his or her impact from our life.* Remembering the deceased and reliving special times will still enable you to get on with your life. Although the "I choose not to forget" stance may seem contradictory to the concept of letting go, it will actually help enhance your recovery and give you some control over a situation that feels out of control.

After a while, your friends and relatives may, in an effort to have you start living again (according to their schedule), encourage you to "let go of the past and move on with your life." They mean well, and they are partially right. However, you may have some unfinished business to do first. We suggest you hold onto the feelings you have about the deceased, that you continue to treasure the memories— that you hold onto the past as you honor the present and move into the future.

Myth #7
I must wear black for a designated time period or I will dishonor the person who died.
The custom of funeral black is ancient. It originated back in the days when people felt that spirits, some of them ill willed and ill tempered, hovered around a corpse. Black was worn to make the living inconspicuous and less apt to be bothered by evil spirits.

By the nineteenth century, definite rules were in place concerning the length of mourning and the clothing one was to wear during each phase. Two years of deep mourning was expected of widows—no more, no less. According to *Death in Early America* by Margaret M. Coffin, "During the Victorian times a woman mourning the death of a father or mother or one of her own offspring wore dark clothes for a year. This mourning period lasted half the time a wife traditionally mourned her husband, but the garb was similar. Mourning garb was worn for six months for grandparents, for brothers and sisters, and for a friend who leaves you an inheritance. Mourning for an aunt or uncle or for a nephew or niece was an obligation of only three months, and white trim was allowed throughout."

Fortunately, American mourning customs have changed considerably and the depth of our loss is no longer measured by the luster of our clothing. Further, the clothing we wear has a definite effect on how we feel about ourselves—brighter colors will help lift our spirits and the spirits of those around us. So don't hesitate to wear whatever clothing makes you feel best.

A woman that Pam knows wore red, white, and blue at her husband's funeral and for many months (on and off) during her mourning. Her husband had served in the war and was an American patriot when he died suddenly. Her choice of clothing clearly helped her to honor him.

Myth #8

I won't have to grieve as much and I will feel better if I use alcohol or medication to alleviate my sadness.

Some survivors will use, or increase their use, of alcohol or antidepressants. Grief does not disappear. It goes underground temporarily and waits to be expressed. People may mistakenly believe that "If I drink (drug) to get over it, then the grief will be gone when I'm sober." Nothing could be further from the truth. When you stop taking these mood-altering drugs, you must start the process of grieving where you left off. There is no shortcut.

Of course it isn't difficult to find a doctor willing to prescribe a sedative, and it's easy to buy a bottle of gin, but using substances as a long-term solution does more harm than good. It will add to your confusion and stall the process of your recovery.

However, if you are experiencing extreme anxiety, depression, or if you cannot get adequate rest to face emotions and decisions, then temporary relief offered by medication may be needed in order to function. It is not uncommon for loved ones to use prescribed sleep aids or anxiety medications short-term during the immediate aftermath of a loss. A competent professional should help make this decision.

You may also want to consider our online resources to find a list of natural, herbal remedies that many people have found helpful.

As Bob Deitz says in *Life after Loss,* "To take control of your grief, you must face your loss head on with all your senses working. You can't do that while you are blissfully tranquilized."

Myth #9

If I talk about the loss of my loved one I'll feel worse.

You've got to talk about it, and talk about it, and talk about it some more. Find someone who will listen and talk until you can't talk anymore . . . at least for the moment. Then when you need to talk again, start all over with your story. You cannot move through your grief unless you experience it. Hiding it or denying it will only prolong it. Meeting and talking with other people who have been through this process will help you. Ellen Sue Stern writes in *Living with Loss: Meditations for Grieving Widows,* "It's essential to allow yourself to talk as much as you want; healing is hastened by reminiscing about your husband [or loved one], processing the last days of his life, the funeral and any other details surrounding his death. For now, choose only to spend time with people who are supportive and understanding, who can lovingly listen as long as you need to talk."

ELLEN'S STORY

Ellen was at the beginning stage of readjustment to the unexpected loss of her husband of thirty-eight years. She felt she had no friends in the community. Her sense of isolation was enormous and overwhelming to the point where she felt she needed medication for the anxiety she was experiencing. She was also dealing for the first time with financial and estate matters she knew very little about. This was creating even more anxiety for her. She attended a support group where she found immediate acceptance and validation. She was literally lifted to a higher, more positive place after attending just two meetings. Ellen is now attending the group regularly and is feeling much less "crazy" and more in control of the process. With the group's support, she asked her attorney and accountant to slow down a bit and explain things more clearly. She put off making too many decisions and found out from a group member where she could get more information about real estate issues, and she allowed the group to give her feedback on her financial concerns.

Myth #10

Shouldn't I be strong enough to "tough it out" by myself?

Don't expect to get through this time alone. You need all the support you can get. Your need for support may be wearing on your family and friends. You may be getting the mistaken idea that after a while you should tough it out on your own. We can only recover from our loss if we are in an atmosphere where honesty and loving acceptance are encouraged and where our burdens are shared. Seek out or develop a support group where you can share your pain, process any lingering guilt, and see hope for the future. One of the best ways to "see" your personal growth is to join a support group that will assure you of "how far you've come." In a group, we see others who are back where we once were in the journey, or ahead of us in their healing, some who are ready to begin new relationships, and others who are at the very beginning of the process. Wherever they are in their grieving you will find many common threads and gain inspiration as you share your experiences together.

Healing from the trauma of sudden loss in isolation is extremely difficult and may even be hazardous to your health. When you're having a problem, isn't it a comfort to talk to someone who has "been there, done that?" There is something comforting about being with others who understand the painful process and life-style alterations you are experiencing. Lots of heads nodding in agreement while you talk of your suffering as well as your accomplishments in the face of it all can be very healing indeed. According to research, one of the benefits that a group can offer is a boost to the immune system! In helping others, you will find yourself moving a little more quickly in the healing process. Groups, large and small, professionally operated or member-run, can provide not only understanding and support, but also an exchange of useful, pragmatic information.

Myth #11

I've done something wrong because some of my family and friends are turning away from me.

There will be times when family and friends turn away from you because they are experiencing their own grief. They may believe that if they interact with you by expressing their feelings they will needlessly compound your grief. Others simply want you to "move on"—they don't want to see you hurt any more. If your family and friends cannot be supportive you will feel uncared for and angry. Don't try to make them do or be what they are incapable of—look for support elsewhere.

Myth #12

I should be relieved that they didn't suffer a long and lingering illness.

You may hear some say, "well at least he died quickly—be happy for that." Perhaps you are thinking this way if the person you lost suddenly was much older or had been suffering. But for most of us, the sudden death was an untimely one—one that occurred much too soon for the person and those left behind. There may be little, if any, relief in the knowledge that they died quickly.

Myth #13

Someday I'll have another (spouse, child, parent, lover . . .) and that person will erase the pain and replace what I have lost.

Yes, you may some day have "another," but to expect that person to be a replacement for the one you have lost not only places an unfair burden on them, but is an expectation that will also set you up for further pain. It is a healthy and hopeful attitude to take comfort in knowing you will love and form similar relationships in the future and at the same time to face the realization that no one can be replaced by another.

Myth #14

Once I am done with one stage of grief, I will simply move on to the next.

With the popularity of the well-known "Five Stages of Grief" (Kübler-Ross), some people mistakenly believe that grief is a linear process. As mentioned before, recovery is not like an elevator that takes you from the basement of despair to the penthouse of peace and understanding. It is more like a maze where you go forward a bit, move back a few steps, cover the same ground again, and find yourself at the beginning. Like a fun house hall of mirrors, you see yourself over and over again, distorted and misshapen until you come out the other side.

Myth #15

If I relive the good times, I'll stay stuck in the pain.

There are memories that keep us blocked or stuck and those that can move one forward into life. Over time you will learn to recognize the difference. For now, don't be concerned that your memories of your loved one will keep you stuck.

Myth #16

Children really don't understand death and probably don't need to be included in the funeral plans or memorial services.

As mentioned in Chapter 9, Helping Children Grieve, depending on the developmental stage of the child, many children do understand death and feel the loss deeply. When the death is sudden and unexpected, a child's trust in a safe world is altered. By all means, depending on age and ability, try to include the child in the funeral plans or memorial service. Invite them to write a short note or draw a picture about how they feel to be placed in the casket. Some small children may be frightened by the sight of a dead person and you will need to honor this fear. Don't ever push a child to do something that frightens or disturbs them. Likewise, if they are clear and coherent in their requests to be included, do not hold them back. It is certainly in the child's best interest to encourage participation in a way that offers them closure and a small measure of control in this out-of-control situation.

Myth #17

To properly honor the deceased, I must have the standard wake and burial.

While many people are comfortable with and will choose a standard funeral, there are many other options. When Brook lost her brother, the thought of a funeral didn't seem right to her family. They felt Caleb would rather have a party or celebration in his memory. They chose to throw a party at his favorite pub and restaurant in town. Over four hundred people came and businesses from all over town donated food and beverages. Instead of a tombstone at the local cemetery, Brook and her mother chose a bronze plaque with a favorite quote mounted on a rock at Caleb's favorite lake. Do what feels best to you. Don't let the funeral home or your clergy-person talk you out of creating a wake, memorial service, or funeral that better fits what you feel the deceased would have wanted. (See the Appendix for forms to help plan arrangements.)

Myth #18

I am scared that if I grieve, I'll "get over my loss." I don't want to forget him!

Grief is not something we 'get over' or heal from as if it were an illness. It is a journey to a new stage of life. The goal is not forgetting or resolving. The goal is reconciliation with life.

In times of pain and loss, we have a tendency to want to hold on to every moment and every memory. Many grievers also avoid disrupting the deceased's personal items. Wives may leave their husband's clothes in the closet. Parents may close the door on a child's room. When you are ready, storing or giving away these items does not mean you are discounting the memories.

The fear of forgetting the deceased or the fear that our memories will fade is a powerful fear, but when we hold on to everything they owned, we stifle, slow, and sometimes even stop growth. Ultimately, the goal is a balance between holding on and letting go. Cherish your special memories, hold them, journal them, and don't give them up. But at the same time, you can look forward to growth and the energy that returns when you are able to let go of some of the material reminders.

Myth #19

Help, I'm stuck on instant replay. I can't get this out of my thoughts—something is wrong with me.

One of the horrors of instant replay is the persistent questioning of the choices we made. For example: Could I have called the ambulance sooner? If I'd known CPR would it have made a difference? Were there warning signs of the condition that I missed? Could I have done anything at all to prevent it? This kind of constant replay over an extended period blocks acceptance and closure.

Instant replay is the mind's way of coming to terms with the unfathomable. Some instant replay is necessary, but too much can keep us stuck. If your own instant replay is becoming an obsession, consider setting a ten-minute timer and obsess for ten minutes, then get on with your day.

Another technique is what therapists call "thought stopping." This is a technique where you consciously stop the thought and deliberately change the subject. This is not a complicated task and is easier to do than you might think.

If the circumstances of the deceased's death were particularly gruesome or statistically unbelievable, you may be replaying it over and over in your mind. If you have a horrible image of your loved one's last minutes or hours that runs over and over like a bad movie, first acknowledge the horror, and then work to shift to an image that is more pleasant, like when you first met, for example.

Paul G. Stoltz, PhD, writes in his book *Adversity Quotient: Turning Obstacles into Opportunities:* "Arm yourself with STOPPERS. Whenever a crisis strikes, anxiety is a frequent—and useless—response. It also spreads like an emotional wild-fire making it impossible to apply rational steps to better cope with the problem. Soon you start to "catastrophize" and feel helpless and hopeless. You squander energy and time worrying. To avoid imagining the worst will happen, use what I call "stoppers" to regain control.

- "When you feel overwhelmed, slap your knee or any hard surface. Shout, "Stop!" The sting will shock you into a more rational state. Some people leave a rubber band around their wrist. When they feel anxiety, they stretch it six inches and let it go.
- Focus intently on an irrelevant object, such as a pen, the pattern of the wallpaper or a piece of furniture. If your mind is removed from the crisis, even for a moment, you can return with the calm you need to take effective action.
- Take an activity break. Just fifteen or twenty minutes of brisk walking or other exercise will clear your mind, raise your energy, and flood your brain with endorphins—chemicals that put you in a more optimistic mood.
- Put yourself in a setting where you're dwarfed by your surroundings. Catastrophizing makes problems larger than life. A shift in perspective will cut them down to size. Drive to the beach and look out over the ocean . . . stand at the base of a large tree . . . gaze up at the clouds . . . or listen to a great piece of music and let the grandeur wash over you."

Myth #20
This kind of thing doesn't happen in my family.

Your life experience to this point may have been death free and now you are suddenly dealing with violent or traumatic death. You may be thinking, *We live in a good neighborhood, we never took drugs, we were church going, God-fearing, so how come this kind of thing happened in my family?*

We are applying what appears to be logical thinking to an illogical situation. This kind of thinking is also a form of denial. The best way to work through denial is to continue working with the situation, absorbing reality little by little as you are able.

A great book about this is *When Bad Things Happen to Good People* by Harold S. Kushner. Rabbi Kushner writes, "Laws of nature do not make exceptions for nice people. A bullet has no conscience; neither does a malignant tumor or an automobile gone out of control. That is why good people get sick and hurt as much as anyone."

Myth #21

There must be something wrong with me. I'm not crying.

Everyone else is, but not me. Maybe I didn't care as much for him/her as I thought!

You may not be crying, but this doesn't mean you have no heart. If you are not crying, you may be blocked by the fear that once you start crying, you will not be able to stop. You may have been taught that strong people don't cry in public, or your cultural upbringing may have something to do with your inability to shed tears. In any case, you may need to learn how!

Shedding tears can help you release sadness that might become "stuck" in your body. Crying has been referred to as "the oat bran of the spirit and the cleanser of the soul." There are sound scientific reasons for the relief and calmness that follow the shedding of tears. Research has shown that healthy people cry more. When you cry, your tears release chemicals that help you cope with stress and pain. According to doctor's reports, tears contain encephalins, which can dampen physical or emotional pain and release ACTH, which has a calming effect.

Myth #22

I'm not grieving right—I should be doing something differently.

Perhaps I went back to work too soon. If I really loved him (or her), I'd be more devastated!

These internal self-judgments can block grief and are harmful and self-defeating. Perhaps you are looking at the way others grieve and are comparing yourself to them. Just as no two people are alike on this planet, no two people will "do grief" in exactly the same way. Some people will function at a very high level and some will not function at all. Some people will become introspective; others will cry, rant, scream, and rage at the drop of a hat. These differences are largely influenced by the stage of grief you are in and your personality type. Cultural differences are also at play here, and men have a tendency to grieve differently than women. Another important variable is the number of losses you have experienced in your life. Multiple losses compound and will influence how you handle your grief. We've said it many times: we all grieve in our own unique way.

Myth #23
I should feel guilty.
If you were not directly responsible for the death, you may be suffering from what is called "survivor guilt." In *Survivor Guilt,* author Aphrodite Matsakis, PhD, writes that "survivor guilt involves asking the existential question of why you suffer less than someone else, or why you lived while others died."

Struggling with the question, "Why them, not me?" can create so much anxiety, pain, and self-doubt that you stay stuck in your grief much longer and more intensely than needed. You may feel that guilt is the way to "pay penance" for surviving, or that intense guilt is a way to honor your lost loved one. However, they want more for us, much more. Process your guilt with a trusted friend, therapist, or clergyperson. The best way to honor the deceased is to move through your guilt, put down the stick you use to beat yourself with, and move on.

Myth #24
I shouldn't feel so angry.
Angry feelings directed at your loved one can be the most upsetting of all emotions. Yet, if you do not express your anger, it will keep you blocked. It may surprise you, but expressing your anger at the unexpected loss can ultimately help you feel less angry. Your spiritual and emotional growth are at stake if you believe there is no room for anger and hateful feelings. You are human. In addition, holding onto anger and keeping it submerged is extremely draining and you need all the energy you can get during recovery. Express your anger. See page 30 for ideas.

Myth #25
I'll never be happy again.
With each hardship or loss we face in our lives, it becomes easier to be pessimistic and negative. One man we interviewed reported three deaths in recent years and the loss of a job. He had become detached and resentful and found little reason for trying. He had come to know this dark place intimately, and although it wasn't appealing, it was home. The more familiar something is to us, the harder it is to leave, even if it's a dark and depressing place. However, these feelings are excuses

to avoid the pain and work of rebuilding. The rebuilding process is slow and hard, but it will always happen when we dedicate our hearts to it. Trust that you will be happy again someday.

Myth #26
After a while I will no longer think or feel anything about the loss.
You may be ambushed by grief when you least expect it. We do not forget our loved one or grow out of grief. You will, from time to time, throughout your life, re-experience feelings associated with the loss.

Myth #27
In order to process my grief effectively I need to advance through the Five Stages of Grief.
Many people turn to the well-known "five stages of grief" to explain this complex process and the path to healing. What many people do not know is that these well-known five stages of grief are based on the work of Elisabeth Kübler-Ross and describe a *dying person's reality* as he or she goes through the process of death. The stages are:

Shock
Denial
Depression
Anger
Acceptance

Written for use by someone who is living while dying, many grievers are perplexed when they do not "fit into the mold." These stages only partially apply to a survivor of sudden death. In addition to these stages, the survivor of sudden death will experience many more stages and rages that need to be worked through.

Phases, stages, and levels of grief are offered as guidelines for us in unknown territory. The human mind thrives on structure and order; in this time of chaos, we look to these models to help us get our bearings and find our way forward. Yet, accepting "stages" or "phases" at face value can force unrealistic self-expectation. You will not necessarily experience each "phase," nor may you experience them in a linear or sequential fashion.

The research shows, and is corroborated by our observations, that the active grieving period when you have lost someone to a lingering death lasts about two to five years, depending on the work one does in recovery. In lingering death there is pre-death grieving, so that by the time the actual death has occurred, family and friends have already been grieving for a period of time. Sudden death presents a different scenario. With sudden death, the various stages can be compressed into a single hour, minute, or day.

In reality, grieving is more like a maze of emotions than an elevator that starts at the bottom and arrives at the penthouse of peace and understanding. Like a maze, we go forward a bit and then back over the same territory. If we learn to love and accept ourselves even as we are emotionally weaving through the maze, we may begin to see our humanness and our brokenness as a threshold to personal growth. In any case, it is important to assure yourself, no matter how "crazy" and lost in the maze you may feel, that you do come out on the other side and that you are not alone.

Myth #28

The final stage of grief requires acceptance.

Acceptance is the hardest concept to understand. When someone is dying slowly, you have an opportunity to reach acceptance—*slowly*. When someone is gone suddenly, acceptance is extremely difficult. Pam had a client in her practice that questioned acceptance.

> "I once had a client who said to me, 'Why do you keep saying acceptance is the final phase in my recovery? The word acceptance feels like a permission giving word. It feels like I've said that the death is okay with me, that I have given my approval. I have *not* given my approval. The death of my husband will *never* be okay with me . . . so what is meant when the final step in the grieving process is acceptance?"

The *American Heritage Dictionary* says acceptance means:

1. *The act or process of accepting.*
2. *The state of being accepted or acceptable.*

3. *Favorable reception; approval.*
4. *Belief in something; agreement.*

Let's not refer to this stage as "acceptance." It is better defined as "acknowledgment." Acceptance is too close in meaning to "approval" and how can one approve of the sudden loss of someone? You will probably be ready to acknowledge your loss in about three to six months, though it may take a year or more. There will be times when you are tempted to return to denial for a while—just to feel a little better. Yet the route to healing is through the pain of acknowledgment.

These are the most common myths and grief blocks we have discovered since the first edition of this book and our decades of working closely with mourners. You will undoubtedly discover others in various shapes and forms. Support groups and self-help exercises are most valuable in moving through these blocks, and we offer you some in the Grief Recovery and Exercises chapter of this book.

PART TWO:
The World Is Upside Down:
Collecting Our Scattered Pieces

As the shock and numbness begin to lessen, we realize our lives have changed forever, and scattered pieces have replaced a solid foundation. In this section we explore the pieces we are left to rebuild with.

While our loss has stopped our world as we know it, the rest of the world continues to move on day to day as it always has and always will. We are challenged when we attempt to reconnect with this world and the thousands of people who have not experienced sudden loss firsthand and wonder why we can't "get back to normal." It can be tempting to hide from this world, but long term this world is full of gifts, future, and hope. We will explore the challenges of relating to others and redefining our lives without our loved one.

We also explore how to help ourselves and those we love—partners, children, family.

Chapter Five
The World Is Upside Down

*"The doorbell rang at around eight-thirty. I wasn't expecting anyone,
so a strange feeling came over my heart. I peeked out the keyhole, and saw
my brother, Denver, and sister-in-law, Allison, standing in the hallway.
I let them in. There was a deep silence, and I knew from my brother's
eyes what had happened. He didn't even have to speak.
He took me in his arms, and my world changed forever.
My eyes moved to a picture of my son as a child, his red hair cropped
close to his head, and his big blue eyes looking out at me. My world
was turning to darkness, and I would never live in it the same again."
—Singer Judy Collins on the death of her son, Clark.*

"I can remember staring at the sun that day and watching it fade behind the trees.
I remember wishing with everything in me that the sun wouldn't go down. I knew
this was the end of the last day where I had known my son alive," said one mother.

Yet as the sun sets on our days with our loved one, the world takes on a new look and we are forced to question our place within it.

Many grievers report feelings of everything feeling "upside down" or "wrong." In a matter of seconds, we learned that the world has changed and will never again be the same. A stage of shock follows. Unlike a lingering death where people may prepare affairs and make arrangements in advance, those facing sudden death are forced to deal with all of these things immediately. Questions and loss of purpose follow as we are forced to interpret and understand death at a time when we are not remotely prepared to do so. Spiritual questions and reassessment of one's religious faith may also occur. In this chapter we will look at the ways in which our world is turned upside down and some ideas on how to cope during this confusing time.

Assumptions Are Shattered

When we grapple with sudden loss, we are forced to reconsider some basic assumptions about ourselves. We may begin to feel vulnerable and a sense that life is tenuous. We may begin to question whether or not the world is meaningful and orderly. We may see ourselves as weak and needy for the first time. Those who haven't had to deal with the trauma of sudden death may also come to question these assumptions, but they are not *forced* to question the basic truth of these assumptions in the same way a survivor must.

We are all forced to confront our mortality. Most people deal with this issue in mid-life. It is then that we begin to see signs of our own aging or we face the imminent death of our parents or grandparents. This is the natural order of things. However, as survivors of sudden death, we are forced to confront our mortality at the time of the trauma—regardless of our age. A heightened sense of the fundamental fragility of life quickly emerges—usually within minutes, hours, or days of the death.

Aphrodite Matsakis, PhD, says in her book, *Trust After Trauma*, ". . . although it can empower them to try to make the most out of life, it can also be frightening and overwhelming not only to themselves, but also to others who, quite understandably, prefer to avoid confronting the inevitability of their own deaths."

You may have thought, "It can't happen to me." But it did happen and you may no longer feel the world is a safe place. Feelings of vulnerability can bring on a sense of doom or an expectation that your own future may be foreshortened. You may also experience an intense fear that the trauma may repeat itself and another family member, lover, or friend will die.

Dr. Matsakis goes on to say, "The just world philosophy cannot explain what happened to you. You used to think that if you were careful, honest, and good, you could avoid disaster. But the trauma taught you that all your best efforts could not prevent the worst from happening. Perhaps you saw others who were also innocent die or who were unfairly injured. So, while you would like to believe that the world is orderly, and that good is rewarded and evil is punished, you had an experience that contradicts these beliefs."

When our foundation is swept from beneath us, we begin questioning the fundamentals of life. As crazy as it seems, this shattering of assumptions is a normal part of grief. *We must re-evaluate what we once held as true, move through the ruin, and create a new foundation based on what we have learned.*

Loss of Purpose

Many grievers feel a loss of purpose. After all, we've known a life that is certain. We were certain that a person would be there, we never questioned. Suddenly, all we have left are questions—questions like: Why did this happen? If a person can die so suddenly—what is the purpose of trying to accomplish and trying to live? Brook battled this concept in the wake of Caleb's death.

"I have always been an over-achiever. I scheduled and organized my life so I could climb mountain after mountain in search of reaching some higher place. When Caleb died, I wondered what the purpose of all the climbing was. I suddenly realized there was no guarantee I would live to be seventy—or even another week. So what was the purpose of all this sowing—if the chance to reap could be taken away?

Lost inside this question, I turned to a wonderful friend and my local pastor, Jeff. We often had lunch together and I always found comfort in his words. I stared at him across the table, and said simply—'What does anything matter?' He relayed a sentence, which was a riddle in itself. He simply said, 'Because nothing matters, everything matters.' I tried over lunch to comprehend the sentence as it twirled through my mind. Finally, I asked him to interpret further.

Jeff explained that looking long term or planning ahead cannot matter. Sure we need to be somewhat prepared for the future, but to become overly preoccupied is foolish since life can disappear so quickly. 'Everything you do at this very instant is what matters,' he explained. 'You should be living life, right now. Anyone who is living for tomorrow isn't really living' At the time, I had been juggling a few thoughts on where to go with my writing career and what project to pursue next. The thought of having a whole book in front of me seemed daunting and purposeless. I was scared to start something, scared perhaps that I would never finish it. Jeff asked me what mattered most at that very moment. "Getting by," was my reply. As our eyes met, I knew that was what mattered. I would write about getting by because that meant something to me, and if life went away tomorrow, I would be content in where I was today."

Since nothing of the future matters, everything in the here and now does. To learn to live in the present, to reap the gifts of the moment, is the best tribute we can give to anyone, much less ourselves.

Redefining Ourselves

When we lose someone, we often lose a piece of ourselves. The closer our relationship with the person, the more of our self we have to redefine. Much of our identity comes from our relationship to others. Take the woman who has called herself a wife and mother for thirty years and then loses her family in a plane crash. This woman whose identity was wife and mother is left without a husband or children. Defining ourselves by others can bring fullness to our lives, but when faced with loss it also means we must redefine the resulting emptiness.

One of the first things to remember when seeking redefinition is that you don't need to know all the answers now. No one should force you or "hold a clock to your head" asking you to redefine yourself overnight. This is a process. It involves soul-searching, courage, and rediscovery. It takes time. Realize that you don't have to let go of who you were—you just need to adapt for the future. In the case above, the mentioned woman will always know what it was like to be a wife and a mother. For the rest of her life, she will remember and relive her role in her thoughts and actions. Even though life turns itself upside down and our role may change suddenly, we can't deny the importance of our history.

Simply stated, the question becomes, "Now what?" After expecting life to take a certain course, it has chosen its own, far from your plans. Again, take it slow. Choose one thing that you know for certain. If you have always loved to paint, know that in the future you can still be a painter. Focus on what you do know about yourself. Look at the things you've always wanted to try and pick one to focus on. Take it one step at a time, and as you're ready, add another "piece" to yourself.

For some, this rebuilding takes months, for others it can take a lifetime, but piece by piece you can rebuild. When you are ready to begin the rebuilding process, turn to the Exercises chapter for ideas to get you started.

What Matters Now?

During the process of redefining ourselves, we may ask "What matters? What is my purpose now?" All the dreams and goals we have made for tomorrow may seem pointless as we realize they can be torn away without notice. "Why live for tomorrow, when it may not exist?" asked one man. In some form or another, many of us can relate to his question.

Each of us is forced to venture down our own soul path and do our own exploring. We must re-evaluate our priorities. If spending time with our family is important, then we should start now. We shouldn't work so hard in hopes of that "better day" when family can be our only focus. Instead, we must learn to incorporate our priorities, needs, and dreams into our daily lives.

What are your priorities? What matters? How could you live differently? Most importantly, how could you make every day count? In many ways, the best tribute we can give to the deceased is to allow them the impact of permanently changing our lives. Allow your life to fluctuate in form. Allow your priorities and loves to surface—and then live by them. When we do this, we are offering the greatest tribute to the one we have lost. In this way, we are showing them that though they have gone, they have changed our life and allowed us to live more fully. Think about that. If you were to die tomorrow, could you think of any better legacy to leave behind than the power of helping others live more complete lives?

Finding a Beginning, Middle, and End

Questions abound when we lose someone tragically. Unlike those who lose someone after a lengthy illness, we have little or no time to question doctors, understand a diagnosis, struggle with our faith, or say our goodbyes.

During our upbringing we learn to understand life in terms of cycles. We understand the cycle of age. We know the cycle of schooling. We know the cycle of work. We know the cycles of diet and exercise. Almost everything can be understood as a cycle with a beginning, middle, and end. Our minds will immediately try to do the same with our tragic loss experience. Our mind will look for the beginning (What happened?), the middle (How did he/she feel, respond, progress?), the end (Was he in pain? Did he have any last thoughts or words?) Yet unless we were present, we are left with question after question. In order to get to a place where we can think about the experience in its entirety, we must know as much of the cycle as possible.

This is why it is so natural to talk with others about our loved one's last moments. Over and over again, grievers tell their stories, attempting to make sense of them, attempting to understand the cycle. Often, there are ways to get more information. Police, witnesses, and doctors can all offer clues to what happened. When we have enough clues we can piece together a story that will allow our questioning to lessen. As our questions lessen, we create more room to heal.

Dr. Ann Kaiser Stearns, author of *Coming Back: Rebuilding Lives After Crisis and Loss,* offers the following suggestion: "Make a conscious effort to identify what is not making sense to you about your loss or crisis. You might ask yourself: What is it about the situation and/or about his or her death that is most puzzling or troubling to me? What part of grief is troubling me? What other things are troubling me?"

Before seeking your own beginning, middle, and end, this can be a useful exercise. Confront your questions. Explore your feelings and record these thoughts. Use this as a guideline to gather the information you will need.

Brook found that she and her mother had many questions.

"For starters, my mother and I had never heard of the term anaphylactic shock—we couldn't even pronounce it. Our initial disbelief was so strong, not a single question was asked at the hospital. But as the days went by, the questions came one after the other. *Caleb had been stung a month before—was this a cumulative effect of venom? A long time ago he had chest pains that went undiagnosed—could his death be connected to that? Had any blood been drawn and a firm allergic reaction determined? If his death certificate said 12:54 and his friends said he was unconscious at 11:15—what happened between then and 12:54?*

I did as much research as I could and then I called the doctor. I immediately put him at rest by letting him know that I trusted he had done everything in his capacity, and I did not, in any way, question his ability. I let the doctor know that my questions were more about figuring out the order of events. We talked for close to an hour.

After combining his comments with my research, I was able to confidently assume that Caleb did die from a fatal reaction to a bee sting. He was dead before the ambulance arrived, or minutes after, and unconscious long before that. He was not pronounced dead until 12:54 because the doctors were praying for a miracle. Being so young and healthy, they worked extensively on him in the E.R. trying anything they could to revive him.

I learned bee allergies are not hereditary. However, I also discovered those who know they are allergic can carry an Epinephrine shot. Epinephrine can relieve the reaction or buy the needed time to get treatment.

With this knowledge and for my own peace of mind, I went to a specialist in the allergy field. I asked the allergist to test both my three-year-old daughter and myself. He took our blood and sent it to the Mayo clinic for analysis. The tests came back negative. Yet, since this allergy can develop at any time, he gave us both adrenaline kits so that we would feel more at ease. While only ten people a year die from fatal reactions to insects, it was important for me to have that comfort."

Talking to others will help you get the information you need to find your own beginning, middle, and end. This information-gathering can be a major catalyst in moving past the grief of "what happened?" to the process of rebuilding. It allows the mind to cycle through the event in its entirety, instead of stopping to question and get lost in the who, what, when, where, why, and how.

Why Did This Happen?

Every griever is bound to question fate and the heavens, wondering: Why did this have to happen? There are, of course, no concrete answers. We can speculate. We can try to create reasons to offer comfort to ourselves and our family—but in the end, we just don't know. Perhaps this is one of the hardest parts about losing someone so unexpectedly. In our Western world we are so accustomed to having the answers. We know two plus two equals four. We know that we can send a spacecraft to the moon and back. We know that our 401K possesses X value or that our gardens will certainly begin to bloom in May. We are a culture that seeks answers and rarely rests without them.

Yet here, we face the challenge of accepting that there is no answer, at this point in time. To leave it be "only questions" is one of the most challenging demands of grief work. As poet Rainer Marie Rilke eloquently states, "Live the questions now. Perhaps you will then gradually, without noticing it, live along some distant day into the answer."

Brook eventually garnered the trust that someday she would understand.

"Many have asked me where that trust was birthed. It came from many nights of trying to figure it out. I mapped out every possibility, every sequence of why this might have happened. None of them brought answers. In fact, few of them brought comfort. Eventually, I realized I was getting nowhere. The only way to get somewhere was to surrender to the fact that I did not know the answers. It is hard to surrender, to quit seeking, to accept the unknown.

One night I simply laid my heart at the foot of the universe. I said to the earth, to the world, 'I do not understand this and I am ready to quit trying to understand. I am ready to accept that the universe knows more than I, and that I will understand as I am ready. Until then, I ask that I am granted peace.'

Peace didn't come overnight, but it did come. And with it came a renewed faith. But it was a different faith than what I had once known. It is a faith that someone is standing by me or over me and will lead me to what I must know as I must know it. It is a faith where I surrender the unknown without expectation. I trust the process and that all will unfold in its own time."

Do We Ever Get Over Grief?

Recovery from a major, sudden loss is a lifetime process. It's true that the pain lessens with time, but expect to be ambushed by grief occasionally. You may be ambushed by grief on the date of your anniversary eleven years from the date of the death; ambushed by grief the year your son or brother would have graduated from high school; ambushed by grief when you see couples meandering through the park or children playing in the sandbox; ambushed by grief even after you are happily remarried—and on and on. In a letter Sigmund Freud wrote to a man who lost his son, he stated, "Although we know that after such a loss the acute state of mourning will subside, we also know we shall remain inconsolable and will never find a substitute. No matter what may fill the gap, even if it be filled completely, it nevertheless remains something else. And actually this is how it should be. It is the only way of perpetuating that love which we do not want to relinquish."

Expect that when you do find happiness, the joy you feel will be intense. It will just be different. Expect that the good days will outnumber the bad and they will. Expect a new sense for the importance of life to emerge. The way we perceive grief changes over time is conveyed in Madeline L'Engle's quote at the start of the book and also Caleb's mother's poem entitled, "Grief:"

> You don't get over it
> you just get through it
> you don't get by it
> because you can't get around it
> it doesn't "get better"
> it just gets different
> every day . . .
> grief puts on a new face.

In Gay Hendricks' workbook, *Learning to Love Yourself,* he offers another way to look at painful events and emotions. ". . . think of a painful feeling as being like a bonfire in a field. At first it is hot, unapproachable. Later it may still smolder. Even later, you can walk on the ground without pain, but you know there is an essence of the fire that still remains. Take your own time, but be sure to walk over the ground again. You must do so because whatever you run away from runs you."

Chapter Six
Relating to Others

"Go away. Don't call. And don't try to talk to me.
I can't hear you and I'm sure you won't hear me.
If you want to help, bring me food. Otherwise, go away."
—*Stephanie Ericsson*, Companion through the Darkness

As we experience grief, and our world changes, relating to others can be difficult—
especially when these "others" have not faced tragic loss firsthand. Our different view
on the world changes us in many ways, and the interactions that once came naturally
may become difficult. Certain situations are bound to be trying. In this chapter we
will look at some of the mountains we will climb while relating to others.

Too Close to Home

For some time after our loss, situations that are similar to what we once had may
be hard to deal with. For instance, a parent who has lost a child may have a hard
time seeing parents with their children. A widow may have a hard time in an

environment where couples are present. It is hard to anticipate situations that will hit too close to home. Some you might expect, other times they might surface out of the blue.

One widowed waitress reported that she felt she was progressing well through her recovery after her husband had died. After six months she had gone back to work. Then, almost a year after his death, a couple came in and the man looked about the same age as her husband. He ordered her husband's favorite wine. "I fell apart right there. I had been fine for months and suddenly I just couldn't hold it in."

If you can manage it, try not to push yourself into these situations before you are ready for them. There is no "time limit," no set "right or wrong" way to deal with others. Don't let others convince you that you need to do "this or that"; instead, follow the cues of your heart and body. If a situation surfaces and triggers strong emotions, excuse yourself from the environment and try to get to a place where you can release and vent your emotions.

You Are a Different Person

Brook found that she emerged a different person after Caleb's death . . .

I remember a phone conversation with a good friend of mine, several weeks after Caleb's death. She was telling me about something . . . though I can't recall what. Then she paused for a moment and said, "Brook, you don't sound like yourself."

My reply came out of my mouth before I could choose it. "I am not the person I was three weeks ago and I will never be that person again."

Surprised by my own response, I relayed it to my therapist who was helping me work through issues surrounding my brother's death. "Of course you're not," she said. "And one of the best things you can do for yourself is to know that you are a different person now."

A fear set in shortly after that, though. I suddenly wondered how I could relate to all my old friends when I now felt so different about the world, life, and myself. Things my friends and I had once discussed seemed so trivial. Their work problems and love life issues that I once discussed intensely seemed silly. I felt like yelling at them. I wanted to say, 'Trust me, if you're breathing, life ain't so bad.' Though my friends were sorry for my loss, they couldn't fully understand. No one understands the effect of tragic loss unless they go through it firsthand.

I told my mom one night that I didn't think I could keep any of my friends that hadn't known Caleb because they just wouldn't understand. My mom told me to give it time. But I withdrew from friends and didn't call to set up lunches and didn't show up for regularly scheduled activities. I didn't want to pretend to be the person I used to be, the Brook I thought they all would expect.

One morning, my dear friend Sara stopped in. She informed me that we were going to have breakfast together and that we could either go out or she would go get a couple of omelets and bring them back. I smiled at her determined attitude. We ended up going out for a nice breakfast and I was amazed at how well it went. We talked about all sorts of things, we talked about Caleb, about work, about my week. We talked and she listened and she absorbed and she was there with me. With the 'new' Brook.

I had other friends who I couldn't seem to cross that bridge with. But what I learned from Sara was that it was so important to give each friendship a chance. Friendship can cross bridges and worlds. Remember that even if you do not consciously seek to change yourself, the experience of loss will change you.

It's Okay to Laugh

In Jacquelin Mitchard's novel *The Deep End of The Ocean,* there is an incredible scene. The book is about a family whose son has been kidnapped. The mother, Beth, is sitting in the office of the chief detective, Candy. The two women have become quite friendly throughout the weeks spent on the search. The mother has been grim, depressed, and withdrawn throughout the search. In the scene, the detective says something that causes the mother to laugh. She laughs only for an instant, before a look of horror comes over her face—horror, that in the face of misery she laughed. Here is an excerpt from the scene:

Candy held up the mailer. "Actually it's a padded cry for help."

And Beth, to her horror, laughed, instantly covering her eyes and feeling that she was about to choke. Candy was on her feet and around the desk in seconds.

"Beth, Beth, listen," she said. "You laughed. You only laughed. If you laugh that doesn't mean that's a point against our side. If you laugh, or read a book to Vincent, or eat something you like, it's not going to count for or against us on the big scoreboard of luck." Beth began to cry. "You have to believe me," Candy went on. "It feels like if you watch a movie, or listen to a song or do anything that makes you feel anything more than like absolute shit, that little moment of happiness is the thing that's going to be punished . . ."

While this scene details the events surrounding a kidnapping, many of us can relate to these feelings. At times, it's hard to laugh—we feel guilty for "going on." We wonder if our laughing makes our grief less real—if our memories will fade—if people will think we don't miss the deceased.

If only there were precise rules on how to grieve, how much easier it would be. How should we look? How should we act? If we look like we are having fun, what might people think? Is it okay to just forget for a while—to try and escape what has happened?

The answers are all within your heart. There is nothing you need to do, or act like, for the sake of others. Don't worry about how anyone perceives you. It's all right to escape for a while, to watch a comedy—to laugh.

The Ten-Day Syndrome

In the immediate days following a loss, we are often bombarded with visitors, food, offers to help, phone calls, flowers, and condolences. Then we see the ten-day syndrome in action. Most major news stories get about ten days of coverage in the media and then it's old news—on with the new. The grief experience is often similar. As the days roll by, the calls, condolences, and comfort lessen. It may appear as if all are trying to get back to "their" world before the tragedy happened. Meanwhile, we are just beginning the long and difficult road of grief—needing more support than ever.

In her book, *Suddenly Alone,* Dolores Dahl writes, "Phone calls, visits, food . . . there was so much activity following your death that I had no time to be lonely, no time to digest the fact that you were gone. I was overwhelmed with the support and the love that filled my home during those first few days of disbelief and confusion. But, as is always the case, everyone returned to their own homes, their own lives, shortly following the memorial service . . . and I was alone."

It's not uncommon to feel annoyed or angry with others who continue on as though life is "normal" when for us it is anything but. It's not uncommon to be upset that other's worlds just continue on, while it feels like your whole world has stopped. Brook and her mother discussed this scenario one evening.

"My mother had finally gone out to do some mandatory shopping. It was her first outing since Caleb's death. While out, she saw some women friends shopping. They were laughing and choosing items and placing them in their carts. From afar, my mother watched wondering—*How can their lives just go on? Don't they know what I'm going through?*

While on the phone, I reminded her of deaths we had faced in the past; deaths where we weren't the family or the immediately close. We thought about all the people we had known who had lost someone before we had experienced loss firsthand. What had we done in those instances? Just as others had done to us, we had sent a card, a call, or a condolence and then returned to our own lives."

There is little one can do, and life must go on. We are not taught how to handle death—so people do the best they can, usually following the standard of passing on condolences through a call, letter, or gift. Only those who have had to walk this painful path will be aware of the agony that waits ahead. Those are the people you need to seek out when the Ten-Day syndrome hits. Whether it is through one of the support networks listed in this book or through a person you already know, ensure you have support throughout the year ahead.

Repeating the Story

One of the most challenging aspects of grief is the retelling of what has happened. We may find ourselves moving through the healing process and having a great week—only to run into someone who doesn't know of our loss. Brook's mother encountered this several times. The rural Wisconsin town where she lives is a summer home for many. Caleb's death occurred in the fall. The next summer, many returning acquaintances asked, "How are your son and daughter?" The grief of the past moved full force into the present as she recounted the cold events of the previous fall and winter.

Unfortunately, there are no ways around this. The best you can do is to decide how you'd like to handle these situations in advance. If you don't want to talk about it, it's fine to say so. "I lost my son over the winter but I'm not ready to talk about it today." It may seem short or abrupt, but it is your right. Others find that telling the story brings comfort.

Awkward Questions

Family is openly talked about in society. "How many children do you have?" or "Do you have any brothers or sisters?" or "Are you married?" are questions we encounter frequently. How to respond can be difficult. Brook experienced this when she moved from Wisconsin to Oregon . . .

"I live in a very community-oriented neighborhood with lots of neighborhood get-togethers and functions. Since I was the "new kid on the block" many people would ask where I moved from, where my family lived and if I had brothers or sisters. This was their attempt to make friendly conversation and get to know me. The first time I answered, "I had a brother but he died six months ago," and the woman with whom I was speaking just quit talking. We had stepped into an awkwardness that neither of us knew how to step out of. After a couple more minutes of small talk she excused herself. I knew that sharing something like this so soon would cause the other person to be uncomfortable—but what was I supposed to say—she had asked the question!

The next time I was asked if I had brothers or sisters, I simply said, "No." Then the person asked me, "What was it like growing up an only child?" Then I had to explain that I didn't become an "only child" until my mid-twenties.

I finally devised two responses that felt natural to me. I would either say, "I have one brother but he's far away and I don't see him that much anymore," or "I had one older brother who died a year ago—but I still feel very close to him." Both of these answers seemed to put the questioner at ease.

At a time when we likely want to curl up and be alone, it is important to relate to others as we are able. Often this is best achieved one person at a time. Take a step out and talk to someone. Go at whatever pace feels right for you. Don't feel shame or guilt for not being able to "jump back into life." Regaining equilibrium takes time. Go easy and be easy with yourself.

Chapter Seven
Difficult Days: Holidays, Anniversaries, and More

"Traditions are like rules; however well intentioned when it comes down to it, they were made to be broken. As children we lived for the opportunity to break rules and traditions, to strike out on a different path. Why not experience that joy? Change the meal, change the location, make new traditions; your life has changed tremendously and so should your traditions."
—*Scott Miller,* Tips For Those Grieving During the Holiday Season

Holidays, birthdays, and other special days associated with the deceased present a special challenge. The loss becomes painfully evident and the feelings associated with the occasion become dulled and gray. Try not to be alarmed by occasional setbacks. This chapter will give you some ideas about what to expect. Knowing what to expect will allow you to create some options for yourself when these situations arise.

Birthdays

The deceased person's birthday is a time for remembering. You may feel your loss anew for many years each time their birthday comes.

Your own birthday may seem different. You may wonder why you are still alive and they are not, and it will be difficult to celebrate your own life for a while. For those who have lost an older sibling, the year when you pass your sibling's age at their time of death can be incredibly stressful. It is an odd feeling to outlive your older sibling.

Many people find a sanctuary by creating a ritual with which to celebrate the deceased's birthday. Perhaps you can surround yourself with other people who were close to the loved one. Perhaps you can go take a walk in nature and just think and cry and rant and talk out loud. In the Exercises chapter you will find some rituals that may be useful.

Anniversaries

Some people find that they may do well for an entire year, only to find themselves virtually incapacitated by grief during the days surrounding the anniversary of the death. You wake up one morning with a heavy feeling, not knowing exactly why you feel so burdened. Then it hits you—the anniversary of one or another dates you shared with the deceased in the past.

On the anniversary of the day of death, many grievers report a short-term depression. It's not uncommon to experience discomfort, sadness, and depression for a couple weeks before and after the date of death each year. You may find some alternative solutions like herbs, vitamins, and therapy to help you through this trying time. The strength of a support network can also be beneficial. Many people do "fine" throughout the year, only to be knocked off their feet as these significant dates occur.

Some religious traditions have a requirement based on the one year anniversary of the death. In Judaism for instance, Judaic law has a prescribed ritual for "death days"—the anniversary of the death. You are expected to need to discharge extra emotions during those days. The headstone is unveiled a year later. Every following year, a special candle is lit in the home. Even if your religious tradition does not dictate it, you will feel some deep or extreme emotion on the anniversary of the death. Try to look at the anniversary of the death as another opportunity to grieve—to feel some of what has been unexpressed up until now.

Other anniversaries where you can expect to feel "extra emotions" include:

the last day you saw your loved one alive
the day you first met
the day you were married or engaged
the day the "plug" was pulled
the day you found out they were dead
the anniversary of a trip you took together

There may be additional anniversaries depending on your relationship to the deceased. If you expect these anniversaries to be challenging emotional times, you will be less surprised. If you know they are coming and when, you will be better able to cope. Mark your calendar and make special plans. If you can, make special arrangements for yourself (i.e. take the day off from work, get a babysitter for the kids, find time and space to be alone, visit the grave, etc.) You may want to consider a ritual for the day of death. The exercises section of this book contains several ideas.

Weddings

If you are mourning the loss of a spouse, weddings can be especially difficult to attend. The bride and groom look so happy, but "don't they know it can be all over in a matter of seconds!" The vows are said and you hear "until death do us part," and then the tears well up. If you have lost a young daughter or son, expect to feel anger and sadness that you will never see them married, and that you will not have grandchildren, etc. If you are in the early stages of mourning, it may be better for you to stay away from wedding ceremonies altogether and attend receptions instead. Or send a gift and stay home. This is a day of celebration for the bride and groom and their families. Don't be surprised if they avoid you in an effort to maintain their joy and experience the celebration. Try not to take their actions personally.

If your adult child is getting married, and their father or mother is deceased, the wedding and its preparations can trigger profound sadness. Pam's son Ian is getting married in less than a year, and "I expect Ian and I will both be missing his father at this special event."

If you are the one getting married, expect your wedding day to be filled with a flood of emotions. Anger might be one of them—"Mom was supposed to be here, sitting in the front row. Now I have to look at an empty chair. It's not fair!"—"My sister was to be maid of honor, my best friend was looking forward to being my best man!" Your anger and sadness may seem unbearable.

Expect to have some tears—for joy and for sadness. Make sure you tuck a tissue in your bouquet or your jacket pocket. Let the officiant know ahead of time what you're going through. It would also be appropriate to ask the officiant to honor your lost loved one by requesting a moment of silence during the ceremony, as you light a candle for missing your loved one.

Pam, in her role as Interfaith Minister, does many wedding ceremonies. The following is an excerpt from one wedding in which the bride had experienced a recent loss. You may wish to incorporate these words or something similar into your own ceremony:

As we light these candles, we sense the love and the presence of all those who have gone before us—especially Denise's mother, Ruth. We feel her with us today, adding her special blessing to this sacred ceremony. It is my hope and my prayer that the families of Denise and Michael, both seen and unseen, will do all they can to help sustain and nurture the bond of these two as they seek to create their own family.

Holidays

With the loss of a member of your immediate family, holidays and special occasions will be difficult. Holidays are often filled with traditions and memories of closeness. As we face these days without our loved one, the empty space looms large in our hearts. By creating new traditions and understanding the common difficulties faced during the holidays, they can be easier to cope with.

AARP offers these tips in their article, "Frequently Asked Questions by the Widowed."

- Plan ahead. It helps to ease the strain.
- Set priorities. This can make it easier to phase out elements less pleasing to you.
- Make new traditions. This new phase in your life deserves some new traditions.
- Include [the deceased's] name in conversation. It helps others talk about him/her.
- Express your feelings. Most people understand and accept your need to cry.

- Find someone you can help. Giving assistance to others is very satisfying.
- Buy yourself something special. You've suffered a great loss. Be good to yourself.
- Cherish your memories. These are yours to keep; they grow more precious over time.
- Be patient with yourself. Allow yourself extra time to accomplish tasks.
- Take time out for rest and relaxation. This will ease the stress of grief.

Most importantly, take your time and be gentle with yourself as you move through the holidays.

Holiday Traditions

Don't try to hold on to your previous traditions or the way things were done in the past. Your family has changed. It's okay to change the way you celebrate the holidays as well. Think of a new tradition. If you always celebrated Christmas at home, consider renting a cabin for a couple of days. If you always put up your tree early in the year, consider putting it up later. If a large dinner was always cooked, go out for dinner instead. Do things differently. The memories will be strong when the holidays come; altering routines is the best way to still find some joy.

Brook's family changed their routine after Caleb's death.

"Caleb died two months prior to Christmas. Both my mother and I had done most of our shopping. As Christmas neared and we were still heavily immersed in sadness, we wondered what to do with all the gifts. We decided to give them to Caleb's friends. To change our routine, instead of celebrating Christmas day at my mother's, she comes to my home. While we always have Caleb in our minds and hearts, we have learned the need to let go of some of the pain and engage in activities and new traditions that can help us move forward with our lives."

When we do what Brook has done we are honoring our lost loved one. It may seem as though we are disrespecting our loved ones or moving away from our memories—but in fact, we are paying tribute by moving on with our lives.

Elizabeth was a newly widowed mother when the holidays came. She shares her story . . .

"The holidays, oh please save me from the holidays…make them go away! I remember my thoughts as a newly widowed mother of two young children sixteen years ago, as I raced around trying to put some kind of Thanksgiving and Christmas together. *Can't we just forget about it this year? Doesn't the rest of the world know how much pain I'm in?* I got together with another sad and lonely woman from my support group. I invited her and her kids to my house to have a turkey dinner for Thanksgiving. It helped to not face the carving of the turkey (which he did, rather skillfully each year) alone. Somehow I did most of it, whatever "it" was, all the while listening to the happy Christmas carolers, fa la la la, la, la, la la.

Christmas day that first year was really strange. I opened the presents with my two children and then sat staring at the tree, imagining how it would feel to hurl the decorations off the deck and set the living room on fire. I must have sat in the green living room chair for two hours after that, not moving."

Where Does One Go During the Holidays?

Does one have to go anywhere? Do you have to pretend to be happy and joyous for the sake of others? Is it okay to celebrate this year if you want to? Like so much of the grief process, we need to listen to our inner guidance in these matters. If you need to be alone, that's okay. You can choose that. You may have to put something together for your kids and that's fine. You might find them a great joy and inspiration and a reason to get out of bed. Other than the practical needs of those who are dependent upon you, you don't need to take care of others by pretending "everything's all right."

If you do visit family and friends during the holidays, feel free to let them know the following ahead of time:

- I may need to leave your home earlier than you expect me to. (I get tired easily these days because I'm under a lot of stress.)
- I may need to take a walk by myself after dinner. (It's hard to be around happy families for too long a time.)

- I may cry unexpectedly when I hear certain music. (I have memories of good times and it's hard to hold back the tears.)
- I may not eat all the food and goodies you offer me. (My appetite hasn't been what it used to be—maybe I'm finding all this "hard to swallow.")

Even without a sudden death in your family or circle of friends, the holidays can bring up all kinds of difficult feelings. Depression is the most difficult feeling of all. You will need to face that it's going to be nearly impossible to stave off depression, especially at this time of year. Everyone seems to be so happy, families are gathering together, and there is a hole in your life. Walking through the mall you may see the perfect gift for your deceased loved one and dissolve into a flood of tears. You may have already bought the deceased gifts and there they sit, wrapped, under the tree, unopened. It would be extremely arrogant of us to suggest there is an easy fix for the kind of sadness that surfaces around the holidays. Both of us still suffer from periodic holiday blues. It may provide some relief to volunteer your time to help the needy and hungry. Giving of yourself to another, less fortunate person or to someone who has experienced a similar loss can take your mind off your own sadness—for a time.

This year, be one of the first people you think about during the holiday season. A support group will be especially useful during this trying time of year. Peers can offer rituals and ideas they use to make the holidays easier, or they can offer a shoulder to lean on in your time of need.

Happy New Year?

You may be at a different place right now and your optimism about the future may have begun to emerge. Celebrate! You are moving along in your recovery. For others, especially those in the early stages of recovery (first, second, and third year), optimism about anything is a struggle. The first full year without your loved one can be especially difficult to move into. Your well-meaning friends and relatives may have a different opinion. You may hear phrases like, "It's the New Year— time for you to start fresh, get a new lease on life, stop crying and feeling sorry for yourself." It is important to remember when confronted with their judgments or concerns that your recovery is your recovery. Your time frame for healing is your time frame, not theirs.

You may simply need to acknowledge that it is a new year and leave it at that. If the death occurred two years ago, you may mistakenly believe that since you are now two years into recovery that you *should* be feeling better by now. Don't be fooled by dates.

It's possible the thought of a New Year's Eve celebration (or any celebration, for that matter) will bring up deep sadness around the loss of good times with the deceased or memories that are less than pleasant (i.e. drunkenness and unsafe driving). In either case, it is important to honor yourself wherever you are. You might make up your own New Year's ritual—light some candles (one for each month/year you have made it on your own), burn some incense (to symbolize the burning away of the old way of being and the sweet smell of a new way), pour yourself a glass of wine or soda and drink a toast to yourself. You may have begun to live! It might be a good time to compare where you are emotionally with where you were last year at this time. (Please see the Exercises chapter for specific ideas to help you do this.) Last year you may have wanted to stay in bed with the covers over your head every day of the week, and maybe now you only think about staying in bed three days a week—without the covers pulled up! These are not small steps. They are large strides on the path of grief recovery and they deserve your praise and recognition.

Next Year

Next year it will hurt a little less—next year there will be a little more joy in your life. Next year you may be able to hear the music. Next year you may have more to give. Next year you may even be more ready to help someone else. Wherever you are in the grief process, there is the possibility of new life. We know it's hard—and we also know it gets less hard. The next time a special occasion, anniversary, or holiday comes around, you will feel a little more in control, a little less pained, the situation will be a little less difficult, and you will begin to celebrate life again—one day at a time.

Chapter Eight
Grieving Apart, Grieving Together:
Understanding How Men and Women Grieve

"Needed: A strong, deep person wise enough to allow me to grieve in the depth of who I am, and strong enough to hear my pain without turning away."
—*Fr. Joe Mahoney,* Concerns of Police Survivors Newsletter

Understanding the difference between men and women's grief is essential to understanding and supporting one another in our time of need. Keep in mind that this section is based on how the majority of men and women respond to the grief experience, but there can be a great deal of crossover. These are general patterns and not written in stone.

Both men and women will go through the majority of patterns, feelings, and emotions that fill the pages of this book during the grief experience. If you are caring for (or trying to understand the experience of) someone who is grieving, we recommend reading this book in its entirety.

Men and women are taught to handle their feelings differently. When it comes to understanding or supporting a member of the opposite sex, being aware of these differences can help replace misunderstandings with communication. The primary differences can be categorized into three areas: (1) Problem-Solving, (2) Processing, (3) Communicating.

Problem Solving and Facing Challenges

One of the main communication barriers is what men and women seek to get out of a conversation. Women often seek someone to talk and explore with, whereas men often look to "solve the problem." Men will commonly put "solving and thinking" before "feeling and expressing." When faced with grief, a man may want to figure out how to support his family and how to be the anchor before exploring his feelings.

Many men believe they are responsible for taking care of the family. This belief can make it hard to show emotion when they feel the need to be providers. This is complicated further in many men by guilt. As the "protector" of the home, a man may feel guilty or feel that he has failed if the death occurred in his immediate family. Taking action or finding answers is the most common response among men facing challenges or problems.

Women are more apt to see relationships as the central point in their lives. Often, women's relationships and emotional ties to children and spouse come before any other priority, including self care. When confronted by a sudden death, many women worry less about the "outside world," and the logistics of "getting by," and more about life within the four walls of home. For women, open and honest talks that focus on connecting are often the most necessary step for problem solving and facing challenges.

Processing Grief

Recognize that you may each define "support" differently and be open to each other's definitions. Society has long led men to believe that they are leaders and should be self-reliant. Men want to be able to take care of themselves and their own needs. Women are often led to believe that they need others and are used to talking amongst other women. Men, on the other hand, are not provided with many opportunities to share their emotions safely. When grief strikes, women are more likely to seek a support group, whereas men are more apt to seek time alone.

Men don't like to "burden" others with their troubles. They may feel that grief is "their own problem" and that they should tough it out on their own. Men may cope better by taking some time to "work through" their grief in a private setting.

While women often find release through talking or journaling, men may benefit from a more physical outlet. A punching bag, running, racquetball—anything physical can help release pent-up emotion.

In the weeks following the death of Brook's brother, her mother wanted to clean out her attic, which was filled with unused clutter from the years. While it wasn't memorabilia of her son, it was a purging of a "very-lived-in" home—an attempt to create order out of chaos. Brook's husband Andy had a semi deliver a large dumpster. About a dozen of Caleb's male friends rushed over to help. Aggressively they threw the unwanted items into the dumpster. They broke glass. They broke doors. They vented. They cleaned. They purged. And in the end, the dumpster was full of no longer needed clutter. The attic was clean, the basement organized, and somehow their souls lightened. While the grief journey had only begun, they were able to release some of their anger through this process.

The release needn't be as extensive. Contact football, a punching bag, anything that allows one to physically exert their emotions in a healthy way can aid this process.

Communicating

Women are much more likely to clearly express their thoughts and emotions. Women generally spend much of their time discussing emotions with other women. Articulating feelings often comes naturally and easily, and it can be hard for a woman to understand why men cannot do the same.

The ability to know what we feel and to express our feelings in words is an acquired skill. For adults who grew up in homes where talking about feelings was part of the daily routine, articulating feelings is easier. If, on the contrary, feelings were rarely discussed, it can be hard to put words to the complex emotions we face.

In men's circles, it is uncommon to express and articulate feelings. When men are pressured to show feelings, everyone can become easily frustrated. Women get frustrated because they feel "closed off," and men feel frustrated because they can't find the words to express themselves in the way a woman wants.

A woman may feel she is not being "heard or understood," when trying to express her grief to a man. With men being taught to handle their feelings silently and stoically, he may not be able to respond in the way she needs. Men may feel their needs are not being respected when pressured to talk or share uncomfortable feelings, when actually the woman is coping the best way she knows how by trying to connect with him.

For men, the job of "just listening" can be incredibly challenging. Men hate to see others in pain—they think that they should be able to prevent or "solve" the situation causing pain to those they care for. But it's important to remember that women need someone who will *just listen*. For women, listening also involves paying close attention to a man's non-verbal communication, such as body language.

I'm a man and it seems like all this self-help and group support stuff is for women. I'm afraid I won't find the help I need.

Men grieve differently from women. They are often silent, solitary mourners who immerse themselves in activity and private, symbolic rituals. They have a tendency to approach grief in a cognitive way, and they may be prematurely judged as cold and uncaring. They feel profoundly, but often they cannot express the depth of their loss—even to intimates.

Men have a tendency to "tough it out" rather than seek support. But when they do find a support network, they most often find a strong bond with the other men and a safe place to express feelings. Ken was encouraged to attend an all-male grief support group. Reluctant, it took him several months to skeptically attend a meeting. After the meeting, Ken expressed great relief, speaking with tears in his eyes. "And I thought I was the only guy in New York whose heart was being ripped out every time I looked at my wife and saw my daughter in her face." There is no "manly" way to grieve, the experts say. There are many ways to cope with loss that have more to do with personality than gender. However, there are stereotypes: a man who loses his wife, for instance, is expected to have two or three months of sadness, then "suck it up" and get on with living.

Among the 13 million widowed people in the United States, there are eight widows for every widower. Little wonder men who lose their wives feel adrift. Society expects men to "walk tall" through their grief yet offers little male-related support.

Jim Conway, a minister and author of *Men in Mid-Life Crisis,* believes in group therapy. Jim joined four grief groups after the death of his wife. Conway likens grief groups to Alcoholics Anonymous. "You don't have to explain what it means when you say, 'I am grieving.' I need to go and sit and listen and cry. I needed to know I'm normal. By the time a year was over, I knew I needed to move on when my primary purpose turned from being helped to helping others."

The internet can come in handy here as well. We found several pages for grief sponsored by men. Read through the Internet Resources section of the last chapter for ideas.

Different Losses, Different Worlds: When One Member of a Couple Experiences Tragedy

Brook's immediate birth family was small—her parents, her brother and herself. In 2007, the birth family of four was just Brook and her mother. Brook's husband, Andy, however, has a large family. Andy has five siblings, most of which have married and are having children of their own. He has two grandparents still living, aunts, uncles, cousins—Thanksgiving of 2006 was attended by forty people and ten dogs!

In the years immediately after her brother's sudden death, Brook had a difficult time attending the Thanksgiving celebration. She watched as all the brothers and sisters interacted, and in the back of her mind, she wondered if they truly understood how lucky they were to have one another. At every opportunity she began encouraging Andy to keep in closer touch with his siblings.

Brook found that while these Thanksgiving get-togethers were intended to be a time of connection, she felt isolated and alone. Amidst the laughter and joking and sharing of this large family, the loss of her own family unit was magnified.

After Thanksgiving that year, Brook expressed her feelings to her husband and asked if she could take a "year or two" off. He understood and explained it to his mother so there would be no hurt feelings.

To date, Andy's family has not experienced any sudden or tragic loss. God willing, they never will. In their thirteen-year marriage, Brook and Andy see the world very differently because she has lived through the grief experience in ways Andy cannot understand. These tragedies have not distanced them, but they have brought them closer. Brook attributes this to:

- Andy's commitment to being present and listening during the times of tragedy
- Andy's ability to listen—knowing that there is not "an answer" or "a cure" to take away Brook's pain
- Andy's commitment to respecting how this changes Brook's perceptions and needs, even when he can't understand it firsthand
- Andy's not putting a "time limit" on the grief experience and allowing Brook space or closeness as needed
- Brook's willingness to share what she is feeling, as well as she can, when she is feeling it
- Brook's honesty about how isolated she feels amongst a family group and other difficult feelings that many people would leave unsaid

Masculine Grief

Terry Matine and Kenneth J. Doka offer the following summary in *Living With Grief After Sudden Loss,* "Masculine grief tends to be private, dominated by thinking rather than feeling, and action-oriented. While most masculine grievers are men, many women adopt this pattern of coping as well. Although traditional therapies have encouraged grievers to openly share their emotional distress and to recall painful events, masculine grievers may respond best to private, problem-solving approaches that respect and encourage emotional mastery."

Martin and Doka offer this outline as the usual masculine grief pattern. Reading this outline can help men identify their patterns and help those close to them create ways to work through the grief process.

- Feelings are limited or toned down
- Thinking precedes and often dominates feeling

- The focus is on problem-solving rather than expression of feelings
- The outward expression of feelings often involves anger and/or guilt
- Internal adjustments to the loss are usually expressed through activity
- Intense feelings may be experienced privately; there is a general reluctance to discuss these with others
- Intense grief is usually repressed immediately after the loss, often during post-death rituals

Since men often grieve differently, it can be valuable to start or attend a support group that consists only of men. In the book, *Men and Grief* (see Resources), there is a comprehensive section on how to start an all-male support group.

Guidelines for Grieving Couples

If you are facing the loss of a loved one as a couple, the following ideas may help you in your journey.

Read This Chapter Together

It's important that you both understand grief and how it affects a couple. Read and discuss this chapter together. Use it as a springboard for questions such as, "Do you experience that?" or "Would you like to try that?"

Find Additional Support

One mistake that many married couples make is the expectation of having all their needs met by one person—their partner. This is unrealistic and puts too much pressure on a partner. Our needs are so diverse; it takes a diverse group of people to meet them. The same is true with grief. We need more than just our partner to help us through.

Discuss Issues Away from Home

The home environment will be charged with emotions and memories. To help overcome complicated emotions and distractions, make time to talk and share away from home. Take a break from the intensity of the situation. Go out for dinner, focus on one another, and talk through joys, problems, pains, and life.

Write Notes to Each Other

Therapist Tom Golden said, "I know a couple who has a terrible time talking about their grief but when they start writing notes to each other they gain a greater understanding. Give it a try." (Tom Golden maintains an excellent website, which has many articles on men and grief. *Tom Golden: Crisis, Grief & Healing.* See the Resources chapter for more information and the web address.) He also shares, "One way to give men more time is to write to them, rather than talk to them. By writing a note it gives the man the freedom to read it more than once, to take it with him . . . and [more] importantly to respond in his own time. Another benefit is that writing takes the non-verbal communication and the "tone of voice" out of the equation.

Convey Your Needs

Miscommunication is the number one problem in any relationship—from work relationships to friendships to marriage. Don't let miscommunications further complicate your grieving process. Don't expect your partner to know what you need—be specific. Try sentences that begin with "Here's what I need . . ." "Are you willing . . ."

Allow Time

It may take a while for men to articulate how they feel. Keep in mind that most men have not had as many opportunities to articulate their feelings in a safe environment as women have. If a woman asks a question, she needs to allow some time for the man to form his response. It could take minutes, hours, or even a day.

Ask Specific Questions

Men often aren't as familiar with their feelings and emotions as women. Questions like, "How are you feeling?" and "How are you doing?" are likely to be answered with, "Stop asking me," or "I'm all right." It's not that men are avoiding answering the questions, but rather they are simply answering them the way they always have. Women can try more specific questions for more specific answers. Questions like, "What was the hardest part of the funeral for you?" "What do you think John would want us to do today?" may help open the communication lines.

Chapter Nine
Helping Children Cope with Grief

"In one of the stars
I shall be living
In one of them
I shall be laughing
And so it will be
As if all the stars
Were laughing
When you look
At the sky at night"
—*Antoine de Saint-Exupéry,* The Little Prince

To help you understand what you might encounter with your own children or those you care for, we have organized this chapter by age groups ranging from babies to young adults. This should give you some guidance as to what to expect and how you can be most helpful, depending on the child's stage of development at the time of the death.

In the past, children were thought to be miniature adults and were expected to behave as adults. It is now understood that there are differences in the ways in which children and adults mourn.

Unlike adults, bereaved children do not experience continual and intense emotional and behavioral grief reactions. Children may seem to show grief only occasionally and briefly, but in reality, a child's grief usually lasts longer than that of an adult. This may be explained by the fact that a child's ability to experience intense emotions is limited. Mourning in children may need to be addressed again and again as the child gets older. Since bereavement is a process that continues over time, children will think about the loss repeatedly, especially during important times in their life, such as going to camp, graduating from school, getting married, or after becoming a parent and having their own children.

A child's grief may be influenced by his or her age, personality, stage of development, earlier experiences with death, and his or her relationship with the deceased. The surroundings, cause of death, and family members' ability to communicate with one another and to continue as a family after the death can also affect grief. The child's ongoing need for care, the child's opportunity to share his or her feelings and memories, the parent's ability to cope with stress, and the child's steady relationships with other adults are also factors that may influence grief.

According to the U.S. Department of Health and Human Services, children do not react to loss in the same ways as adults. Grieving children may not show their feelings as openly as adults. Grieving children may not withdraw and dwell on the person who died, but instead they may throw themselves into activities (for example, they may be sad one minute and playful the next). Often families think the child doesn't really understand or has gotten over the death. Neither is true; children's minds protect them from what is too powerful for them to handle. An adult might grieve nonstop for days, whereas children experience their grief in shorter time increments, sometimes hours and sometimes minutes at a time.

Childrens' inability to understand death, coupled with lack of vocabulary to articulate feelings, often leads to self-expression through behavior. Strong feelings of anger and fears of abandonment or fears of death may surface in the behavior of grieving children. Children often play death games as a way of working out their feelings and anxieties. These games are familiar to the children and provide safe opportunities to express their feelings.

As children grow, they will need to re-experience the loss at each stage of development. For example, at age five, a child's understanding of death has moved from fantasy-based to reality-based. As they learn and understand more, they may need to review and re-experience the loss. When children realize the finality of death, they need to re-interpret what the death means to them. It's important to know this so that you don't feel you are "taking two steps backward," if your child becomes preoccupied with the loss at different stages of his or her development.

One of the biggest challenges for children is the loss of their assumption that childhood is a safe place. Until this moment, young children believe they are immortal and invulnerable and that nothing could hurt their friends, parents, or siblings. This deep trust is destroyed when they experience tragic loss at a young age.

A child's actions may change. It is not uncommon for a child to emotionally and physically regress during the grief process. The child may lash out, throw temper tantrums, do poorly in school, become shy or introverted, perform badly at once-perfected skills, have nightmares, and the like.

Patience and love are the keys to helping your child move past regression. This patience and love is only possible if you are doing your own grief work and renewing yourself emotionally so make sure you continue to take care of your own needs as well.

Babies (Birth to Eighteen Months)

Naturally, babies can't ask questions, however they do experience a visceral response to loss. They feel it in their bones and sense it in their environment. An infant's view of the world is self-centered, and they believe that all things exist for them and because of them. You may experience the baby as more cranky and irritable. This will depend upon their relationship to the deceased. Naturally, babies will feel more of a loss if it is one or both parents than if it is an uncle or other close relative that died.

Babies often become fussy, hard to calm, and fearful of separation. They may develop sleep problems or night terrors. By maintaining children's regular patterns, we help offer a safe parameter within which they can experience their grief. During this time, it's important to offer extra comfort, holding, and soothing time. Keep in mind that older babies often understand what you are saying, even if they are unable to speak. Offer soothing statements and avoid talking about details of the death within earshot.

Immediate physical comfort and a commitment to help the child cope as he/she ages are the best actions you can take. If you are the infant's primary caregiver, it can be challenging to care for the baby's needs as well as your own. If at all possible, find someone outside the family to assist you in caring for the infant so you can give yourself the necessary time to organize your life and to grieve.

Toddlers (Eighteen Months to Three Years)

During this phase of development the parents' or caregivers' main task is to set limits with the child. If your world is upside down because of a sudden death in your home, it is hard to keep up with previous limit-setting. However, it is essential to the child's well-being. Toddlers may also regress and become extremely fearful of separation from their caregivers. If the toddler was toilet trained at the time of the death, they may have a setback. You may experience them as unduly demanding, whining, and needy. They may not want to eat the way they had previously or they may not sleep well. Keeping children on a regular schedule will help to alleviate these fluctuations.

Toddlers know something has occurred in their lives, but they have few, if any, words to express themselves. They have no concept of death and expect the loved one to come back. They will worry about their adult caregivers and may cry when you cry. It is okay to put words on your experience and to tell the child, "I am sad because _____."

It is also important to answer any questions openly and honestly. Telling a child that the dead person is "just sleeping" or "God came and took him," can create enormous fear and anxiety. The child may be afraid to sleep or fear he will be snatched away by God. It's okay to use the word "dead" and to look for ways to illustrate the point (i.e. when the dog died; our goldfish was floating in aquarium, when the bird fell out of the nest).

Direct questions from toddlers are also challenging. At a time when you may be emotionally drained, direct questions can be hard to cope with and to answer. Brook's daughter went through an intense phase of questioning.

"Samantha was three when my brother died. At first, she didn't ask many questions, but a few months after the death they started coming. 'Why are you and Gramma Wendy sad?' 'Why did that bee bite Caleb?' 'What's 'lergic' (allergic) mean?' 'Is a bee gonna bite me?' 'You and me don't have to die, right?' I found the best way to answer these questions was honestly. I explained that usually people die when they are older, but sometimes people die when they are young. I explained that she wasn't allergic—we checked with a doctor. When she asked where dead people went, I told her that I didn't know but I thought it was a good place."

For toddlers, the concept of death is hard to grasp. They have experienced little that will prepare them for the concept. In their favorite cartoons, characters "die" and then return in the next episode. Finality is unfamiliar. Until now, death has been something that just happens in movies or in cartoons, yet nobody really dies. Children at this age often confuse death with sleep and may experience anxiety as early as age three. They may stop talking and appear to feel overall distress.

One of the best things we can do is to use age-appropriate materials to help our children understand what has happened. In the Resources chapter, you will find a list of books that can help guide your child through the questions and emotions of grief.

Young Children

Until children are about four years old, they cannot conceptualize death, and because developmentally they believe the world revolves around them, some will even worry that they may have somehow caused the death (i.e., *If I were a better kid, Daddy wouldn't have gone away*). Sometime between the ages of five and nine, children begin to understand death and realize its finality. They will feel abandonment quite keenly and will worry that their needs may not be taken care of (i.e. *Who will feed me? Where will I go?*). Most adults begin the first stage of mourning almost immediately, but children usually begin mourning several weeks or months after the death. According to Dr. Roberta Temes in *Living With An Empty Chair: A Guide Through Grief,* "Children should not be criticized for caring, selfishly, about their own personal needs at the time of parental death. The child who asks 'But who will take me to the ball game?' or 'Who'll braid my hair for me each morning?' or 'What's for dinner?' when everyone else is weeping, is not being unduly selfish. She is responding as a child should respond."

Children's grief expresses three primary questions:

1. Did I cause the death to happen?
2. Is it going to happen to me?
3. Who is going to take care of me?

Did I cause the death to happen? Children often think that they have magical powers. If a mother says in irritation, "You'll be the death of me" and later dies, her child may wonder if he or she actually caused the mother's death. Also, when children argue, one may say (or think), "I wish you were dead." Should that child die, the surviving child may think that his or her thoughts actually caused the death.

Is it going to happen to me? The death of another child may be especially hard for a child. If the child thinks that the death may have been prevented (by either a parent or a doctor), the child may think that he or she could also die.

Who is going to take care of me? Since children depend on parents and other adults to take care of them, a grieving child may wonder who will care for him or her after the death of an important person.

Age Three to Six Years

At this age, children see death as a kind of sleep; the person is alive, but only in a limited way. The child cannot fully separate death from life. Children may think that the person is still living, even though he or she might have been buried, and they might ask questions about the deceased (for example, how does the deceased eat, go to the toilet, breathe, or play?). Young children know that death occurs physically, but they think it is temporary, reversible, and not final. The child's concept of death may also involve magical thinking. For example, the child may think that his or her thoughts can cause another person to become sick or die. Grieving children under five may have trouble eating, sleeping, and controlling bladder and bowel functions.

In American society, many grieving adults withdraw and do not talk to others. Children, however, often talk to the people around them (even strangers) to see the reactions of others and to get clues for their own responses. Children may ask confusing questions. For example, a child may ask, "I know grandpa died, but when will he come home?" This is a way of testing reality and making sure the story of the death has not changed.

Children between the ages of three and six do much of their learning through repetition. For this reason, it's common for children to ask the same question over and over or to alter it slightly. While this can be draining for you, take the time to answer the questions. Keep in mind that the child's peers will have little information on death and will not have the emotional maturity to help their friend. The only support children of this age group can get is yours—or other support you provide.

Age Six to Nine Years

Children at this age are commonly very curious about death, and may ask questions about what happens to one's body when it dies. Death is thought of as a person or spirit separate from the person who was alive, such as a skeleton, ghost, angel of death, or bogeyman. They may see death as final and frightening but as something that happens mostly to old people (and not to themselves). Grieving children can become afraid of school, have learning problems, develop antisocial or aggressive behaviors, become overly concerned about their own health (for example, developing symptoms of imaginary illness), or withdraw from others. Or, children this age can become too attached and clinging. Boys usually become more aggressive and destructive (for example, acting out in school), instead of openly showing their sadness. When a parent dies, children may feel abandoned by both their deceased parent and their surviving parent because the surviving parent is grieving and is unable to emotionally support the child.

Age Nine and Older

By the time a child is nine years old, death is known to be unavoidable and is not seen as a punishment. By the time a child is twelve years old, death is seen as final and something that happens to everyone.

Grief and Developmental Stages		
Age	**Understanding of Death**	**Expressions of Grief**
Infancy to two years	Is not yet able to understand death.	Quietness, crankiness, decreased activity, poor sleep, and weight loss.
	Separation from mother causes changes.	
Two to six years	Death is like sleeping.	Asks many questions (How does she go to the bathroom? How does she eat?).
		Problems in eating, sleeping, and bladder and bowel control.
		Fear of abandonment.
		Tantrums.
	Dead person continues to live and function in some ways.	Magical thinking (Did I think something or do something that caused the death? Like when I said I hate you and I wish you would die?).
	Death is temporary, not final.	
	Dead person can come back to life.	
Six to nine years	Death is thought of as a person or spirit (skeleton, ghost, bogeyman).	Curious about death.
		Asks specific questions.
		May have exaggerated fears about school.
	Death is final and frightening.	May have aggressive behaviors (especially boys).
		Some concerns about imaginary illnesses.
	Death happens to others, it won't happen to ME.	May feel abandoned.

Grief and Developmental Stages		
Age	**Understanding of Death**	**Expressions of Grief**
Nine and older	Everyone will die.	Heightened emotions, guilt, anger, shame.
		Increased anxiety over own death.
		Mood swings.
	Death is final and cannot be changed.	Fear of rejection; not wanting to be different from peers.
	Even I will die.	Changes in eating habits.
		Sleeping problems.
		Regressive behaviors (loss of interest in outside activities).
		Impulsive behaviors.
		Feels guilty about being alive (especially related to death of a brother, sister, or peer).

Adolescence

Pam's son Ian was twelve when his father died. She shares her story . . .

"My twelve-year-old son, Ian, was anxious to show his dad the new braces Dr. Mathews had installed that day. This was a new experience, a rite of passage if you will, and Ian needed to share it with his dad. Although George and I had been divorced for many years, we were friends and joyfully shared in the day-to-day life of our son. I drove Ian to his dad's office, he smiled broadly at his dad, showing off his new hardware, and George embraced him. It was the last embrace. George was dead just one day later. Ian, at age twelve, was at least able to communicate and express his sadness and anger verbally, although minimally. Imagine experiencing all the intense emotions of a sudden loss, without the ability to express your feelings in words. This is the younger child's plight."

Adolescence is a time of mood changes, and under the best of circumstances, a challenging time for all involved. Add to this the sudden death of someone close when they are least prepared and it's no wonder children find themselves wondering about the meaning of life.

Peer support is extremely important to the adolescent. If the adolescent child has lost a close friend, they should be encouraged to meet with and spend time with their peers and to use the time constructively.

A grief support group comprised of children experiencing a similar type of loss may help immensely. A group will help a child develop a safe way to express his emotions, especially anger. If there aren't any existing support groups, encourage your child to start one through school or church. Pam saw the benefit of school support with her son.

Another challenge of this age group is the need to be independent. It is around this age that children begin pulling back from their parents, seeking their own identity and independence. Barbara D. Rosof writes in *The Worst Loss,* "In order to grow toward psychological independence, [adolescents] must loosen the ties of dependency that have bound them to parents all their lives. This is a long process, one that proceeds by fits and starts over the next ten years. As they begin to pull away, the prospect of sharing with you the intense and painful feelings that the death of a sibling [or other close person] stirs up may feel dangerously regressive: It threatens to pull adolescents back into the very dependency they are working so hard to outgrow."

For this reason, an outside support person becomes essential. If you cannot organize a support group through church or school, talk to a school counselor or other professional about being the support person for your child.

"We were fortunate that our school system had provisions for one-on-one grief counseling for Ian. He attended sessions with a school staff social worker faithfully for almost two years after his father died—most of them without my prodding. I believe the school's awareness and intervention was responsible for Ian's coping as well as he did. However, there were times when he acted out his anger in the home. With no words to express his enormous grief, Ian acted out physically, as many boys do, on the day of the funeral. Without saying a word, he left our house with a religious book his stepmother had given him. I watched as he threw the book onto the rain soaked street and kicked it for over an hour. He walloped that book over and over again until it broke from its binding in shreds. One final blow sent the soggy book sliding into the sewer. When he came back to the house, he looked spent—and relieved. Fortunately, he didn't hurt himself or anyone else."

When the deceased is a sibling, adolescents and teens may want to be away from the house and spend more time with friends than family. There are a couple of reasons for this. First, parents may be so absorbed in their own grief that children do not want to intensify their own emotions and grief by being around their parents. They may feel an obligation to comfort parents, yet they may not have the emotional energy to do so. Second, the house carries many memories of the relationship with their sibling or other family member and they may not be ready to face these memories. While it's important to maintain communication with the child and discuss feelings, offer the child his or her needed space, provided it's a safe space.

Teenagers to Young Adults

Teenagers and young adults may experience a sense of unfairness (i.e. Dad was supposed to be at my wedding; Mom was supposed to be present at the birth of my first child; John at my college graduation). They will also experience a keen sense of their own mortality and may worry that they will die in the same unexpected way as their parent, friend, or close relative. Again, a support group of peers can be extremely helpful in preventing the submersion of intense feelings, which can erupt in impulsive or destructive behaviors.

"At age nineteen, Ian is a well-adjusted young adult entering his second year of college who recently asked, 'Mom, I wonder what kind of man I would have turned out to be if my father hadn't died when I was twelve?' Choking back tears, I answered the only way I knew how, 'I don't know how you would have been different, I only know he would have been proud of the way you turned out.'"

Teenagers experience many of the same stages of grief as adults. However, they also have experiences unique to their age. These include:

Private Grieving

Teenagers often aren't as familiar or comfortable displaying strong emotions. For this reason, many grieve privately. They may cry in their rooms or in the shower.

Unhealthy Anger

Teens may choose unhealthy venues for releasing their anger. They may destroy things or engage in self-destructive behavior. It's important to remember that teens do not have as many healthy outlets open to them as adults do. For this reason, it is imperative that we offer healthy outlets to teenagers.

Sexual Activity

With the loneliness that accompanies grief, teenagers may be left feeling lonely and scared. They may feel family members don't have the energy or ability to comfort them, since they are facing their own grief. For these reasons, it is not uncommon for teenagers to become sexually active in an attempt to ease the loneliness.

Guilty Feelings

From an early age, children long to please their parents, family members, and those close to them. Often they interpret an argument as their failure to please. Furthermore, they may feel responsible for the death because they didn't behave well, caused too many arguments, were a source of stress, or didn't meet parents' expectations. While parents find this reasoning inconceivable, it is common in a teenager's mind. It is important to reiterate over and over again that the teenager was in no way responsible for the death.

Does Your Child Need Professional Help?

Grief is unfamiliar territory to children, just as it is for many adults. Changes in emotions and behaviors, especially in the initial months, are to be expected. However, it is important to remember that a child has less tools and resources to seek help or understand the types of help available. Observe both verbal and non-verbal communications carefully. If a child talks about or acts out in way that inflicts self-harm or harms another, consult a mental health professional immediately.

The behaviors below, excerpted from *Helping Children Grieve* by Ruth Arent, MSW are offered as guidelines for when to seek professional help.

Is your child. . .

- Depressed, immobilized, or feeling hopeless?
- Showing emotional swings that are greatly exaggerated, with extended periods of anger or fear? Acting out with anger and hostility?
- Continuing to yearn for the dead loved one, to the detriment of schoolwork?
- Showing new symptoms of trauma, or showing recurring manifestations of old symptoms after they had subsided?
- Refusing support from family or others?
- Abounding in physical complaints, weight problems, sleeping problems, nightmares, or nervous habits?
- Prone to suicidal thoughts?
- Threatening to quit school or run away?
- Defiant, obstructive, or creating non-stop stress and problems in the family?

Keep in mind that a professional may recommend medication, which would be ordered and supervised by a mental health physician.

Physical Outbursts

Since children and teenagers are often not mature enough emotionally, they are much more likely to act out their emotions physically. This can take the form of tantrums, fighting, screaming, tattooing, body piercing, or other physical expression. Watch for these physical signs. When you see one, realize it is probably caused by emotional repression. Take this as a red flag to find a support network or professional intervention for your child.

Suicidal Thoughts

If the teenager was especially close to the person they have lost, they may see suicide as a way to rejoin their loved one. Also, when teens are not dealing with their emotions in a healthy way, they can quickly become overwhelmed. Suicide becomes an escape route from these turbulent emotions. When a teenager details *any* part of a suicidal plan, this is an *immediate* sign to seek professional help.

Linda Cunningham offers some helpful ideas for adults to help encourage teenagers to work with their grief. In her article entitled "Grief and the Adolescent," she writes: "Teenagers often give us mixed messages. They tell us that they need and expect our help in providing them with food and a nurturing environment but also tell us, on the other hand, that they can run their lives on their own. Because people do not always know how to respond to teens, they frequently back off, resulting in a teen who is left to grieve alone or with very limited support . . ."

Some other ideas to help grieving teenagers include:

- Ask to see a picture of the person the child has lost. Ask questions about the person. Ask them to share their favorite stories and memories.
- Be inquisitive about the death. Ask the child what happened. Ask how the child feels about what happened. Often, as a teenager tells their story, we can listen carefully for clues of what they are confused about or feeling guilty for.
- Talk to your teenager about grief and the common emotions he/she is likely to feel. If it is the child's first time with these intense feelings, they can be extremely frightening. Choose a book or two from the recommended resources list to help the teenager familiarize himself with the emotions of grief.
- Encourage the teenager to make a collage. Help to gather magazines and pictures. Cut out words, pictures, and notes that carry special memories. Place the finished collage in a place where the teen can see it often.
- Consider framing a picture of their loved one and hanging it in their room.
- Help the teenager identify his needs and relate them to others. A teenager may feel unsupported, but it's hard for others to support him when they don't understand these needs. Identifying what would help most is a way to alleviate the unneeded pain of isolation.
- Encourage your teen to start a support group with other grieving friends. Offer your home as a safe place to hold the meetings. Do whatever you can to help. Perhaps you could carpool and pick up other kids, provide appetizers or beverages, photocopy handouts, etc.

Grief by Proxy

According to Ruth Arent, MSW and author of *Helping Children Grieve,* "Grief by proxy occurs when a person empathizes with the victims of a tragedy and experiences the same emotional reactions and symptoms of traumatic stress. With acts of terrorist violence and natural disasters occurring around the world, trauma by proxy is almost universal, affecting adults and children as well."

Whether tragic events touch your family personally or whether newspapers or television bring them into your home, you can help children cope with the anxiety that violence, death, and disasters can cause.

Listening to and talking to children about their concerns can reassure them that they will be safe. Start by encouraging them to discuss how they have been affected by what is happening around them. Even young children may have specific questions about tragedies. Children react to stress at their own developmental level.

The *Caring for Every Child's Mental Health Campaign* offers these pointers for parents and other caregivers:

- **Encourage children to ask questions.** Listen to what they say. Provide comfort and assurance that address their specific fears. It's okay to admit you can't answer all of their questions.
- **Talk on their level.** Communicate with your children in a way they can understand. Don't get too technical or complicated.
- **Find out what frightens them.** Encourage your children to talk about fears they may have. They may worry that someone will harm them at school or that someone will try to hurt *you.*
- **Focus on the positive.** Reinforce the fact that most people are kind and caring. Remind your child of the heroic actions taken by ordinary people to help victims of tragedy.
- **Pay attention.** Your children's play and drawings may give you a glimpse into their questions or concerns. Ask them to tell you what is going on in the game or the picture. It's an opportunity to clarify any misconceptions, answer questions, and give reassurance.
- **Develop a plan.** Establish a family emergency plan for the future, such as a meeting place where everyone should gather if something unexpected happens in your family or neighborhood. It can help you and your children feel safer.

General Guidelines for Helping Children

- To help the child begin to mourn, a surviving parent needs to continue the daily routine as much as possible.
- Work on listening. Communicating with a different generation can be difficult. Do your best to listen and be present without telling the child what to do. If you have a hard time listening objectively, find someone who can.
- Continually express your unconditional love and acceptance.
- The child's environment should stay the same—this is not the time for a new school, a new house, or even a new babysitter.
- When you sense the child's readiness to grieve, it is okay to pray together, cry together, and reminisce together.
- Allow the child to talk, and talk, and talk about the death with you. Help him or her understand that the intensity of grief will lessen over time. Not talking about death (which indicates that the subject is off-limits) does not help children learn to cope with loss.
- When discussing death with children, explanations should be simple and direct. Each child should be told the truth using as much detail as he or she is able to understand. The child's questions should be answered honestly and directly.
- Children need to be reassured about their own security (they often worry that they will also die, or that their surviving parent will go away). Children's questions should be answered, making sure that the child understands the answers.
- A discussion about death should include the proper words, such as car accident, died, and death. Substitute words or phrases (for example, "he passed away," "he is sleeping," or "we lost him") should never be used because they can confuse children and lead to misunderstandings.
- When a death occurs, children can and should be included in the planning and participation of memorial ceremonies. These events help children (and adults) remember loved ones. Children should not be forced to be involved in these ceremonies, but they should be encouraged to take part in those portions of the events with which they feel most comfortable. If the child wants to attend the funeral, wake, or memorial service, he or she should be given in advance a full explanation of what to expect.

Remember that no matter how old the child, they have experienced the worst possible tragedy. They will feel terrible. They should not be encouraged to forget or deny. They must learn, with your help and guidance, that they can overcome emotional catastrophes. Allowing the child to feel the full power of the sudden loss will help increase coping ability for the rest of the child's life.

Part Three: Sharing Our Stories

"All sorrows can be borne if you put them into a story or tell a story about them."
—Isak Dinesen

This was by far the hardest section of this book to write and compile. As authors, our goal was to create a valuable resource and guide, yet in doing that, we were stumped when it came to this section. We wanted to cover the different people we lose in our lives—parents, spouses, friends, children, siblings, etc., but just as there are no rules to grief, there are no rules to handling different types of loss. In reflecting on our own experience, we realized what we needed most was to hear that other people went through what we did, and although changed, came out the other side. We also needed general guidelines, poems, quotes, and other materials to support the grief journey. We collected stories, quotes, songs, poems, and prayers that moved us. We divided this section by chapters of one's relationship to the loved one

117

(parent, child, sibling, etc.). We encourage you to read through each chapter, since relationships are not easily classified into one area or another. A husband can also be a friend. Our siblings can be friends and parental figures, etc. For this reason, we believe you will gain quite a bit from the offerings in each chapter.

In this updated edition, we have added stories and thoughts in several areas, including suicide, military casualties, mass tragedy, and the unique challenges we have been asked about time and time again from grieving readers.

We searched for real-life stories and real-life grief experiences. And over the years, we have continued to add to this knowledge and extrapolated stories from those we have encountered in our journey. Additionally, we've added common emotions and questions that those who are grieving have brought to us.

> *"When loss is a story, there is no right or wrong way to grieve.*
> *There is no pressure to move on.*
> *There is no shame in intensity or duration.*
> *Sadness, regret, confusion, yearning, and all the experiences of grief*
> *become part of the narrative of love for the one who died."*
> —*Patrick O'Malley, psychotherapist and*
> New York Times *columnist*

Chapter Ten
Losing a Friend

"There is only one way for you
To live without grief in your lifetime; that is
To exist without love. Your grief represents
Your humanness, just as your love does."
—*Carol Staudacher*

True, deep, abiding friends are hard to come by, and like all sudden losses, extremely difficult to understand. Our connection to friends, newly hatched or life-long, may be more intimate than the connection we have to our families; or a family member may be the closest friend we have.

In later life, most of us begin to ease slowly into the fact that due to death, we will need to let go of those we love and are close to. As we age, it's natural to expect that friends will eventually become ill and die. As Judith Viorst would say, our second half of life becomes a time of "necessary losses." However, when we lose a friend through the tragedy of sudden death, the slow process of letting go is aborted.

Many friends fulfill particular roles. A friend is rarely "just" a friend. Most friendships include elements of other relationships. For instance, in cases where we didn't have functional parenting, our friend may have become like a parent to us. In this case, the chapter where we discuss losing a parent will be additionally helpful to you. If your friend was much younger than you when he/she died, it may be that you served a parental role or were a significant mentor. Perhaps some of what is included in the chapter on losing a child will be helpful. If your friend was also your romantic love, the chapter on losing a significant other will give you some insights and support as you grapple with your loss. We hope this chapter will provide you with some useful ways to navigate the loss of a friend.

Reaching for the Phone

I keep reaching for the phone. I want to tell my friend something or ask her advice.

You may find yourself reaching for the phone to call your friend, to tell them about an occurrence, to invite them to a movie, to sit with you and tell you about their most recent accomplishment. Yet there is no one at the other end of the phone — only a dial tone.

When a close friend dies suddenly, it is natural to feel cut off from your source of advice and companionship. Thrown into the ever-present reality of the moment, there you are with your questions, your fears, and your celebrations, and your friend isn't there to share them with you. In the past, your friend would have been beside you at a moment like this.

Pam offers an idea for internalizing the voice of a friend.

"I had a therapist years ago tell me that the goal of therapy was to internalize the therapist's voice and make it a part of my own inner dialogue. Perhaps you can do this with your friend. Close your eyes, imagine their response to your call—you may feel them with you—internalize them— make them part of your life for the rest of your life.

I received a card from a friend when my father died and in it she wrote, 'Now you will have him with you—always . . .' I believe that's true."

My friend and I were closer than family and shared everything together. I am finding the grieving process very challenging because there is little support or acknowledgement for the bereaved whom are not related by family ties. I am watching the support extended to everyone else and want to scream: "What about me!?"

You might have been the loved ones confidant, closest person, or you may know the person better than anyone, but you are not formally or legally automatically included in the death process. This can be extremely challenging when you see families carrying out plans or rituals that contrast what you believe your friend would have wanted.

Friendships tend to come and go throughout life, whereas family bonds are permanent. Even when families are estranged, a death often brings relatives together—at least for a time. If the family and friends of the family are not aware of your close friendship ties, you may find yourself grouped with "other caring people and well-wishers." You may feel the special closeness of your bond with the deceased is not understood or being respected.

It is important to remember in the aftermath of sudden death it is hard to care for one's self, let alone think clearly enough to keep everyone's best interest at heart. If the family is not aware of the depth of your friendship ties, it would be impossible for them to anticipate or consider your needs.

When Caleb died, Brook's mother Wendy was amazed by the number of friends Caleb had whom she had never met. She remembered many of the names from stories but hadn't realized how profoundly her son had impacted their lives. In the weeks, months, and even years following Caleb's death, it wasn't uncommon for one of his friends to stop by the house and introduce himself. Wendy loved these visits and hearing "Caleb stories" she had never heard before. By the time the friend would leave, both Wendy and the visitor had forged a new friendship based on their love for Caleb.

Consider paying a visit to one of the family members your friend spoke fondly about. Share stories and memories. This connection is likely to be valued and cherished by you and the family member. You may even emerge with a new friendship that cherishes your friend as the common bond.

What can I say to the family that will convey what my friend meant to me?

Almost more than any other person, your relationship with the deceased was unique. He probably revealed to you more of his true nature than to anyone else, including his family. Your reminisces and impressions of who he was will be more valuable because he was so real with you. In fact, you may know him better than his family because you spent more time with him over the years. What can you say? You can offer to share your stories. Brook's family found this extremely comforting.

> "Caleb had more friends than anyone I've ever known. When he died, our house was flooded with his friends. My mother, Caleb's friends, and I would sit in our living room recalling memories and stories. We did this for days. We laughed together, we cried together, we grieved together.
>
> Several of his closest friends had special stories they wanted to share. Some were funny, some were odd, and some were metaphysical. These friends offered to share their stories with us in private. We welcomed each story and my mother and I discuss them to this day. Do not be afraid to offer your story to a grieving family. Sharing our memories with one another is one of the best ways to keep our memories alive."

Is it appropriate for me to ask the family if I can participate in the funeral or memorial service?

Yes, by all means ask. They may not want you (or anyone outside the family) to participate, but most families welcome input from friends of the deceased. Personal stories illustrating your friend's humor or kindness are usually well received. If you are denied the privilege to read something at the service, perhaps there will be an opportunity if the family receives guests in their home following the funeral. Another way to convey your thoughts and feelings about your friend is to put them in a letter or card and send this to the family.

I want to place something in the casket—a memento of our friendship. Do I need to check with someone before I do this?

It is a good idea to check with the family before you place an object in with the deceased. The funeral director can also guide you. When Pam's friend, Eleanor died, Pam wanted Eleanor's family to place in her hand a small golden goddess Pam had given her when she was alive. Pam knew this had great meaning to Eleanor, the family agreed, and the funeral director was glad to comply.

I've been asked to participate in the memorial service. This is all so sudden and I haven't had a chance to prepare.
First of all, you are not expected to be a perfectly stoic performer. This is not a performance, it is meant to be a meaningful send-off for your friend. If you are at a loss for words, you might want to select the lyrics from a song you both enjoyed as a way of conveying the depth of your relationship. Or you may simply want to say, "I have no words except, I will miss him. He was one of my best friends."

Pam read the following at a friend's funeral and prefaced it by saying, "As I read this, try to imagine these words being said by the departed . . ."

"Relatives and friends, I am about to leave:
my last breath does not say 'goodbye,'
for my love for you is truly timeless,
beyond the touch of bony death . . .
I leave my thoughts, my laughter, and my dreams
to you whom I have treasured
beyond gold and precious gems.
I give you what no thief can steal,
the memories of our times together:
the tender, love-filled moments,
the successes we have shared,
the hard times that brought us closer together
and the roads we have walked side by side . . ."
—Edward Hays, *Prayers for a Planetary Pilgrim*
new section here after the sec break

When Friends Die

As I write this, my husband and I just buried two of our closest friends within weeks of one another. They took our shared histories with them. Just like that. Two people, husband and wife, close friends, and off they went with the stories of our lives together. Who knows us as well as they did? How do we replace them? Thirty years of problems, kids, and wonderful grandchildren; thirty years of religious and political arguments and agreements; thirty years of shared tears and joys. We spoke in a kind of shorthand, a private language where we could finish one another's sentences.

It's a universal truth: as we age, our friends die more and more often, and many times suddenly. We can't replace them. That's a ridiculous idea and a wish that can't be fulfilled. But we must try to find new friends who we can confide in, who will hold us up when we are down—friends who will be there for us and who we can offer ourselves to. Someone once said to me a few years ago, "Pam, you've got to make younger friends—they last longer!" Well, that didn't work—three of our four friends *were* younger.

I remember reading *The Bridge of San Luis Rey* by Thornton Wilder. The book is about a bridge that collapsed in Peru back in the eighteenth century, suddenly killing five people. The tragedy is witnessed by a monk as he was about to step out onto the bridge and he's left wondering, as we tend to do when bad things happen, if there was some purpose to this event or was it just random? The truth is always more complicated, and I agree with narrator who concludes: "But soon we shall die and all memory of these five will have left the earth, and we ourselves shall be loved for a while and forgotten. But the love will have been enough; all those impulses of love return to the love that made them. Even memory is not necessary for love. There is a land of the living and a land of the dead, and the bridge is love, the only survival, the only meaning."

The following, an excerpt from *The Prophet,* by Kahlil Gibran, was read by Pam for a friend who enjoyed singing and dancing:

"For what is it to die but to stand naked in the wind and to melt into the sun? And what is it to cease breathing, but to free the breath from its restless rides, that it may rise and expand and seek God unencumbered? Only when you drink from the river of silence shall you indeed sing. And when you have reached the mountain top, then you shall begin to climb. And when the earth shall claim your limbs, then shall you truly dance."

The following is a reading that anyone can use—and if your friend is a woman, feel free to change "he" to "she."

A Friend

What is a Friend? I'll tell you.

It is a person with whom you dare to be yourself.

Your soul can go naked with him.

He seems to ask you to put on nothing, only to be what you really are.

When you are with him, you do not have to be on your guard.

You can say what you think, so long as it is genuinely you.

He understands those contradictions in your nature that cause others
to misjudge you.

With him you breathe freely—you can avow your little vanities and envies and absurdities and in opening them up to him they are dissolved on the white ocean of his loyalty.

He understands. You can weep with him, laugh with him, pray with him—through and underneath it all he sees, knows and loves you.

A Friend, I repeat, is one with whom you dare to be yourself.

–Author unknown

When honoring a loved one, go with what feels intuitively right to you. What touches you deeply will likely touch others. When Brook was in her teens, she lost a friend in a car accident. At the service, the friend's father got up to speak. Barely able to get the words out between gasps and tears, he delivered a few minutes that moved everyone in the room. The deceased was a performer and he ended his talk with, "Always a performer, let's give him one more standing ovation for the time he gave us." Everyone in the room stood, clapping with all their might, tears streaming down their faces as they honored their friend. Typical? No. But it moved everyone more than any other spoken words could have.

Naturally, the best way to honor a friend is to speak from the heart—your heart. What you say doesn't have to be eloquent or full of fancy epitaphs. Simple, straightforward, and heartfelt words are what the family is longing to hear. If you're feeling stuck as to where to begin, look to the form we have provided in the Appendix. This form is intended to give you a place to start and should help you cover the most important aspects of your friend's life and your relationship. Again, there is really no right or wrong way to eulogize a friend. You can sing a song, write a poem, dance a dance, or read what someone else has written. Use your imagination and trust your instincts. If you are intuitively drawn to a particular reading or creative act, it may even be your departed friend who is gently nudging you, instructing you on how to celebrate his life.

Some Things You Can Do

Internalizing Your Friend

The loss of a friend takes an enormous toll on the soul. You may feel like their loss has taken a part of you away. One of the best ways to honor your friendship is to take some aspect of your friend's life or the way he lived his life and incorporate this part of his personality into who you are.

Contributions

Did your friend love children, lost animals, parks, the theater? Find an appropriate way to contribute time or money to an organization that promotes one of those special values.

Helping His Parents

If your friend was the child of aging parents who cannot drive, or who may not be able to care for the grave site, assure them you will, with fresh flowers, weeding, etc. From time to time, take a photo of the grave site to show them.

Friend Support Group

Many support groups exist for those who have lost a partner or a child, but there are few that exist for the loss of a friend. One person that Pam knows formed a support group with the deceased's friends. This is a wonderful way to keep a friend's memory alive while working through grief. We have included in the Appendix the letter this woman used to begin her group.

Chapter Eleven
Losing a Parent

*"... I learned to attend viewings even if I didn't know
the deceased, to press the moist hands
of the living, to look in their eyes and offer
sympathy, as though I understood loss even then.
I learned that whatever we say means nothing,
What anyone will remember is that we came ..."*
—*From the poem, "What I learned from My Mother" by Julia Kasdorf*

We expect to lose our parents—someday. We expect them to become frail and fragile and gradually "melt away" over time. And yet, few of us are really ready for our parent or parents to die, much less tragically or suddenly. We believe there is "always tomorrow" to say what needs to be said, to express what we feel. There is always tomorrow to express the anger, the pain, the love, and the gratitude. Then we are cut short, mission aborted, and we are left holding a bag full of feelings that may feel heavier than we can bear. The unsaid gratitude becomes outrage. The unexpressed anger turns inward and we are depressed. The unspoken pain they caused us becomes a stone we carry in our hearts or perhaps guilt at the relief we feel in their passing. We waited for the right time, and when sudden death occurs, that right time is gone forever.

Many of us look to our parents for guidance and acceptance well into our adult lives. We rely on their opinions. We rely on them for our roots. When we lose a parent, a part of our history disappears. We can no longer ask opinions or hear stories of when we were younger. We lose a piece of our foundation. Melissa Rivers's father, Edgar Rosenberg, committed suicide twenty-seven years before the passing of her mother. "When one parent dies," says Melissa, an only child, "it's a comma. When the second parent dies, it's a period." The following story details a girl's loss of her father and how that affected her throughout life.

DADDY

He was the center of my universe. He was my hero.
September 17, 1975

I was blissfully ignorant of what was to unfold. The phone rang. An employee of our riding stable. The horses had not been fed. Where's Frank? Where's Daddy?

Never would such a thing happen. Even as my mind raced to reach a sane and rational conclusion. I knew! Hopeless. Helpless. It was another fifteen minutes before I fully understood, and felt the impact of these words. His car; parked at the church where he would meet a friend and run. Not jog. Run. There was something sinister about that car being parked there at this time. Still not fully grasping, understanding. It's locked and his shirt lay on the front seat. The car is never locked.

He's in trouble, passed out. I start to run down the trail. Halfheartedly. I knew that I couldn't help him alone and would need help. I tried to shout out for him. No strength. No use. Helpless. Hopeless. I weep.

Into my car and back towards the house to call. Who? The ranger. Find him. Help him. I pass Bonnie and my brother heading towards the church. My brother is pale and Bonnie is crying. And this I know is true: *My father's dead. How am I ever going to live!*

It will be many years before I pull that thought out to examine it.

Beat a tree: "Damn You For Dying!" And recover.

My good friend Naomi comes right away. She was my anchor then. To the barn to be with my horse and the woo-woo begins. Naomi's horse Greg has a nameplate on his stall door: "Casablanca, Naomi A." A moth lands on the first "a" in Naomi. It looks like: N*omi. Daddy always called Naomi, "Nomi." Signs are somehow important to me at this moment, although I have no conscious knowledge of their existence. This sign sets a tone that will come to be woven throughout the years.

Pickle is my best horse and my heart. He senses my overwhelming grief and lowers his head against my body. I embrace him and we stand like this forever. Such a magical moment to be comforted by my best friend in this way. I drink it in. Actually I let it out. Such unconditional love.

Later, as I walked away from his stall, something caught my attention. The bottom corner of my jacket had been chewed off! No wonder Pickle stood so patiently. No wonder he'd been so loving. It was the best kind of "step in the pants," as my father would say. Pickle brought me back to the joy that was/is my father. Ever the tease. Always the coyote. A part of me that lives.

This joy defined the shape and depth of my grief. The grief was huge, but it carried with it the best I knew of my father and myself. I went on, one step at a time.

Days later I'm folding laundry that's been in the basket for a while. In the middle of the clothes basket is my father's shirt. The one that he had worn on the last morning of his life. I pick it up carefully, tenderly, tearfully. A large moth falls out. Dead, if I remember correctly, but a moth just the same. A powerful sign. Daddy was all right. And I grieved.

Cigarettes. Marijuana. Alcohol. In excess, but somehow over the years I work my way through it, and I come out the other side alive. So alive! and wanting to understand what motivated me, what dictated the choices I was making, had always seemed to make.

The wrong man; always the wrong man. And I found my way to a light. And she was Pam. She shined that light on me and I could see the beauty, and the strength, and the value of me. Me! She walked beside me as I explored the paths stretching out before me, and the ones that I had left behind. The choices I had made since my father died, and the ones I had made while he lived.

And now, twenty-four years since he died, more than half my life-time later, the Spirit of my father is strong with me.

So say the ones that knew him in this life.

So say the ones that know him in the next.

So say I. I know him in both.

I feel the best he can be.

Beautiful.

Pure, with the perfection that only Spirit can inspire.

I am grateful for the sequence of events that has brought me to this place in time. I would not trade who I am or what I have experienced for the world. I was also grateful that my father died suddenly, without prior illness. He died in the middle of the land he loved, doing what he loved to do. I clung to this image whenever I needed to shift out of my grief. I read somewhere that when a person dies suddenly, it's because they've completed what they came here to do and have no reason for prolonged illness. I like this thought.

Years later a psychic told me that my father had actually stuck around longer in order to stay with me. That really made me feel special, at a time when I was terribly insecure. I needed so much. I have it.

—Rita Grenci

Generation Shifts

In addition to the loss of foundation and emotional challenges we face, there are other challenges. For one, roles may shift. If we have lost our last living parent we move from the middle generation position (you are a child and you have children) to the older generation position.

Additionally, if you lose one parent suddenly, like Rita, you may be left with the responsibility of caring for the surviving parent. Without warning or prepara-tion, you must assume the role of caregiver. You become responsible for working with an attorney, the insurance company, maybe even a criminal trial in the courts.

If you and your parents were on the younger side (you in your twenties and they in their forties) at the time of death, you may have deep regrets over what you did and didn't get to do with them. If you and your parents were older (you in your forties and they over sixty) you may still have regrets, but it's more likely you have more memories to cherish.

"It is understandable that shock and denial follow sudden, unexpected death. There is a small corner of the mind of every distraught mourner that hopes against hope for a reversal of reality—for the curtain to be pulled back and the dead parent to step forward, beaming, *It was all a big mistake!*" Lois F. Akner, CSW, *How to Survive the Loss of a Parent: A Guide for Adults*

Martha faced the unexpected death of her seemingly healthy mother just shy of the Christmas holiday.

My mother died on December 23, 1990, just thirty days after collapsing from a burst aneurysm. She was a sixty-one-year-old woman with *no* health problems whatsoever. She was very healthy, slim, followed a good diet and never suffered from any serious illnesses. According to doctors, she died of Adult Respiratory Distress Syndrome—which resulted from complications of two brain surgeries to repair multiple aneurysms that were found around her brain.

Apparently she was born with an AVM-Abnormal Vein Malformation, which she never knew about, neither did we. I am the oldest of three sisters, two of us were pregnant at the time. My father, who was sixty-three at the time, was devastated at the sudden loss of my mother and his companion whom had never left his side in thirty-two years of marriage.

It was the Sunday after Thanksgiving when she collapsed at 6:45 a.m. I lived two houses down from her. I had to call the paramedics, something I had never ever done before and that was very traumatic. I also had to ride with the paramedics and decide which hospital to take her to, without knowing how serious her condition was.

The last conversation I remember was the Monday before Thanksgiving when we were shopping for our family dinner. We spoke a lot about my baby, which she was so anxious to meet. Once she collapsed and after the surgeries, she was placed on morphine. I never had a normal conversation with her after that Thanksgiving dinner.

Even though it has been almost eight years since her death it is hard to say what stage I am in. My sisters and I have become even closer and have helped each other through the pain, although we are unable to speak a lot about it. Our children help us through it. Two of them were lucky enough to have been watched by her, one was a-year-and-a-half, the other just six-months-old. It is very difficult to go to the cemetery without breaking down, but the kids go with us and understand that she is buried there. We talk about her to the kids and keep her pictures to remind them about how wonderful she was. This has helped although I have yet to completely cry all the tears because I am terrified about not being able to stop. That deep pain one feels which touches the very core of your being is where I need to go because I know I will cross into a different stage. That is where I think I am now, ready to face the fear of feeling that pain and getting to a point where I can speak to my mother directly about things that happen to me or to ask for her advice.

I carry her with me every single day and with every action I take, I remember her wisdom and values as I teach my own child about how to be a good person who helps others.

What I have learned from the grieving experience and facing tragic death is that you never know when you will die. One must enjoy every day and enjoy family. Our family and children need us. It is important to keep my mother alive in her memories, I see a lot of her in me, I even see her expressions in me and that is good because I keep her legacy alive and I am passing it on to my son.

I went through a rough time when my father passed away three years later. It is scary to know that you are all grown up and are truly responsible for your actions. I am my mother now . . . I never realized what she meant when she said, "Just wait until you have your own

family, you will understand why I am so strict and demanding of you."
She was preparing me to take her place . . ."

"In the end, the way your father or mother died is not a complete statement about their lives. There is much more that remains to be remembered. To concentrate only on the manner of the end deprives not only your parents of their total identity, but *you* of a broader perspective." Fiona Marshall, *Losing a Parent*

Some Things You Can Do

Letter Writing

Write a letter to your parent expressing your true feelings and place it in the casket before burial or cremation. If the body was not recovered, you can burn the letter on a beach or some other outdoor place. As the smoke rises, imagine the words are being carried on the air to your parent.

Photographs

Find a photo of your parent that you have not yet framed. Take it to a photo store to be enlarged, have it framed, and hang it in a special place.

Listening

Keep "listening" for advice and guidance from your parent. Your parent may have died, but she was a powerful influence in your life. If what you "hear" is negative, now is the time to turn DOWN the volume on negative influences and turn UP the volume on positive influences.

Seek a Mentor

There may be someone else in your life that you can find who will help nurture and encourage you the way a good parent would. With the help of this surrogate parent, you may be able to get some of your unmet needs addressed.

Seek Out More Information

Talk to your parent's friends, work associates, or others involved in their daily activities and ask them to share stories of their times together.

Lessons Learned

Make a list of all you learned from your parent, good or bad. It can help to know that their life had meaning to you and that you received some very important life lessons from them. Even if your parent died an untimely death and was in your life for only a short time, you can surely find the meaning in your relationship. This can truly help you accept the loss and move on in your grief.

Chapter Twelve
Losing a Child

> *"I've learned that I am much stronger than I ever gave myself
> credit for. I've learned patience, because grief does not go away
> just because you want it to. And I've learned that helping other
> people is sometimes the best help I can give myself."*
> —Donna F. Mother of a seventeen-year-old daughter who committed suicide

It has been said that there is no loss as devastating as the loss of a child—
regardless of your age or the child's. Sudden death is a mix-up of everything we
know to be true in life. Losing a child to sudden death is a break in the natural
law and order of life. The child we have spent our time loving and caring for and
planning to watch well into adulthood has been taken. It is a heartbreak like no
other. If the death was a suicide, the recovery is filled with another set of difficult
emotions (see Chapter 16 on suicide). Those who live through and survive such an
ordeal without becoming bitter have the strongest, most loving souls of all people
walking the planet.

In her book, *Surviving Grief,* Doctor Catherine M. Sanders writes, "The reason parental grief is so different from other losses has to do with excess. Because loss of a child is such an unthinkable loss, everything is intensified, exaggerated, and lengthened. Guilt and anger are almost always present in every significant loss, but these emotions are inordinate with grieving parents. Experts estimate that it takes anywhere from three to five years to reach renewal after a spouse dies, but parental grief might go on for ten to twenty years or maybe a lifetime. Our lives are severely altered when our child dies and there can be no replacement. Substitutes offer little respite. This is not to say that there is no hope for happiness. It is just that the shock and severity of this kind of loss leaves us feeling completely helpless and full of dark despair."

As Dr. Sanders points out in the previous excerpt, our emotions are intensified with the loss of a child.

Extreme Emotions

There are so many dramatic changes and hardships to understand and overcome with the loss of a child. It has been said that after losing a child, we embark on a lifelong healing process. Understanding these unique challenges can help us to understand how to work through them.

Disorder

Disorder seems to be more prevalent after losing a child as compared to any other loss. While we may face disorder in our physical and emotional lives, we also feel disorder within the world. When we have children, we expect them to outlive us. We build a future around our children. We build dreams and fantasies and goals. In short, we build a world. When a child is lost, these fantasies and dreams come crashing down without warning. Basic logic seems to have abandoned the world as we know it.

A Piece of Ourselves

Children are an extension of us. They carry many of our physical and personality traits forward into the world. We see ourselves in their eyes. Through our children, we envision a better future. When we lose a child, we lose this extension, and we lose this hope.

Guilt

Guilt runs strong in surviving parents. As a parent, we expect ourselves to be able to take care of our child. From birth, most parents promise their children they will protect them. When a child dies, we may feel a sense of personal failure. We may think we weren't "good enough" as parents. These distorted thoughts are the mind's attempt to make sense of the unfathomable.

Anger

Although anger is present in most types of grieving, it is different when we've lost a child—it's often much more intense. Parents simply cannot passively accept this devastating loss—they must express their anger at someone. It might be God, it might be the doctors, it might be whoever was present—but the anger will come. Obsessive anger needs to be talked about with a professional. In order to function, it is imperative that parents funnel this anger into a healthy or creative outlet.

Stress

In her book, *The Worst Loss,* Barbara D. Rosof writes, "The death of a child is a loss like no other. *The Diagnostic and Statistical Manual of Mental Disorders,* psychiatry's diagnostic bible, does not overstate the case when it calls the death of a child a 'catastrophic stressor.' It robs parents of what they love most, isolates partners from each other, and deafens them so that they cannot hear the cries of their other children."

The stress experienced by a parent is unimaginable. It is important that each parent recognize and seek ways to deal with this stress. For women, who tend to find comfort and healing from discussion, joining a support group is a wise decision. The Compassionate Friends is a support group that deals specifically with child loss. They have over five hundred chapters. See the Resource chapter to find out how to locate a chapter near you.

Men also need to find support. Some men find this in a support group setting and others prefer one-on-one counseling or handling their grief privately. Later in this chapter we take a detailed look at men's grief. We also cover grieving as a couple in Chapter 8.

Losing an Adult Child

Losing an adult child carries unique challenges. A parent has put so much time and energy into raising a child. You spend hours, days, and maybe years lecturing children on how to be safe. "Don't talk to strangers." "Stay away from drugs and alcohol." "Look both ways before crossing the street." After all this careful care and attention throughout their youth, you assume you are "out of the woods"—that now you will reap the rewards of watching your child develop as an adult. You wait for them to marry or follow a career or have children. When you lose a child at this life junction, although you have many precious memories, you are robbed of the future experiences you have expected.

In the brochure titled, *The Death of an Adult Child,* The Compassionate Friends write, "If the adult child dies as the result of an accident or an illness, parents are often told (while being comforted by friends or family) that they should be grateful that their child lived as long as he or she did. Of course you are grateful to have had your child for twenty-five, thirty, or forty years, but that does not mean your grief is lessened! Many parents have stated their relationship with the adult child had become one of friendship. They feel that they have not only lost their child, but a friend as well."

The following poem by Brook's mother, Wendy, details the emotions and trials of losing her son when he was twenty-seven years old.

Three Weeks to the Day
PART ONE: Saturday
it is three weeks to the day—to the hour—to the minute
to that split second—when daylight-savings-time
became eternity
What day is that you ask?
the day the sun rose for the last time
the day my son rose for the last time
What hour you ask? It was around noon I am told
What minute? We can give or take a few of those
What second you ask? The second was that split segment

of the smallest minute of measurement
when a life—my son's life—Caleb's life
spilled over that edge of earth time
into an all time—beyond time
(as we know it anyway.)
'Caleb is dead,' the doctor said
And I said no.
'Your son died,' he said yet again
And my scream came—loud—and raw—and uncontrollable
Grief such a small word—only five letters
such a soft, sad, quiet word
I thought I knew so much about it
how to shape it. Form it. Manage it.
Yet it thrashes through my brain waves
like a tide pounding, pounding—circling around and around
coiling, squirming like some screaming ugly snake.
Until its death rattle shakes and hisses me in the eye
striking so fast I'm not ready.
Are we ever?
I went home.
I anguished.
I languished
numb from shock.
I slept
exhausted
dreamless
unrefreshed
people answered my phone for me
people cooked for me
people understood for me
I became an animal—instinctual—senses heightened
muscles tensed—with an acute awareness of the very
air I breathed
the wafts of incense from his room
his footsteps up into the attic

the clean, soapy smell from an untaken shower
his bottle of cologne, still full
His ghost spirits moved through the house as he made his good-byes.
almost brushing against my shoulder with a last wispy hug.
and people answered the phone for me.
and people cooked for me.
and people understood for me.
My dearest friends cared for me
when I didn't care.
I try to understand, what isn't understandable
He was only twenty-seven, just half my age.

What is most important to remember is that you will need time, lots of time, to get back on your feet. Be patient with yourself. Ask for patience from those around you. Make sure you are moving forward, no matter how small the steps might be. At the end of this chapter, you will find some specific ideas for working with your grief. Additionally, many of the exercises in Section Three will be helpful. The Resources chapter also contains many books with great thoughts and guidance for parents who have lost a child.

Your Relationship with Your Partner

The most intense challenge to the equilibrium of a relationship is the loss of a child. Studies have shown that married couples experience extreme stress during the three-year-period that follows the loss of a child.

Tonya lost her five-year-old son when he got in the crossfire of a robbery. She explains what she went through with her husband. "We were both so drained. It was like staring at each other through a thick fog—we kept trying to reach out to each other, knowing we needed each other, but we couldn't reach. He saw my pain and I saw his, and yet there was no energy to console each other."

Tonya's experience is a common one. A couple who previously worked as a team is left unable to function or help each other. The grieving process of couples is further complicated by history, gender differences, and expectations.

In his book, *When Goodbye is Forever: Learning to Live Again After the Loss of a Child,* John Bramblett shares his experiences after the death of his son. One story exemplifies the differences within a couple. In this story, he and his wife were at a Rotary party. While discussing unusual events surrounding his son's death with a small group of people, he noticed his wife staring at him through the sliding glass door. He writes, "I knew what she was thinking; she knew what I was talking about. I wanted to communicate my experience; it was part of my way of coping. She felt that talking about those striking episodes in our family's life cheapened them. Neither of us was wrong; our approaches were just different."

Understanding and respecting the differences in our individual grieving styles is necessary to work through grief together. Read through Chapter 8 on the grieving styles of men and women for additional guidance.

Another complication is blame. If one parent was present when the death occurred, that parent may blame themselves or the other parent may blame them. Blame creates guilt, conflict, anger, and resentment. It is destructive and serves no purpose—yet it's a natural human emotion. In losses where one parent was present and blame occurs, seeking professional help is strongly advised. A third party to help navigate complex emotions is often needed.

Compromise

Barbara D. Rosof offers this advice to couples, "In many areas of your life together, such as socializing, family activities, holiday observances, one of you will be more ready to reengage than the other. If your partner wants to do something and you feel unready, you may need to push yourself. There is a balance to be struck in your efforts. Your child and your loss will always be with you. But giving up your life with your partner and the pleasures you have had together will not lessen your loss. Your balance has to do with holding onto your child, yet finding a way to live your life for yourself and with your partner. Your balance will not be arrived at quickly. Expect false starts and uncertainty. You need your partner's patience and your own."

At some point, in order to effectively move forward, you will need to nudge one another and learn the art of compromise.

Stay Connected

Even though you are wrapped in your unique grief, do not give up your connection as a couple. Make time to spend with each other. Don't shut each other out or you will be strangers when you get to the other side of grief. Schedule at least thirty minutes a day to sit together. Try and talk to each other about your feelings and the challenges of the day. If you can't talk about that, try talking about memories. If talking is too difficult right now, just hold hands or hold each other. This daily communication, whether physical or verbal, lets each partner know that the other is committed to working through the tragedy—together.

Single Parents

The loss of a child carries unique challenges for the single parent. If the deceased was the only child, a single parent may find themselves living alone and the silence unbearable. There is no partner with whom to share the grieving process.

Perhaps the only challenge more difficult than the loss of a child is facing that loss alone. Yet that is the prospect faced by many single parents. For single parents, it is especially important to find a support network, whether it be in-person or online (see Resources, page 267). Finding other parents who have survived the loss of their child will be a vital component in getting back on your feet. Also, it is common for the single parent to have a longer haul on the road of grief. What some people recover from in months may take years for the single parent. Be especially sensitive to your needs and emotions and seek the help of a professional or a support group.

For Parents with Surviving Children

In her book, *The Bereaved Parent*, Harriet Sarnoff Schiff touches on one of the hardest issues, that of grieving children. ". . . a recurrent theme appears to be that the living children received precious little by way of comfort from their parents."

Surviving children often feel their parents have abandoned them. A parent's grief is strong and often they cannot emotionally cope with the grief of their surviving children as well. This happens with many forms of loss, but when the loss is a child's sibling, the intensity is increased.

While you are engaged in acute grief, which will take at least a year, and for the loss of a child usually much longer, it's important to remember the perspective of your other children. Children are trying to cope with the loss of a sibling while also coping with an unfamiliar distance from their parents. It's important that surviving children understand that you are facing grief, and your behavior does not mean your love or feelings toward them have changed.

A common scenario after losing a child is an attempt to "make it right." Some parents will start an organization, fundraiser, or other memorial in the child's name. It is an admirable goal to keep the child's memory alive for generations to come. However, it is all too common for these memorials to become all-consuming. The parent spends so much time wrapped in the details of preserving his child's memory that he forgets to enjoy the children that are living!

Likewise, parents may constantly talk about the child who has died. Other children may quickly feel inferior, ignored, or unimportant if their parents focus so heavily on the other child. It is common to talk about the deceased frequently throughout the first six months to a year, but after that, there should be a point of letting go. While we can, of course, discuss emotions with friends or a counselor, within the family the letting go process has to take place if the current family unit is to remain healthy and intact. This doesn't mean that we forget. It means we begin to look toward the future and not dwell on the past. We bring balance into the home. We keep the memories of the past alive while creating new memories.

Some Things You Can Do after the Loss of a Child

Develop a Living Memorial

Many parents find comfort in developing a memorial, informational pamphlet, or organization in their child's name. In our interviews, we have found parents who have published information on drunk driving, drug use, suicide, gangs, etc. and distributed them in their local community and sent them to newspapers around the country. Other parents have developed or founded organizations that are now national in scope. Other parents have found peace in starting a scholarship fund in their child's name and awarding the scholarship to a child who wants to pursue an interest similar to their child. Brook's family started an annual water-ski tournament in his honor. Caleb was a nationally recognized water skier who enjoyed tournament skiing. Each year, they hold a tournament at the lake at which Caleb loved to ski and award cash prizes and plaques.

International Star Registry

"Honor your loved one by giving them the stars! What a beautiful way to memorialize your child, by naming a star after him or her! Since 1979, the International Star Registry has been bringing these dreams to earth by offering a unique and magical opportunity to name a star. Plus, when you purchase your star through MISS, a portion of the proceeds will be donated directly to the combined efforts of MISS and the Arizona SIDS Alliance." The star kit includes a certificate, a telescope coordinated for locating the named star, a large sky chart with the star circled for easy identification, an astronomy booklet, and a memorial letter. See the resources section in the back of this book for details.

Donations

In her book, *A Handbook for the Living as Someone Dies,* Elizabeth A. Johnson suggests, "It may be very therapeutic and rewarding for you to donate your child's toys and other belongings to a children's home or to the children's wing at a hospital or hospice. In this way, the energy of your child's possessions is passed onto other children. A part of him continues to brighten the lives of others."

Memory Books

In *How to Support Someone Who is Grieving,* June Cerza Kolf writes, "Souvenirs, memorabilia and even some clothing can certainly be kept. In fact, putting old photographs in albums can be a task that is very rewarding at this time. It helps the bereaved recall happy memories." See the exercises chapter for ideas on how to create a memory book.

Online Memorials

The Internet has created new ways to share, cherish, and remember our loved ones through online memorials. Videos, text entries, recordings, music, and photographs can be combined into a permanent web page to memorialize and remember the deceased.

This also helps for younger members of a family when they are growing up and may want to know about a deceased relative who died when the child was very young. For more information visit legacy.com" or muchloved.com.

Chapter Thirteen
Losing a Partner

"Trying to put my pain behind brought me to many dead ends… Sometimes I wondered if I was losing my mind. The old rules did not apply anymore. I felt as if I had been dropped by parachute into a different country where I had no map and everyone spoke a foreign language."
—*Cathleen L. Curry,* When Your Spouse Dies

The loss of a partner or spouse is devastating on many fronts. Our partner is often our confidant and best friend. We have both our emotional and physical highs and lows with this partner—day in and day out. To live without this "half" leaves us feeling incomplete, confused, and shortchanged.

This is often intensified by the length of time we have spent with our partner. If we have been with our partner for many years, we may find that our partner completes our thoughts and is a compliment to our actions. We are left feeling as if we have lost half of our self in addition to our partner.

Added stressors arise at the life changes that often accompany the loss of a partner. We may have a significant financial change to endure, we may need to move, we may need to comfort our children, and have few people to comfort us.

Loss of Identity

Our partner makes up a significant portion of our history. With our partner, we interpret the world, daily events, and the ups and downs of life. When we lose this partner unexpectedly, we lose many of the foundations of our identity. We are left to rebuild at a time when we are both emotionally and physically depleted. This rebuilding process will take time. Our friends and children may encourage us to move forward before we are ready. This is only to be expected, since those who care for us hate to see us in pain. Many people feel that by "getting back into life," our pain will be alleviated. These are good intentions, but this route does not work in reality.

As we grieve, we will need to rebuild our foundation, one brick at a time. In his book, *Loss,* John Bowlby writes, "Because it is necessary to discard old patterns of thinking, feeling, and acting before new ones can be fashioned, it is almost inevitable that a bereaved person should at times despair that anything can be salvaged and, as a result, fall into depression and apathy. Nevertheless, if all goes well, this phase may soon begin to alternate with a phase during which the bereaved starts to examine the new situation and to consider ways of meeting it. This redefinition of self and situation is as painful as it is crucial, if only because it means relinquishing all hope that the lost person can be recovered and the old situation re-established. Yet until redefinition is achieved no plans for the future can be made."

At first, nothing will feel comfortable. Each day will bring new realizations and troubles. But in time, you'll find yourself engaging in a memory or hobby or thought that you enjoy. It may be only a minute of "peace," but peace nonetheless. This becomes your first brick. Seek out these sources of peace and record them in a journal. Notice what you like and what you don't. Form new opinions. Pursue a new interest. You may not be able to move quickly on these things. You may want to take a "getaway," but not have the emotional energy. That's fine. Order a few travel brochures on the internet and page through them. A step is a step—no matter how small.

In the exercises chapter, you'll find a Redefining Ourselves exercise that can help you in this process.

Circles of Friends

While living as part of a couple, there is a tendency to make friends as a couple. Many widows experience a troubling problem after the death of a partner. Frequently friends that the couple has known are lost when the couple dissolves into a single person. There are many reasons for this. It may be awkward to relate with other couples as a single person—especially when these other couples knew you as part of a duo.

Memories also play a large part in the loss of friendships. When we are with other couples we have shared with, we remember times passed. The other couples may be uncomfortable discussing or remembering these events or continuing to discuss the past when we are ready to move on. As we explored earlier, we are not a society equipped to deal with loss. It's unfortunate that this means one loss will often lead to other losses, due to others' resultant discomfort with death.

For younger couples, the loss of a partner is often unique to their experience. It is rare that others in our immediate circle will have experienced the sudden death of a partner. Although our friends experience the loss with us, they do not have the firsthand knowledge of what it is like to live through this kind of death. We resurface, torn and viewing the world through different eyes. We return to these friendships a different person, with a change in status. It is this difference in viewpoint that accounts for many dissolving friendships.

Another reason that friendships fade is that our loss reminds others that tragic loss can happen to anyone, to people they know—and maybe even to themselves. These explanations offer little comfort or justification for the actions of friends. However, there are a few things to remember. First, don't assume friendships won't work out. Give each friendship a chance. Secondly, if friendships dissolve, it is challenging to face these losses in addition to your partner, but know this leaves room for growth. When you are ready, focus on making new friends. The AARP publishes a great brochure for those who have been out of the friend-making loop for a while. See the Resources chapter for ordering information. Lastly, do seek out a support group of people in like circumstances. Create a group of close contacts who are at different points on the grief path. Use them as your touchstone. Share your concerns. It may be that you are too depleted to actually attend an in-person support group. There are many groups for widows and widowers that offer online chat, see the resources section in the back of this book.

Lingering Memories and Images

Many widows and widowers report seeing images of their loved one and feeling their presence. You may have dreams in which your partner is still living. According to studies, about one-third to one-half of widows and widowers have had these experiences. Realize the images are normal and needn't disturb you. You may feel your partner's presence with you constantly, like that of a guardian angel.

Many widows and widowers find it helpful to internalize an image of the deceased. In a 1974 report of Boston Widows by I.O. Glick, he found that "Often the widow's progress toward recovery was facilitated by inner conversations with her husband's presence." When we continue to talk and communicate with our loved one, we open ourselves to their presence—whether real or imaginary is irrelevant—and we open ourselves to their guidance. Learning to talk, and listen, to our loved one can be immensely comforting as we progress through our grief work.

MARILYN'S STORY

"We planted tulips and daffodils in the woods by our beautiful new house, our dream home, the place where all the kids and grand kids would come, the place where we would grow old together. We had lived there for five months when Gary died suddenly of a brain aneurysm and my world became a dark, terrifying, lonely place, where just days before it had been full of joy and wishes come true. No words can fully describe the shock and horror of sudden death with its untimely issues, especially when your loved one has never been sick. He'd served with the Marine Corps in Vietnam and came back without a scratch. *How could he be dead now?*

A case of the flu . . . that's what we thought the night before he "officially" died; the night before the transplant arrangements were made and life support removed; the night before my heart felt the unbearable crush of a tremendous stone of grief. We had both been married before, divorced, and finally (we thought) got it right. Seven years was all the time we had together, but we had no idea that death would come so soon for one of us. We always said we could deal with anything as long as we had each other. We'd discussed death: my son, Dan, had served in the Army Signal Corps during the Persian Gulf War; I was a Hospice volunteer; and my friend, Kathy had died suddenly two weeks before, followed by my Hospice patient one week prior to my husband's death. I said a eulogy at Kathy's funeral, encouraged by Gary, who was so proud of my seminary studies. I never dreamed that I would be doing the same thing for Gary in the same chapel two weeks later . . . three weeks before Christmas. What I could not have known was that my grandmother and another dear friend would both also die within months of Gary.

The support groups . . . yes; I went to them all. I even eventually facilitated one myself. I cried and ranted with the others, yet I felt that because of the unexpected nature of Gary's death, it was different for me; different for those of us who did not have a chance to make final plans, to get things in order, to say good-bye. I was mad at God. I felt that the loss of four people I dearly loved all at once was a cruel joke and I thought I was losing my mind. But, worst of all, I lost my faith and so, felt truly abandoned, adrift, punished, terrified. I had dedicated my life to serving God, yet I was in hell. Things got worse. People expected me to 'get over it.' I awoke in the middle of every night and was haunted by a replay of the events of the night Gary fell in the bathroom and the emergency people couldn't find the house; how I frantically ran up the road looking for them and how I had to leave Gary lying there, alone on the bathroom floor. I tortured myself with 'what-ifs,' feeling like a failure, as if I could have saved him. The doctors told me that his aneurysm was so massive that even if it had happened in the hospital, they would not have been able to save him. Yet, I continued to have the repetitive thoughts replaying every event leading up to the removal of life support; the night terrors; the panic attacks; the chest pain; the disorientation; the absolute abandonment. I sank deeper and deeper into a clinical depression. I couldn't work, I couldn't pray, I couldn't do anything. I felt like I was an absolute failure and that I was dying. That I was next. Then the blizzard came. I was lost in a surreal world and I was certain I had lost my mind.

I asked my therapist, 'How did you ever make it through everything after your wife died suddenly?' He said, 'I went crazy.' Those three words probably helped me more than anything. If my psychiatrist went crazy when his wife died unexpectedly, and he was still alive and functioning, then maybe there was hope for me. I went to see him every week; I tried different medications; I looked for information on sudden death in books, but only found a sentence or two on the subject. I continued to attend support groups. Why is death such a taboo in America, I thought. It's as if the available literature was focused on "neat and tidy" death . . . the kind people prepare for, but that's not what happened to me.

Finally, after seven months, I was able to move Gary's shoes from the floor where he had put them. That act of moving the shoes made me realize he was really dead and my depression worsened and at around the same time, my son's Gulf War illness worsened and he had to be hospitalized repeatedly. I screamed in my car. I screamed until my throat and neck were aching. I cried and cried and cried. How is it possible to cry that much? The flowers we had planted bloomed beautifully the following Spring, as if nothing at all had happened. The world was still doing what it always did. How could that be when my whole world was changed forever? I wanted to die, but I had to be there for my son, who was, and has been so ill, and desperately needed me.

Therapy continued and after eleven months, I was able to return to work, yet I was not really 'emotionally present,' I was so alone. Comments were made: 'things must be better now, since a year has passed.' People treated me as if death were catching. They didn't know what to say, so they said nothing. They had no idea that I was still in hell and that I felt like a freak. I covered it up. Switched to drinking coffee; couldn't drink tea any more because Gary had made my tea every morning and placed it beside the bed, a small loving act, a kindness that I missed so very much. Months dragged on; then years; I finally was able to pack up Gary's clothes and give them away, but even now, after five and one-half years, I still find things of his in unexpected places and I cry. The dream house is sold, his car is sold, his books have been given to the library, clothes and mementos have been given to his friends and family, and Gary's ashes lie in Virginia's Quantico Cemetery and I have the flag on my closet shelf.

Depression still follows me, but looking back I can see that I have come a long way since the awful day when my world disintegrated. Gary's organs have helped others to have another chance at life. That was what he wanted. I dreamed about him on our anniversary last year. He kissed me and had a bottle of champagne in his hand. I think he wanted to tell me that he loves me and that he wants me to make a life for myself. Now, I know that's possible, at least a day at a time. I believe I can make it now, but it's been a long journey to hell and back again. Where I am now can be summed up in a poem I wrote:

PATHFINDER
You learn to take a little bit
extra on the in-breath

just in case you come up short
when heartbreak comes.
You learn to lean a little
less than most, just enough
to catch yourself and keep a balance
should you start to fall toward the abyss.
You learn to love a little
more intensely should life
send grief to poke you in the eye
and a golden moment pass unseen.
You learn to speak the language
of the heart more clearly
to the ones you love just because
there's so many ways the night can come
and stop you in your tracks,
so many ways the boot
can crush the rose."
Marilyn Houston—Springfield, Virginia

"For two years—I was just as crazy as you can be and still be at large. I didn't have any really normal minutes during those two years. It wasn't just grief. It was total confusion. I was nutty, and that's the truth. How did I come out of it? I don't know, because I didn't know when I was in it that I was in it."

Helen Hayes, actress, after the death of her husband

JOAN'S STORY

Joan was a thirty-two-year-old divorced and remarried woman when her ex-husband, the father of her two children, was killed in a gruesome, alcohol-related auto accident. Thirteen years later, her eyes still well with tears as she relives the sudden impact his death had on her life and those of her children.

"We were married almost eighteen years, but Tom and I were divorced at the time of his death. Even though he had a drinking problem, we had managed a friendship after the divorce, mostly for the sake of our two children. We had even spent a Christmas together. But, before New Years he was drinking again and each time was getting worse. I was remarried at the time although that relationship was rocky as well. Tom had called me earlier on the night he was killed. My son was supposed to go with him that night to the movies and I didn't allow him to go—Tom sounded drunk. Anyway, I got a phone call or two from him at a bar asking me to meet him which I refused to do. I also got a call from the bartender, or maybe it was a friend at the bar asking me to come and get him.

I began praying very hard because I knew what kind of battle Tom had been fighting with alcohol and I remember praying to Jesus to take him if he was going to be so tortured in this life—especially if he was going to be unable to conquer his alcoholism. I knew that my children couldn't take much more of his behavior. It had been so hard dealing with their father's disease.

I knew Tom was intoxicated. My husband of two years was asleep next to me at the time, so I suggested to the person at the bar that he call Tom a cab. I don't remember what the response was. It was probably three or four hours after that—by then my husband had left for work and it wasn't time for my kids to leave for school; they were still asleep. I got a call from the police department saying, 'This is Sergeant Smith, I'm calling to let you know that Tom McKenzie was killed in an auto accident. I apologize. Normally we would have come to the house to tell you, but we couldn't find the house.'

It felt like my insides had dropped to the floor. What crossed my mind was that I had prayed for this just a few hours before. How would I tell his children! I knew what their reaction would be and I began to feel enormous guilt. So, I not only felt guilty for not picking him up but for praying that he be released from his life of torture. I don't know if it's strange, but I immediately thought, 'Who would walk my daughter down the aisle when she got married?' My thoughts went in all different directions.

Although I was in disbelief, I picked up the phone to call my mother. I said, 'Are you sitting down . . . Mom, a police officer just told me that Tom died in a car accident last night.' I kept thinking, I have to talk to Tom—I didn't know what I was going to tell him. I felt crazy. I wanted to ask him 'Is this real? Are you really dead?' And the guilt.

I was angry—why are they telling me this over the phone? Couldn't they have told me in person. I was angry with the police department.

Jenny was thirteen and my son Paul was sixteen at that time. I remember agonizing over what I could say and was grateful they were still asleep. Jenny was the first to awake. I wasn't ready to talk to her, I needed to calm myself first. But there she was. I decided to put my own grief somewhere else because I had to be there for my kids. I knew they'd be devastated. I jumped from hysterical to concentrating on Jenny and Paul. When I told her, she cried out in disbelief. I begged her not to wake her brother, but we had to. We went together to tell him. To this day, I'm not sure exactly how he meant it, but he jumped out of bed, pulled on a shirt and said, "Damn it, I knew it! I should have gone to the movies with him." He was already feeling guilty.

I immediately thought, I must call the school and tell them my children won't be coming in and I had to call my work.

The policeman knew we were divorced, but wanted to know if he should call family members or did I want to. I asked him to call Tom's brother so they could give the news to his mother.

My kids were emotionally a mess. We spent the hour trying to calm each other. An hour later Tom's brother called to reassure me that I would be part of any arrangements they would make. Even though we were divorced, I wouldn't be left out.

I could only focus on my children. At the time, my son's best friend had lost his own father and sister in tragic accidents and I remember my son only wanting to be with him. I knew it was the right thing to do. He needed to be with someone who could understand the experience of sudden loss.

Without my children's input, Tom's family decided to have him cremated. This was hard on Jenny and Paul, I think. Anyway, even though it was a closed casket the kids insisted on seeing their father before the cremation. I guess I'm glad they did. It helped make it more real.

I think back now and I'm glad we had made some amends before he died."

Learning to Do Things Alone

Suppose you were dependent on your partner to travel with you, to drive the car, to make the plane reservations, to pack your bags—now is the time to begin seeking a network of others to help you with these tasks. As you move through the first months of acute grief, it's best not to take too many new steps.

In time, it will be helpful to learn to do these things alone. Some people say it builds character to travel to new places and face what comes on your own. Others would prefer to travel with a friend. Both offer opportunities for growth.

Some people depended on their significant other to *do* for them—others depended on the significant other to *be* with them—and some both. Some needed their partner for a sense of identity and belonging in the world. Whatever you can do at this time to loosen your dependency-hold on your deceased loved one can only be beneficial in the long run. But remember, do this at your own pace—no one else's. The most compassionate message you can give yourself is to drop the expectation that recovery will be an easy, logical process.

For most, it is only with time and enormous personal or spiritual introspection, coupled with the wisdom gained, that the true meaning of the relationship will emerge. There will never be an answer as to why the one you loved died—but, perhaps you can answer for yourself why they were in your life and how their life and death added something positive to your own journey.

Funeral Arrangements

MaryAnn, thirty-seven years old and a mother of two young children, laments, "I knew my husband very well. We talked about lots of things, especially our plans for the future. We never talked about what we wanted as far as funeral arrangements were concerned. Who does at our age? When it came time to make decisions, I did the best I could. I will always wonder if I did the right thing, if I chose what he would have wanted."

This scenario is more common than not. One can only do the best they know how under very stressful conditions. If you are able to make even one choice on behalf of the deceased, you are among the small few. Give yourself some credit.

What can you do when your significant other's family wants their wishes honored over yours and what you believe to have been the wishes of your loved one? In the absence of a will or other document that clearly states what the deceased would have wanted, you must remember that if you were legally married at the time of death, you have the right to do as you wish.

In other cases where you were living together under no formal arrangements, it is more difficult to assert your rights. Sometimes a professional mediator or funeral director can help with these kinds of conflicts. Take the opportunity to resolve the dispute with the help of a neutral person trained in mediation skills, domestic violence issues, financial issues, and other topics. You might visit a mediator or therapist who is not a judge or an arbitrator who imposes a decision on people, but who is trained to assist people in negotiating their own resolutions to their problems or concerns.

Although mediators may come from a variety of professional backgrounds, including attorneys, psychologists, social workers, marriage or family counselors, clergy people, accountants, and financial specialists, they have received specialized training to become mediators.

For Widows with Surviving Children at Home
Emotional Demands

When you lose a spouse before your children are grown, the path ahead is emotionally and physically demanding. You are responsible for not only your own well-being but also that of your children. This responsibility is especially challenging when your emotional and physical resources are limited in the direct aftermath of loss.

During the first weeks of grieving, it is important to have alternate contacts children can turn to for support. Any energy you do have will be needed to propel yourself forward through the day. Ask a close friend to help you with your children and consider having that friend stay at the house.

Be careful, not to spend so much time focused on the children that you forget your own needs. You still have many of your own issues to work through. Make time for this. You may choose to join one of the support groups listed in the Resources section or you may find that just a night out by yourself each week offers the needed space to explore your grief. It's true that you must take care of yourself before you can take care of your children. Single parent Terri Ross said it best in *The Single Parent Resource,* "Just like with airplane oxygen masks—'Put yours on and then help the child next to you.' You have to get back on your feet before you can truly be of help to your child."

Communicating with Children throughout the Grief Process

One question many widowers ask is, "How do we act around our children *during* the grieving process?" As we explored earlier in the book, everything we thought to be certain changes when we experience tragic loss. There are no hard and fast rules to make life appear normal again, but there are guidelines that can help your family get through this process in a healthy way.

First, it is a good idea to let your children see your grief. Many times a parent will assume it is his responsibility to remain completely controlled and collected. This isn't healthy. Kids will not know how to deal with their own grief without an example. If you show little or no grief, the children may feel their emotions are inappropriate. Do not be afraid to let your children see your emotions. Silence is harder for children to take than emotion. It also shows children that it is okay to face grief head on—it need not be suppressed. The only caution is to make sure you don't fall into a pattern of leaning on a child for support. When children are preteens or teens, parents sometimes find themselves talking and sharing their grief like they would with a friend. No matter how mature a child is, if they are not an adult they should not be the sounding board or support line for a parent. Avoid saying things like, "You're the man of the house now," to your young son or burden your daughter with the responsibilities of homemaker.

Lastly, don't avoid talking about what happened or mentioning past events that involved the deceased. The best way to keep a memory alive is to not focus so much on the death, but to tell stories about the deceased's life. Children often won't know whether or not it's okay to discuss their parent. They may fear that bringing up mom or dad will cause you pain or sadness. Take the initiative and set the example. Don't avoid saying your spouse's name. Even if it's difficult, talking does lead toward healing.

Additional Responsibilities When the Partner is a Parent of Minor Children

If the partner was also the mother or father of children, the surviving partner often becomes the key decision maker and provider for the children. He or she will be in charge of decisions on college, finances, rules, curfews, limits, and all other responsibilities. Both parent and child will need time to adapt to these new roles.

The newly single parent should consider all outside help that is available. There are many organizations and resources for single parents (see Brook's book, *The Single Parent Resource* for a comprehensive listing). Immediately work on seeking out support and information. Find a confidant who is a single parent that you can use as a mentor.

Involving children in restructuring the home is one idea that many parents have found helpful. This works best with children that are ten and older. A month or two after the services, explain to them that with one less family member, your family will need to use teamwork and cooperation. Offer ideas on how you think the family could run smoothly. Brainstorm ideas beforehand. Try things like chore distribution, helping with dinner, doing something together as a family on one day each weekend, etc. It may seem hard to be talking of functionality so soon after losing someone, but although someone's life has stopped, our lives don't.

Children need a stable base in order to thrive. Part of creating a stable base is consistency, boundaries, and limit setting. Often, we are so emotionally depleted that maintaining consistency and boundaries is challenging at best. Keep things as regular as you are able. This will help children find a safe, stable environment in which to grieve.

Will I Ever Love Again?

"Will I ever love again?" is a common question. "Why commit to another person? Why should I risk losing another love?" Committed love can provide numerous opportunities for growth as we struggle to stretch ourselves to bring our best to bear in relationships. The experience of sudden loss of love and the recovery process that follows can provide a basis for growing and expanding us as human beings in ways we never thought we were capable.

Some widows look forward to a new relationship but are unsure of how to initiate it. Others feel "guilty" at the thought of a new partner. Is there a right time, a guideline? In an article titled, "Starting Over," that appeared in *People* magazine, author and psychologist Froma Walsh shared that the signs of readiness are subtle. You're not thinking about your partner all the time and you no longer dream of them or picture them when you're with another person. "There is no such thing as totally getting over a loss, but over time you will have those pains less and less often. When you can appreciate the unique qualities of a new partner and not mold that person to fit an old image, then you know you're ready to love again."

Sexual feelings will also resurface. For some, this will happen sooner than others. In the AARP brochure, *On Being Alone,* they offer the following insight, "When you lose your spouse, you lose your sexual partner. It is a painful fact of widowhood. Although sexual feelings are common after being widowed and should not make you feel guilty, there can be a conflict between societal taboos and your personal needs. You need to sort out those conflicts and do what you feel most comfortable doing. If you are considering taking a new sexual partner, you may want to think about what you are really looking for: sex, intimacy, companionship, admiration or cuddling. Knowing what you want can help you know how to go about getting it."

Seeking Purpose

Finding purpose in the relationship can be effective in understanding the death. You're in pain, nothing makes sense, and you may feel totally alone. Trusting there is some ultimate benefit to be found takes an innate trust in the process of healing, at a time when your trust in life itself may have been broken or destroyed. "Why did the relationship need to begin?" can seem like an odd question to ask oneself at a time like this, but the answer can help put the death of your loved one into a meaningful framework. In an attempt to give an easy answer, you might say, "Wasn't it just love and a sexual passion coupled with a desire to have a family and a partner in life that drew me to my lover or spouse?" But, ask again. Why might it have been "necessary" on a spiritual level to begin the relationship? Perhaps it grew out of a pressing psychological need, or maybe a spiritual exigency, or maybe, if you believe in the possibility of past lives or reincarnation, perhaps it began in response to some karmic requirement. A step toward healing the wounds your loss has created can be taken regardless of which understanding you choose. You may have all along wondered "Why him?"—maybe from the minute you said, "I do." No matter which of these "pulls" it may have been, what matters is that you try to see that your relationship (including its ending) was meant to serve a specific purpose in your journey toward becoming a more whole person.

Some Things You Can Do

As you move on with your life, remember this: The love you have for your deceased partner will always have a special place in your heart and history even if/when you have another love relationship and/or remarry. Buy a special box for your momentos and revisit this box on special days if you want to.

Donate

Donate time, money, or special items to a charity that was important to your deceased partner.

Incorporate Traits

Incorporate some special trait or behavior of your deceased partner into your own life so that every time you exhibit that trait or behavior, you will be honoring the loved one's memory.

Write Letters

Many widows and widowers have reported letter writing to be a valuable way to release their emotions and remember their loved one. Begin a notebook and write a letter whenever the urge strikes. Release your emotions, your thoughts, your words.

One of Pam's clients, the husband of a woman who died in a skiing accident, keeps a "love letter journal" where he writes to his wife each day. There will come a day when he doesn't do this at all, or as much, but for now this gives him a great deal of comfort.

Place an Ad

Place an "In Memory Of" ad in your local paper, in remembrance of your deceased partner and have it signify the closing of one phase of your life and the beginning of another. The ad can contain a favorite poem, song lyrics, special graphics, or thoughts about your deceased partner. You can choose any date that was meaningful to both of you.

Chapter Fourteen
Losing a Sibling

"My big brother was so good to me.
When we were kids, he always let me go first.
The night he died, he looked up at me,
Smiled his little crooked smile, and said,
'Sis, this time let me go first.'"
—Connie Danson, eulogy for her brother, Frank Darnell

No matter your ages at the time of death, the loss of a sibling carries many unique challenges. First and foremost, when we lose our sibling, we lose one of the people who knows us most intimately. This person grew up as we grew. We laughed together, schemed together, cried together, fought with each other, hated each other, and loved each other. It is one of the only relationships that experiences, and endures, such a full spectrum of emotions day after day.

In *The Worst Loss,* Barbara D. Rosof writes of siblings: "They are playmates, confidants, competitors; they may also be protectors, tormentors, or have special responsibilities. Siblings know each other more intimately than anyone else.

Siblings know, as no one else in the world does, what it is like to grow up in your particular family. Relationships with a brother or sister help children know who they are and how they fit in the family. The bonds between siblings are woven into the fabric of each one's life."

When we lose a sibling, we lose a piece of ourselves, a piece of our family, and a reflection of ourselves. We lose a precious link to our history and an ally in our future.

Being Overlooked in the Grieving Process

One of the hardest parts of sibling loss is being overlooked in the grieving process. A person can find evidence of this by opening the many books on grieving in a bookstore. Pages upon pages are devoted to parents and spouses. However, the loss of a sibling is not listed as often—and when it is, the coverage is often short. For the Resources chapter of this book, we had a hard time finding anything geared specifically to sibling loss. One young adult who lost his sister wondered why everyone always asked, "Well how are your parents taking it?" and never asked how *he* was taking it. An article in the *Journal News* titled, "Forgotten Mourners," offered the views of many surviving siblings. One person quoted in the article said, ". . . I was so mad. It was as if everyone thinks, *Oh my gosh, losing a child, that's the worst thing in the world,* and they don't even consider there are siblings."

Double the Loss

In addition to losing a sibling, the surviving brothers or sisters often lose a piece of their parents. Parents become wrapped in their grief. For years to come, they may have difficulty relating like before with the surviving children. Many of these surviving siblings don't feel they can go to their parents. "My father had enough on his mind," said one man we interviewed, who sadly watched his relationship with his father deteriorate. One thirty-five-year-old woman named Lee said this in the *Journal News* article, "I don't think society understands what sibling grief is all about. It's a misunderstood grief because it's a double-edged sword. You have your own pain and your parents' pain."

A support group or person will help you to move through these pains. Be careful when selecting your group and make sure they understand the difficulties specific to sibling loss.

In the initial months following a loss, all any of us can do is attempt to navigate grief's path as much as possible. The world is not perfect, nor are we. We often make decisions that are focused more on getting by day to day than on thinking long term. Somewhere between the second and twelfth month, we begin to acclimate back to longer-term thinking and are often surprised to find many of our relationships have changed. There is a tendency to blame this on grief. Usually grief played a part—it catapulted us into a new world in which we thought differently and were concerned more with day-to-day survival than long-term quality of life. Each of us lives this day-to-day survival life for a different length of time, depending on our previous experience with grief, our support network, the level of shock, how present the loved one was in our day-to-day life, and our ability to grieve in healthy ways.

When one person is living day-to-day and another is not, a gap forms in the relationship. The person thinking day-to-day may not have the emotional energy or foresight to think of anything or anyone besides what they physically come into contact with. The longer two individuals remain on different tracks, the wider the gap in the relationship can become.

After a death a widening gap occurs when parent and surviving child enter shock and survival living. The parent often has the widest network. Energies of supporters are often focused primarily on helping the parent, which can (doesn't always) enable the pattern of "survival living" for a longer period. The surviving sibling often has little support. Without support, the surviving sibling will move back to longer-term thinking/living more quickly in an attempt to support himself or find support elsewhere. The parent continues in this survival-living mode for a couple of months or half a year or more. The parent becomes accustomed to focusing only on challenges right in front of them. The surviving sibling is no longer living with their parent and not "right in front of them." The surviving sibling feels isolated, lost, and alone. Meanwhile, the parent has lost all track of time. Because the parent has people coming to her recognizing and validating her loss in this unfamiliar territory, she does not realize that the surviving sibling is grieving alone.

If a gap exists in your relationships, it is important to articulate it and take steps to close the gap, or it will continue to grow. You may feel that your parent should reach out to you, but this expectation will not help matters or solve the problem. If you were close with your parent before, then seek to restore the relationship.

It can be helpful to set up times to visit and to focus on your relationship outside of the loss. During these times, keep the majority of the conversation about you or the parent—not the loss of your sibling. Set aside other times to talk about the loss. Try and develop a routine—for example, talk about the loss when you are at your parent's house, but when in public, try to direct the conversation toward you or the parent. You do not need to share this routine or intention with your parent, just use it as a guideline for yourself to restore a healthy relationship. In time, your parent will likely follow your lead and adapt.

While we cannot hold back grief with rigid boundaries, we can guide it. Guiding it with specific times for grief-talk and specific times for parent/child talk can help everyone get their needs met. In this fashion, we can honor our loved one yet also honor each other equally.

Idealizing

If parents begin to idealize the deceased child, a surviving child's feelings of pain. Idealization involves seeing what we want to see versus reality. It is often used in grief to try and ease pain or to make a memory stronger or more solid. Examples of idealization might be a parent saying things like, "She was an angel. She was taken early because she was too precious for this world." While these are seemingly innocent statements, as a surviving sibling you might think, *Does that mean I am not precious, that is why I am here?* Perhaps you know otherwise because of your close relationship to your sibling, and you can see through this statement, but out of respect, you do not say anything. A parent may also "forget" the annoyances and challenges she faced with your sibling and focus on only the strengths and joys. This can create an incredibly high bar for any surviving sibling and a feeling of resentment toward the grieving parent.

In the book, *When a Friend Dies,* Marilyn E. Gootman writes, "Sometimes people are afraid to say anything bad about someone who has died. They turn the dead person into a saint. Every person in this world has strong points and weak points, even those who have died. Loving someone means being honest and accepting the whole person, both the good and the bad, even if the person is dead."

Guidelines for Young Siblings

When helping your children cope with grief, it's important to remember the dynamics of a sibling relationship. Siblings typically have a love-hate relationship until well into adulthood. While still kids, it's not uncommon for them to be best friends one minute and worst enemies the next. This double-sided relationship often complicates the grief process. The living sibling may wish he had been nicer, more forgiving, or less jealous. Blame and guilt can reign strong for surviving children. The Compassionate Friends offer the following in their brochure, *Caring for Surviving Children* (see the Resources chapter for how to obtain this brochure): "Remember, grief will exaggerate the positive and negative feelings between your children; encourage them to discuss these feelings. Children often feel guilty and/or responsible for their sibling's death. Reassure them that fighting and negative feelings between brothers and sisters are common and do not cause death."

Identity through a Sibling

Siblings define one another. We become "Joe's sister" or "Frank's brother." It's common for a sibling to also explain themselves in relationship to their deceased sibling, or a parent (i.e. "I act more like my mother and my brother has my father's traits."). When we lose our sibling, this identity is taken from us. Within familiar environments where we are known as "Joe's sister" or "Frank's brother," a bittersweet memory remains.

Birth Order

Additionally, our birth order is altered. Mothers Against Drunk Driving offer the following in their brochure, **WE HURT TOO.** "When a brother or sister dies, you now experience a gap in the birth order. If the oldest sibling was killed, the second oldest is now the oldest. If there were just the two of you, you are now an 'only child.' It is difficult to know whether or not you should try to assume a new role, but you are painfully aware of the void left by your sibling's death."

Is He Still My Older Brother?

When we lose an older sibling, it's as if we experience a warp in time. First we experience a new type of day—a day where this person who has always been there is not. Then, as the years go by, we age—eventually passing up the age our sibling was on the day of their death. Brook faced this challenge between the first and second editions of this book.

The four-year age difference between me and Caleb always seemed an eternity when I was a child. When I started sixth-grade, Caleb was starting high school. When I started high school, Caleb was preparing to graduate. Being older, he seemed to experience everything first—he learned to ride his bike first, he earned his driver's license first, he bought a car first, he went to college first, he traveled alone first, he stayed out later. I had become comfortable following four years behind, assured by the knowledge that I could lean on (and count on) the wisdom and help of my big brother.

When Caleb died from a bee sting at the age of twenty-seven, I didn't have the wherewithal to look at the path ahead. Four years later, I found myself in one of the most difficult places of my grief journey. On the eve of my twenty-seventh birthday, I began to wonder, "Am I older than my older brother?" Were we now the same age? Was he younger? While it might seem a minor question, it was a detail that had defined my life. I wrestled with grief's time machine.

Now, at age thirty-three, technically, I suppose I am older than Caleb. In my heart, his memory has always lived on and he remains my older brother. If you care for someone who has lost a sibling, be aware of this complex redefinition in the grief journey. Offer time, space, and understanding.

The Hot and Cold Nature of Sibling Relationships

Sibling rivalry is a natural part of growing up. In some families it's exaggerated, and in others it's practically nonexistent. You may have fought with your sibling, said terrible things, or thought terrible thoughts. No matter how crazy, outrageous, or hateful these things seem to you—be assured, this is *natural*. Inside our guilt, we magnify these bad times—we narrow in on our regrets. There is no need to do this. One way siblings learn about one another and their place in the world is through these rivalries. For each rivalry you focus on, remember a wonderful shared moment, no matter how small or how simple.

Siblings often have a love-hate relationship until well into adulthood. While still kids, it's not uncommon to be best friends one minute and worst enemies the next. This double-sided relationship often complicates the grief process. You may find yourself wishing you had been nicer, more forgiving, or less jealous. Blame and guilt can reign strong for surviving children. Grief exaggerates both the positive and negative of any relationship. Because the relationship can no longer evolve or change, it is frozen in time and we tend to hone in on specific moments in a way we would not do with those who are living.

Imagine if you were to try and hone in on the specific moments of *all* your important relationships. You will likely be able to quickly see that placing relationships under a microscope is not practical or purposeful. Relationships are not comprised of individual one-time moments, but rather a garland of moments over time. If we pick out specific moments, we disrupt the entire garland. Focus on the whole and not the individual parts.

Grieving an Adult Sibling

If you have moved on to a family of your own, the loss of a sibling can create difficult issues in your current family. Many times, when we move and marry, our siblings are not that involved in our "new" family. When we lose a sibling at this junction, it can be hard to find the support we need. Our "new" family will often be sad for our loss, but they may have a hard time understanding the impact. They may be anxious to keep the family unit intact and have a hard time watching you experience your grief. Support groups will be especially helpful if this is your situation—especially if you live far away from other parents, siblings, or friends who knew the deceased.

When we lose a sibling, we are left with few places to release emotion. We may find it difficult to share emotion with our parents, as they are consumed with their own grief. We may hesitate to share our emotions with our spouse, as they may not have known our sibling as intimately and they may not understand. Our emotions are valid, and we need to share them somewhere. In these cases, a trusted friend, clergyperson, or support group can help.

Terri's Story

"Jim and I were like most brothers and sisters. On some days we were best friends, and on others we were enemies. With Jim being five years older, at times I was a tagalong and at others, a welcomed friend. There is something about a sibling relationship that is different than any other—a special bond. Jim and I knew each other inside and out. We could show each other our darkest parts and our brightest—and never fear that we would turn away from one another.

Jim and I explored the world together. We were adventurers. From early on, we sought rhyme and reason together. We built forts and ponds trying to be "brave explorers." We held bake sales and lemonade stands trying to raise money for new games. In many ways, he was my life preserver.

I remember when he left for college and I was just starting high school. I was so lonely. I wondered how I'd make it without him. The pain was intense—but nothing like the pain that would come two years later.

I was sleeping that night when the call came. I heard my mother begin screaming as I struggled out of bed. She held the phone receiver in her hand, her face white. My dad stood rigid next to her. David, Jim's roommate, had called with the news of Jim's death. Halfway across the country, my brother had been returning from his job at the video store when the cars collided.

I knew immediately what had happened. I said nothing. I simply turned around, walked back into my room, and hid under my covers. I wanted it all to go away. I wanted to wake up from the nightmare.

The service was incredibly difficult. Jim's body was so mangled my mother would not let me see him. I still wish I would have gotten to see him. Somehow, I think it would have helped.

The blackness that covered my world was thick. My friends were all choosing colleges, getting drivers licenses, going to prom—excited about finishing their junior year and entering their senior year. They all seemed so young and naïve. I had seen truths of the world that they, hopefully, wouldn't know for many, many years.

I moved through those last two years of high school like a robot. It wasn't until I left for college and got away from many of the places where Jim and I had shared memories, that I was able to begin rebuilding. The process was slow. I sought out a local pastor at college. At first we talked once a week and now it's once a month. Sharing and caring with another has been immensely helpful in working through my grief.

I graduate this year and am excited for that—though I still am saddened greatly by the fact that Jim and I won't get to experience the rest of our lives together. Sometimes I feel shortchanged, but I try not to get caught up in self-pity. Life's too short.

I talk to Jim a lot now. I feel he is with me and he can somehow hear me. This thought is comforting for me. I'll always miss him, but now I can smile at his memory and appreciate the wonderful gifts he gave me while he was alive."
—Terri, Idaho

October by Brook Noel
excerpted from *Shadows of a Vagabond*

I stand within this room
blanked and stripped of your essence,
wishing you might turn around
call my name
say it's a joke
praying for something
to take it all back
to rewind to yesterday
when you were still here.
You walked on water,
we dreamt inside stars
trading childhood dreams
and day into night—
you held my hand

and now I hold yours.
searching for a way
to erase what I witness
to erase what I see.
And inside October's fall light
you let go
while all of us
try so desperately
to hang on.
Brushing your pictures with .
hands that once held yours.
Rock—paper—scissors–
learning to snap…
those days we were too young
to realize how we had so little
while having it all.
There are no words
to frame your soul
to capture this gold
as we helplessly watch
these days slip away
searching for your face, a sign
a world still with you.
I want to revisit the past.
Take you back, take me back,
replay the scene a bit differently.
We look for reasons in forests
where none exist.
We look for answers
while eagles drift by.
Only questions rest on wings.
And though I can't understand
what has happened here—
I tuck our pictures
between your palms.

You have always held me
and I want you to still.
My brother, my father, my friend
I know you will
I know you will.

Some Things You Can Do

Forgiveness

If your parents were unavailable to you when you experienced your grief, or if they didn't know how to help you through it, it's important to forgive them. When we hold onto angry feelings, we don't leave the room needed to heal. One effective way to forgive is to write a letter. Explore all your feelings on paper. Write out your anger, your fears, and your hopes. When you finish, put the paper in a drawer. Periodically over the next month, pull it out, and read it. Feel the pain that you experienced. After a month, add a note of forgiveness to your parents. Then burn the letter and let your feelings of anger rise with the smoke.

"Communicate" with your sibling

In your mind, talk to your sibling like you always did. No matter what your relationship with your sibling—good or bad—you are bound to be tied by the closeness of growing up together in a family. Talk to your sibling and internalize his spirit. When you have a question or doubt, find a quiet place and think about your sibling and what advice he might have given you.

A memory notebook

Consider keeping a notebook for memories, cherished moments, and times together throughout the years. When you are seeking time with your sibling, work in this memory notebook. You may want to list ages at the top of the pages—for example, have one page for when you were two and your sibling was five, another couple of pages for when you were three and your sibling was six. Leave more pages for the years where you have more memories.

Get away for a while
Take a weekend getaway to explore your grief. Often we don't want to share our strong emotions with our parents or partners. If we are married, we may feel like we are putting too much on the shoulders of our spouse or children by sharing with them. A weekend where you need only worry about yourself, and not day-to-day demands, can be especially cleansing and self-nurturing. Take with you a journal and this book and work on some of the exercises. Take long walks outside and "commune" with your sibling.

Chapter Fifteen
Fallen Heroes

Death ends a life, not a relationship.
—Jack Lemmon

Tens of thousands of lives have been affected in these years, in which war has returned to the forefront of our focus. While the risk of death is a burden that servicemen and women assume is known and shared by family, friends, and community, that knowledge does not ease the grief process. In many cases, these families must move immediately away from their friends and support systems and rebuild a life that was once devoted to military service but which is now focused on surviving their traumatic loss.

"There are things I will never forget. The knock on the front door that November morning, the solemn look in the eye of the Army officer who came to deliver the news, the morning paper that bore the headlines, "Soldiers killed . . .," and the feel of the heavy cloth of the folded flag that was gently placed in my arms at the graveside. And I shall never forget the mournful notes of the bugle drifting out over the rows of silent headstones as the final honors were rendered at the cemetery. Those memories are with me forever," writes Bonnie Carroll, who founded the Tragedy Assistance Program for Survivors (TAPS) following the death of her husband, Brigadier General Tom Carroll, in 1992.

Limited Circles of Support

You may find that there are few people in your community who knew your loved one closely. The ability to share memories and process grief with those who are also feeling the loss of your loved one may be limited. After Bonnie lost her husband, she shared, "Tim had been in the military for two decades. Many people knew 'of him' but few people close by 'knew' him."

The frequent relocation of military families presents other challenges. "Shortly after getting as settled as one can during life in the military, we lost George. My two boys were still grieving the loss of their friends from the move when we learned of George's death. Now we are preparing for another move. George had only been here only once and the stay was so short—sure, people can empathize, but when me or my kids try to talk about it to anyone, it feels like we have to tell his whole life story because they didn't know him."

Even with the support of those who offer it, it is common to feel intense isolation, separation, and sadness. The concept of "not having to grieve alone," is welcomed in theory, but if the ability to interact in the initial months with those who truly knew our loved one is limited, some of your grief is processed alone.

When Gina found herself feeling isolated and alone in her grief, a friend encouraged her to reach out to those within her husband's unit. "I had received some letters but hadn't responded. I didn't know what to say. It took a couple of months, but I finally sent letters out. I wrote about me and the kids and what Adam meant to us. I shared his hobbies and a funny story. I figured someone other than family had to be grieving—not because he was a fallen soldier, but because they, too, had an absence in their life. I asked people to write back if they could and if they could share any stories or pictures I would be very grateful. I was amazed at the response. I didn't receive notes, I received pages of stories. I can't explain the type of relief I felt. I have saved the letters to share with the kids when they are older and have kept in close touch with many of those who wrote."

Deepened Denial

A military family might statistically include one soldier who is on active duty, but in many respects, the entire family is on active duty, supporting, praying, and caring for their deployed family member. "In some ways I think Jack's death hit me harder. Although we know the risk is there and live with it every day, I think I had to go into some sort of denial in order to live for all the years he served our country. It would have been impossible to manage our home and family if the fear for his life was constantly on my mind. It was at first—but over time it subsided. We entered an ongoing denial that allowed us to enjoy life here, enjoy his leave, and function," said Jack's wife Carolyn.

Many surviving family members have shared similar stories, and it makes sense that the human mind would be unable to face the reality of death daily for years on end. Some families have been surprised at the depth of their shock, thinking they should know better, but death is not automatically forecasted for enlisted servicemen and women. It carries a higher fatality rate than other careers but certainly not the expected outcome of a life of military service. Death is a possibility, not a probability, and as such it would be unrealistic to expect the shock to be any less than any other type of sudden loss. Indeed, the initial months are especially challenging, because the family has learned to suppress the reality and risk of death in order to function as a healthy family unit. The lifting of shock and denial may take additional time.

Political Challenges

Each loss leaves a unique path for the survivors. While there are commonalities, the loved ones of fallen heroes may face an especially challenging mixture of private and public grief. The story of each soldier is rarely told throughout the nation, yet coverage of the war and opposing opinions are prevalent in day-to-day life. "People don't know what it's like to just try and get a haircut or go to the doctor and glance down and find the magazine next to you has something about the war. Or you are sitting down to watch a movie and it is interrupted with something about the war. It is hard to find a space to heal or move forward when you are blindsided at even the most common places," said Denise, who lost her husband early on in the Iraq war.

Any war is marked by opposing sides and views. In Vietnam, we saw a country vocally divided over the choices of the United States government. In the Iraq war, embedded journalists, advanced video and satellite capabilities, and twenty-four-hour cable stations devoted to front-page news heighten awareness, visibility, and public knowledge of the brutality of war. By nature, the media focuses on conflict and problems with very little attention to the positive strides the military forces make, and little recognition is paid to the lives these heroes touch and the help they give. Military personnel reach out to innocent bystanders of the opposing side, willing to make the ultimate sacrifice in support of their country.

When opinions about the war become more deeply divided, the grieving process of survivors is often complicated. A new grief can emerge if the deaths of these heroes become political symbols. Jackie shares her experience after losing her husband to an IED. "It was only a week after I lost John when I left the house for the first time on my own. I remember just needing to get out all of a sudden . . . feeling so stuck. I actually thought observing the freedom of strangers without military ties might help me. Maybe a child's laugh or people discussing a decision and the freedoms John died for would give me a minute or two of something other than the indescribable pain I had in my heart. I went to a bookstore café and had a coffee. I don't even like coffee but he did, so I ordered his favorite drink. It was nice for a bit and then there was this group reading some magazine with coverage of the war and then they started talking about how stupid the war was and senseless deaths. I knew then to them and others John was only a number. On some channels his picture flashed, but most it didn't. To these people John was just a number that supported their viewpoint. I try to tell myself they had no way of knowing my pain a couple of tables away or that they didn't know any better—but I'm still angry. One of them had to make a call to see who was picking up their son—her or her husband. I wanted to go over and tell her John would never pick up my son again. I wanted to tell them something to make them understand they could sit in this café and talk about stuff like this because so many people had died in wars whether they believed in them or not. I didn't say anything because I'd fall apart. I didn't finish my drink, I couldn't. I suddenly had to get out of there more than I had to get out of my home. I have become really antisocial now. Everyone has an opinion. It would be nice to see people give up half of their news and debate time to sending packages or letters to support the people who defend them."

Rose had a similar experience several months after her son died in Afghanistan. "I think I'm most bothered by the trendiness of the Middle East. It goes in phases of support—really popular at the outset and a couple years later many people opposed what they once supported. Our son and daughters don't get to do that. They stay no matter what. The ironic thing is Andrew didn't agree with the war, but he was too busy defending freedom to talk politics."

Joseph speaks of his frustration with public opinion in light of the death of his sister Michelle. "Michelle chose to enlist and was deployed after the war began. She wasn't drafted or forced—she believed in this country enough to walk into danger. There is all this talk about bringing troops home and Michelle knew about it. The last time I talked to her I remember [her] defiantly saying, "Don't they get it? We don't want to come home—we aren't finished yet." She said her viewpoint was shared by many soldiers and it was discouraging to hear how much of the progress they made wasn't covered. I can't even watch anymore—at least not yet—maybe someday."

While we cannot avoid running into those who speak strongly about a war, try to remember there are many people who aren't speaking but *acting*. Thousands of people not affiliated with the military support the troops over any political view. Organizations like Soldier's Angels and Books for Soldiers are just a couple of hundreds of examples where citizens who care are trying to reach out and offer support through established avenues.

Tragedy Assistance Program for Survivors

www.taps.org

The Tragedy Assistance Program for Survivors, Inc., (TAPS) is a one-of-a-kind non-profit Veteran Service Organization offering hope, healing, comfort, and care to thousands of American armed forces' families facing the death of a loved one each year. TAPS receives absolutely no government funding, but through the Departments of Defense and Veterans Affairs, all families faced with a death of one serving in the Armed Forces receive information about TAPS and our military survivor programs.

TAPS was founded in the wake of a military tragedy—the deaths of eight soldiers aboard an Army National Guard aircraft in November 1992. In the months and years following the loss of their loved ones, the survivors turned to various grief support organizations for comfort; but when they turned to each other for comfort and to share common fears and problems, they found strength and truly began to heal. They realized that the tragedy they shared, losing a loved one in the line of military duty, was far different from other types of losses. They shared pride in their family members' service to America, and tremendous sadness at the ultimate sacrifice their loved ones made.

TAPS provides many vehicles of support, including an 800 number that can be called any time (800–959-TAPS), forums and message boards, weekly internet chats, camps for children, and in-person functions.

Military Losses Outside of the Public Eye

During the decades in which a war isn't daily news, if you lost a loved one in the military, for the most part those not affiliated with the military would ask questions. When war infiltrates the media, these questions may be replaced with assumptions. Outsiders may assume that your lost soldier died while deployed in the war zone they see on television. While these assumptions are not intended to create pain for you, the human mind draws conclusions based on what it is exposed to the most. When your loved one dies outside of a war zone during a time of war, you may encounter strained reactions from others.

In a society that is only beginning to learn a vocabulary for grief, anything outside of an outsider's assumptions places them in foreign territory in which they may be unsure of how to respond. While a simple "I'm sorry for your loss," would suffice in that moment of awkwardness, many people will speak before thinking.

Patricia remembers when she told an acquaintance of her husband's death. "I didn't say he had died in a training exercise because it hadn't occurred to me to share that information. I believed that if someone wanted to know more they would ask. This woman assumed he died on the front lines and grief filled her face. I explained that was not the case and she looked almost relieved. The words she said next still shock me to this day. She said, 'Thank God you don't have to picture him dying in that awful place.' I must have looked shocked because she kept talking. 'Could you imagine if.' I don't remember any of the rest of the sentence. I put my hands up and yelled, 'Stop.' and tried to walk away. She followed me and I turned to her and said, 'Don't you get it? He would have rather died at war.' I was almost yelling and people had stopped and were looking but I didn't care."

In his article, *A Father's Grief*, Lee Vincent writes, "In peacetime, most of the deaths seem to come from highway accidents, training incidents, and airplane crashes. Military airplanes are more complicated than civilian aircraft. Pilots must constantly practice, and mishaps are just part of reality. And every weekend there is a multitude of servicemen and women driving great distances to see loved ones and have fun. Then they rush back hundreds of miles to meet their curfew. Almost every weekend someone dies.

We are bombarded with thoughts of futility, of someone's mistake, of what "should have—would have—could have been." These thoughts don't do anything for you but double your pain. But you must forever know there is no futility or shame in the death of one whose living had so much merit. We must never stain their merit with negative judgments. And we must never let what they *could have been* take away any of the glory of what they already were."

I Should Have Said . . .

In any sudden death we are plagued by the words left unspoken. The loss of a soldier may intensify these feelings. In hindsight, you may feel that you knew each time your loved one left that the risk of death was present. You may find yourself thinking you should have told him or her everything you felt—just in case. This is a common reaction amidst our pain, an attempt to find something to focus on, some thought to obsess on, some way to blame ourselves, to distract ourselves from facing the totality of our loss. Yet if we were to treat each goodbye as if it truly were the last, reciting all of our thoughts and emotions, displaying all of our affection, we would create a sense of imminent death that would not support our loved one, ourselves, or our family.

Each year thousands of lives are taken by automobile accidents. We would not think to go through all of our details, emotions, thoughts, and affection each time we parted with a person to leave for work. In order to function, our focus has to remain on life, not death. Realize that this type of thinking, like any "should have" thinking, is an unhealthy belief that can only do harm to you and your family.

Standing with Pride

Regardless of the circumstances, location, rank, timing, or any other factor, one fact remains. Any fallen hero and their family has heard and heeded the call to support their country. In his article, *A Father's Grief,* Lee Vincent articulates this beautifully. ". . . every one of those we love had already risen far above the rest of our society in character, courage, honor, and ability. And not an atom of their achievement can ever be lost or taken back. If they had lived, they would be proud today of who they are and what they are doing. Now it's our duty to be proud *for* them."

Some Things You Can Do
Connect with Others Who Are Grieving the Loss of a Soldier
While general grief support is a good step, connecting with others who have experiences that share similarities with our own often create the most helpful environment for working through grief.

Hold a Memorial
You can hold a memorial at any time to say the words you would like to say about your loved one. It can be the anniversary of the enlistment date, date of death, birthday, Veteran's Day, Memorial Day, Thanksgiving, or any day. This could also be an opportunity to reach out to the community as well and encourage efforts to support troops.

Reach Out
Consider writing to soldiers who knew your loved one as Gina shared in this chapter. Consider sending a handheld recorder overseas so people can speak their memories to send back to you.

Bonnie Carroll, founder of TAPS shares that "We truly do honor those we love by cherishing the extraordinary lives they lived, regardless of the circumstances or geography of their death. A TAPS Mom shared these words of Ralph Waldo Emerson, "It is not length of life, but depth of life." The decision made to join the military and protect and defend freedom, even if it means going into harm's way, is a courageous one and it speaks to the character of the individual. Their life had depth, and even if cut short, was lived fully and richly.

Chapter Sixteen
Suicide

"Gradually, I came to understand that while it may be
possible to help someone whose fear is death, there are no
guarantees for a person whose fear is life."
—Carla Fine

Over 90 percent of people who die by suicide have a mental illness at the time of their death. According to a study released by the Centers for Disease Control and the National Institute for Mental Health, suicide is the eleventh leading cause of death in the U.S., with 32,000 deaths recorded in 2004 and over 800,000 attempts. This approximates to around one death every sixteen minutes. There are more suicides than homicides each year in the United States. From 1952 to 1992, the incidence of suicide among teens and young adults tripled. Today, it is the third-leading cause of death among young people (after motor vehicle accidents and unintentional injury).

A U.S. Centers for Disease Control survey of high-school students showed that 34 percent of girls and 21 percent of boys have considered suicide, actually *during the last year* 16 percent of high-schoolers made a "specific plan," and 8 percent "tried suicide."

Suicide is one of the most devastating types of loss. In her book, *How To Go On Living When Someone You Love Dies,* Therese A Rando, PhD, writes, "This can contribute to a profound shattering of your self-esteem, with strong feelings of unworthiness, inadequacy, and failure. Like homicide, this death was not inevitable. It was preventable. You must recognize that you are particularly victimized by this type of death, and are susceptible to intensified and conflicted bereavement reactions."

But we are not at fault for someone's suicide. In the end, in the final moment, they made the choice alone. In *No Time to Say Goodbye: Surviving the Suicide of a Loved One,* Carla Fine writes, "Like most survivors, I was haunted by the infinite regrets that are woven into the fabric of suicide. I would replay the chronology of events leading up to Harry's death, searching for lost opportunities to reverse the inevitable outcome. Only as I began to accept the idea that my husband's choice to kill himself was his alone did the powerful grip of "what-ifs" of his suicide begin to loosen. Gradually, I came to understand that while it may be possible to help someone whose fear is death, there are no guarantees for a person whose fear is life."

Diana lost her seventeen-year-old daughter to suicide. She hanged herself in the bathroom. Diana was kind enough to share the story of her grief. The following writings come from her journal.

"One year ago today, on a day quite similar to this in fact, I found out my seventeen-year-old daughter had committed suicide. The person who had to tell me this was my husband. He has never been the same since that day. I have never been the same since that day.

I have never felt pain like this in my life. I am an impatient person, to say the least, I do not like enduring something that shows no sign of going away anytime soon. I want this over and I want it over now. Immediately. But it doesn't stop.

Some days are better than others. Some days I can go through the day and feel halfway normal. Other days, I could very easily just crawl into a corner somewhere and just stop. Stop everything. Stop thinking and stop hurting and stop breathing.

I am at this point of trying to deal with the anger. I'm trying to deal with this anger at her, for quitting. For not thinking beyond that moment in time, and I've been there, that moment in time where it doesn't matter anymore. Where absolutely nothing in this world means a damn thing except what's causing your pain. And all you want is for that pain to go away, like I do right now. I know the moment intimately. I've been there a few times, I'm there now. But something inside me steps through that moment and won't let me end the pain that way. I have to live with it, I have to go and carry it and hope that over time it will be absorbed and become part of me that is just there.

The grief books give you stages. Yeah, you go through them. But more than likely, not in the order they are listed. This is not an exact science, I am becoming more intimately in tune with the effect of grief than I would care to be. And I can't stop it, I can't ignore it, it's there. It doesn't go away, it's there and all you can do is deal with it.

Some days 'dealing with it' has been laying on the bed and running through the entire channel selection on the remote for hours at a time, with no real coherent thought processes going on. Other times it has been a search and destroy run on a room in the house. Or standing outside staring straight up at the sky until my neck hurts, hoping for some kind of a sign, something to flash across the sky that will make sense of it all.

Pitching a fit and placing blame would be easy. It has been easy, that's why I've done it a few times. I blame me. I blame her father. I blame the schools. I blame the doctors. I blame the counselors. I blame _____ . Blame is easy. What's hard is getting past the blame and finally accepting the fact that, no matter what pushed her to do this, Anna took her own life. Anna killed herself. She did this, not me, not her father, not society. It was by her own hand and her choice.

I get through it, I struggle. I fall. I cry. I scream. I rant and rave. And I pace and pace and pace. But I am going through it. One day at a time. Which is all that we can do. Some of us can quit. Some of us can't. I can't quit.

There are no rules. It's been a year today. I will be expected to start 'snapping out of this' and going back to the way I used to be. Sorry, it ain't happening. I will never be the same again. I'm going to be different from now on. That's part of the process. Like it or not. Hell, I don't like it. I don't like looking at bunnies and feeling pain instead of, 'Oh that's so cute, Anna would love that!' I don't like seeing special Barbie dolls and knowing there's no reason to buy them anymore—especially the drag queen Barbie I saw last night. She would've loved that one. I don't like knowing I will never have a grandchild of my own or a continuing relationship with the person she was becoming. I don't like laying awake at night remembering what she looked like laying in that coffin to make this a reality for me. I don't like knowing that for twenty-eight days after coming home I couldn't get into the shower, because every time I did, I saw her hanging from the shower rod and I didn't even see her like that. Grief is a viscous thing and it does horrific things to your mind. After that you are never the same. Everything changes, brutal fact of life. All I can equate this with is an animal licking its wounds. I'm wounded and I need time to heal—and I will heal—in my own time and in my own way.

The last few days have been the yelling at God stage. *What is expected of me? Why do I have to be so strong? How come other people get to go through life and never experience half of what I've gone through in my life?*

I need peace. Peace of mind, peace in my soul and peace in my heart. I have no illusions. Anna and I loved each other dearly, and when we were together it was special time. There were also some very bad times, but we can't predict the future and we can't go back and change what has happened. I know there are things I would most definitely do different if I could.

I held my Godson last night. I watched him be born, what an emotional experience that was. It's funny, in the last few months there have been five new babies born into my immediate circle of friends. People expect this to be painful for me, but it's not really. I never thought I could be optimistic again. Especially right now, but I am. My child is gone but with each new baby that comes into this world, there is a new hope. One new chance for things to go right.

It's a long and slow process. Sometimes for every two steps forward, you drop back three. But other times you get to take two more steps forward without falling back. You just have to keep putting one foot in front of the other and keep going. And that's exactly what I'm doing, one step and one day at a time."

Common Reactions to Suicide
Shock, Guilt, Grief, Anger, Depression, and Denial

Shock, guilt, grief, anger, depression, and denial work overtime when someone commits suicide. In the minds of many people, suicide is seen as *preventable*. With this being the case, many survivors feel intense guilt and anger, since they were unable to prevent the suicide. When the one who has died is your child, the emotions intensify further. The Compassionate Friends write, "The suicide of one's child raises painful questions, doubts, and fears. The knowledge that your love was not enough to save your child and the fear that others will judge you to be an unfit parent may raise powerful feelings of failure. Realize that as a parent you gave your child your humanness—your positives and negatives—and that what your child did with them was primarily your child's decision.

Why?

"Why?" is the question that survivors of suicide ask over and over again. "Why would he (or she) take his life?" The "need to know" feelings are intensified when suicide occurs. The Mental Health Association in Waukesha County, Wisconsin, published a pamphlet titled *Grief After Suicide,* which states: "Why would anyone willingly hasten or cause his or her own death? Mental health professionals who have been searching for years for an answer to that question generally agree that people who took their own lives felt trapped by what they saw as a hopeless situation. Whatever the reality, whatever the emotional support provided, they felt isolated and cut off from life, friendships, etc. Even if no physical illness was present, suicide victims felt intense pain, anguish, and hopelessness. John Hewett, author of *After Suicide,* says, 'He or she probably wasn't choosing death as much as choosing to end this unbearable pain.'"

Recently Brook was invited as a support person to attend the funeral service of a woman in her mid-thirties who had committed suicide.

> I spent most of the time listening to the conversations of family members and close friends. The first and foremost thought on everyone's mind seemed to be: *Why did she do this?* Again and again loved ones tried to put themselves in her shoes, trying on idea after idea to gain some understanding of what had driven her to make this decision. Sometimes they would reach general conclusions that they could agree upon—but

a moment or two later they returned to asking: *Why?* I don't believe we can answer that question easily. I feel that when someone chooses to end his or her life, that person is in a place we do not and cannot fully understand, a place that allows the decision of suicide to be logical at that point. For most of us, the concept of ending one's own life is beyond comprehension. Just as the journey of grief can only be understood when experienced firsthand, I believe the choice of suicide is something that we cannot see or comprehend from the paths we are on.

While you will never know the complete thought processes of the person who took his or her own life, know that you are not alone in your questioning. Many support groups, both in-person and online (via the Internet), can help you explore your questions and feelings. Please see the Resources chapter for support ideas.

Religion and Suicide

There are many mixed emotions, thoughts, and feelings on suicide and religion. For those affiliated with churches that take a harsh view of suicide, this can be an especially difficult time. In Eva Shaw's book, *What to Do When A Loved One Dies,* she writes: "While suicide is mentioned throughout the Bible's Old Testament, there is no opinion, condemnation, or condoning. Saint Augustine said it was a grievous sin and the Catholic church and a few Protestant denominations have, at times, taken a harsh view of suicide. All major religions have abolished the philosophy that suicide is a cardinal sin, however, you may have to forgive [or ignore] a few people who make comments about the religious aspect of suicide."

The Stigma

The Compassionate Friends offer the following on the topic of suicide, "Cultural and religious interpretations of an earlier day are responsible for the stigma associated with suicide. It is important that you confront the word *suicide,* difficult as it may be. Keeping the cause of death a secret will deprive you of the joy of speaking about your child and may isolate you from family and friends who want to support you. Rather than being concerned about the stigma surrounding suicide, concentrate on your own healing and survival. Many parents prefer to use the phrase "completed suicide" rather than the harsh "committed suicide" when speaking about their child."

The people around us may also have a hard time understanding and accepting suicide. Therese A. Rando, PhD, writes, "The normal need to know why the death occurred will be intensified in suicide." You will need to work hard at answering the questions in your own mind, so that when you are ready, you can talk to others about your child comfortably.

If you have lost someone from suicide, get more information. The Internet has many valuable resources and online support forums; additionally, many books are devoted to the topic. If you are comfortable in a support group setting, there are many for suicide survivors. Check the Resources chapter or call your local church, hospital, or college for ideas on local groups. You will need to come to a point where you can remember your lost loved one realistically—both the positives and the negatives.

Tattered Kaddish
by Adrienne Rich

Taurean reaper of the wild apple field
messenger from earthmire gleaming
transcripts of fog
in the nineteenth year and the eleventh month
speak your tattered Kaddish for all suicides:
Praise to life though it crumbled in like a tunnel
on ones we knew and loved
Praise to life though its windows blew shut
on the breathing-room of ones we knew and loved
Praise to life though ones we knew and loved
loved it badly, too well, and not enough
Praise to life though it tightened like a knot
on the hearts of ones we thought we knew loved us
Praise to life giving room and reason
to ones we knew and loved who felt unpraisable
Praise to them, how they loved it, when they could.

Rachel Warnke, now fifty years old, tells her story . . .

"He didn't have to die. Some chemical imbalance that made him depressed contributed to my father's suicide. It was Christmas Eve and I was fourteen years old. Somehow I knew that Christmas Eve day, while I was busy baking cookies, that there was something terribly wrong. I had finished wrapping all the presents for my father when he gave mom a very hard, clinging hug. Then he disappeared from my life, forever. Self-inflicted, carbon monoxide poisoning from his car's exhaust.

I was a shy person to begin with and we had just moved. I was in a new school. I dealt with this tragedy by becoming an adult—at fourteen years old. Many of the kids were cruel and said things like, 'Do you know your father is going to hell because he committed suicide?' These comments disturbed me very much and I prayed for his soul every night.

I never had counseling for the loss. Instead, I coped by doing everything for dad—like shooting baskets in basketball. I became very needy in relationships as I grew older, and extremely afraid of losing someone. I still feel anxious when someone leaves the house, like they may never come back. I always make sure the last thing I say is 'I love you.'

The best healing for me happened six years after he died. I had a dream where he came to me and said, 'Thank you for your prayers, I'm with God now and at peace.' My mother told me she had a vision of the same thing on the same day! The dream and mom's vision had great meaning and healing for me."

> In *Singing Lessons,* author Judy Collins writes about her personal journey of recovery after her son Clark's suicide . . ."On the anniversary of Clark's death, I woke from a dream at midnight. In my dream I had been trying to persuade Clark not to die—striving to convince him that he didn't have to die, he didn't have to end his life. My son smiled and looked at me with love in his eyes. 'Mother. . . ' he said, 'death is not an ending.'
>
> Today, I don't have to stay in depression. I know I have tools:
> I read a spiritual book
> I call a friend who has a kind word, a lift in her voice.

I think about the good things in my life—often writing them down. There is so much in my life for which to be grateful.

I smile with my husband, my friends, my mother and my sister.

In the moment of silence, there is the sound of God bringing me strength—bringing me healing."

Some Things You Can Do

Learn as much as you can about suicide, especially the myths. Understanding the facts can help relieve guilt.

If you discovered your loved one, be acutely aware of the possibility of Post-Traumatic Stress Disorder. Consider talking with a mental health professional.

Write out on paper your thoughts, questions, and anger. When we keep our complex emotions locked within, we further torment ourselves. Make time daily to "let it out."

Find others, either online or in person, who have lost a loved one to suicide. Ask questions. Find guidance and strength from those who have survived this path before you.

Confront the reality of life. We are all human. There are things we tried to do and there are things we did not do. In hindsight, we often see only the things we did not do or "missed signs." We cannot do everything for everyone. We cannot see the future. We cannot know that recognizing the "missed signs" or doing things we did not do would have changed the outcome.

If guilt is plaguing you, write down specifically what you feel guilty about. Write a letter to your loved one sharing the truth and intensity of your guilt. Write another letter back to yourself offering forgiveness.

Remember you did not have a choice about or control over your loved one's decision to commit suicide. However, you do have control over how to live your life today and going forward.

Chapter Seventeen
One of Many: When Tragedy Causes Multiple Deaths

"Occasionally now I drive by Ground Zero. I find it difficult to think of downtown Manhattan any other way than I see it in my head. There will always be that huge airplane tire lying in the street. There will always be the pieces of airplane lying amid tons of dust and rubble. We just clean up and move along with our lives, a bit wiser, with a bit more respect for each other."
—La Femina, *New York City Policy Officer as reported in "The Tragedy Inside Our Lives,"* Time Magazine Online, *September 8, 2006*

The effect of a disaster or traumatic event goes far beyond its immediate devastation. Just as it takes time to reconstruct damaged buildings, it takes time to grieve and rebuild our lives. Life may not return to normal for months, or even years, following a disaster or traumatic event. There may be changes in living conditions that cause changes in day-to-day activities, leading to strains in relationships, changes in expectations, and shifts in responsibilities. These disruptions in relationships, roles, and routines can make life unfamiliar or unpredictable. A disaster or traumatic event can have far-reaching effects in several major areas of our lives, making rebuilding our emotional lives extremely difficult.

The number of mass losses permeating our news coverage has continued to grow since this book's first release. From tsunamis killings tens of thousands to Hurricane Katrina to 9/11 and other acts of terrorism to the Iraqi war, the awareness and impact of sudden loss in our lives as a nation and as individuals—the collective as well as the personal grief—has grown. In this chapter we address some of the additional challenges faced in high-visibility losses that cause multiple deaths.

Trauma

Historically, grief has been considered a form of depression, but studies conducted over the past ten to fifteen years have shown that it is just as accurately defined as a form of trauma, reports the United States Department of Health and Human Services. Historically, the trauma is particularly severe when it is associated with a large-scale catastrophe.

The kind of severe, traumatic distress that is experienced may be characterized by persistent, intrusive, and disturbing recollections of how the person died. You may have recurring dreams of the deceased, episodes of reliving the experience of their death accompanied by strong out-of-character reactions. You might experience an ongoing state of arousal and irritability. Angry outbursts, over-vigilance of one's surroundings, and an inordinately startled response to stimulation are frequently reported.

A wide variety of thoughts, emotions, and symptoms are normal responses to traumatic events. These highly publicized tragedies affect us as a nation and as individuals. Our personal reactions have been shaped by our individual natures, heritages, and our past and present experiences. Each person's response will be somewhat different, and most likely each person's response will impact the way he or she copes and resolves their unique grief issues.

Specific reactions, as well as stress levels, grief, and trauma will differ based upon our individual experience of the event, including our biochemical and physiological make-up, temperament, personality, and the potential for long-term personal impact. For those who have had previous traumatic experiences, symptoms may be reawakened by these events. Guilt or grief may complicate reactions or increase symptoms.

After tragedy, people's specific beliefs about the world as they knew it, human nature, spirituality, and themselves are challenged. The inner world cannot continue in the same way as before and mourners must go through some transformation in order for them to "find their place" in a "new world." Although many will assimilate or accommodate new values, some will not be able to return to their old values and beliefs.

The darkest and hardest days of many tragic losses are reported in the immediate aftermath through the first several months following a death. In instances of mass violence, this period often lasts throughout the first year. As grieving individuals and families work toward healing, they can be catapulted back into the world of grief through news coverage, overheard conversations, and a variety of other external factors outside of their control. It can be tempting to close one's self off from the external world to limit these external ambushes. However in order to assimilate and eventually move forward, such separation is not a long-term solution. Most tragedies of this magnitude have specific resources and support groups formed to assist survivors. Seek help and support from others traveling a similar journey.

Obsessed with Revenge and Retribution

If your loved one died a violent death, initially you may be filled with thoughts of revenge and retribution. The death may have been caused by malice, carelessness, or someone's irresponsible behavior. Keep in mind that obsession is a way we avoid feelings, and consider moving from obsession to some constructive actions like a memorial fund, volunteering for an organization such as MADD, etc. One way to slow or stop thoughts of revenge and retribution is to realize how much energy, and how much of yourself, you are giving to the person or circumstance your anger is directed at or to. When we realize how that person begins to control our thoughts and our lives, we can take steps to let go of these destructive thoughts. In the Exercises chapter of this book, there is a visualization exercise that can be helpful for working through revenge. Focus instead on how you can commemorate the life of the one you lost. If the death was unintentionally caused by another individual, they are likely suffering their own pain and guilt.

In the book, *Get Out of Your Own Way* by Mark Goulston, MD, and Philip Goldberg, the authors tell the story of a client whose daughter was brutally murdered. The client was preoccupied with thoughts of suicide and anger. The author urged her to get on with her life. "I can't go on until I get over this," she said.

"It's just the opposite," the author replied. "Unless you go on with your life, you won't get over it." I explained, "that only by pushing herself into activities and building new memories would she be able to dilute the impact of the excruciating thoughts that hounded her day and night."

Talking to Children

When talking to children and adolescents about traumatic events following the death of a loved one, gentle courtesy is important (e.g., choose an appropriate setting for the discussion). Telling the truth is a must. It is also important to give the child age appropriate information that is within her/his ability to comprehend and process. Distorting the facts or withholding information may result in future confusions and in distrust. Here are additional guidelines for helping grieving children. (See Chapter 9, Helping Children Grieve, for additional information.)

- Spend more time with your children.
- Avoid stereotyping people or countries that might be home to terrorists.
- Children might regress emotionally and socially for a while. They need the reassurance that you love them and that they are safe.
- Encourage adolescents to talk to you or their friends about their thoughts and feelings.
- Watch for signs of prolonged isolation, persistent sadness, detachment, and academic dips.
- Let children know that our government and law enforcement are actively working to protect us.
- Keep regular family schedules for mealtimes, leisure, recreational activities, and bedtime to help restore a sense of security and normalcy.
- Provide an open and safe atmosphere for discussion, encourage questions.
- Tell the truth.
- Give age-appropriate answers.

- If you are unsure how to help your child(ren), seek professional assistance from a qualified mental health professional.
- Avoid giving too much information for the child to handle at one time.
- Do not go into too many details that can increase feelings of fear and worry. Let your child's questions guide you in disclosing information.
- Ask children about what they hear at school and see on television.

Mental Health Aspects of Terrorism

Sources National Institutes of Health: Mental Health Information Center

- No one who sees a disaster is untouched by it.
- There are two types of disaster trauma—individual and community.
- Most people pull together and function during and after a disaster.
- Stress and grief reactions are normal responses to an abnormal situation.

Typical Reactions

fears and anxieties	irritability
crying, whimpering, screaming	confusion
excessive clinging	disobedience
fear of darkness or animals	depression
fear of being left alone	refusal to go to school
fear of crowds or strangers	reluctance to leave home
problems going to sleep	behavior problems in school
nightmares	poor school performance
sensitivity to loud noises	fighting
alcohol and other drug use	

Post Traumatic Stress

Viewing yourself or others as a "victim" of terrorism or any type of traumatic, painful, or extraordinary stressful event isn't always helpful and in fact, discounts the person's survival skills. Although the person may feel like a "victim," the "survivor" is someone who is resilient, knows how to ask for help, and has the ability to develop positive coping behaviors.

An acute stress reaction is an ordinary response to an extraordinary traumatic and stressful event. At least 50 percent of those persons directly affected by horrific events will acquire some degree of post traumatic stress and may need counseling to effectively deal with the stress. The emotional responses exhibited are a human response to a very inhumane act that has occurred outside the range of ordinary human experience.

The Path toward Healing

We heal at different rates. There is no set time limit for a person to feel normal again or to get back to a regular routine. You will have "good days" and "bad days." Allow yourself time to mourn the loss you have experienced and be at peace with the things you cannot control.

Talking and listening to others will help you express feelings in a helpful way.

Try to focus on day-to-day routine things that you are able to do, and try to keep regular schedules such as exercise, mealtimes, etc. Be sure to ask for support and establish regular contacts with friends and family members.

The most important resource you may have is someone whose loved one was also lost in the same event. You can lean on each other for courage and comfort.

Don't hold yourself responsible for the disastrous event or be frustrated because you feel that you cannot help directly in the rescue work.

Take steps to promote your own physical and emotional healing by staying active in your daily life patterns or by adjusting them. A healthy approach to life (e.g., healthy eating, rest, exercise, relaxation, meditation) will help both you and your family.

Participate in memorials, rituals, and the use of symbols as a way to express feelings.

Use existing supports groups of family, friends, and spiritual/religious outlets.

Chapter Eighteen
Other Unique Challenges

"All I have is a piece of paper saying I have a deceased husband."
—*Elsa, a military widow*

The Challenge of Closure: When Our Loved One's Body Is Not Recovered

When the deceased's body is never recovered, such as in the 9/11 tragedy, it can be extremely difficult to begin, much less complete, the grieving process. Often the grieving process itself is slowed. It can be hard to confront the idea that a person who was healthy is now gone without any form of "proof." Our after-death rituals are also altered as we struggle to "put to rest" a loved one who is not physically with us.

Helen Fitzgerald, author of *The Mourning Handbook,* offers this: "If you have lost a loved one under circumstances where there is no body to view or bury, you may be left with lingering doubts as to whether that person really died, complicating your grief, and possibly delaying your recovery . . . In your case, if there is no body, you may not want to have a memorial service to publicly mourn the loss.

You may not want to give up all hope that your loved one could still be alive. Still, you do need to put some closure on this part of your life, and you have the right to have a memorial service when you are ready. Far from an act of disloyalty to the deceased, such a service can help you celebrate your loved one's life . . . You can also include in your memorial service a cenotaph, which is a monument erected to honor the memory of someone whose body is elsewhere. It can be placed in a cemetery, if you wish, or on your own property."

If there are no remains, a memorial can be built. A bench in a park with a plaque, a carved stone or stack of stones placed by a beautiful lake, a statue, a scholarship fund: something visible and real is very important. A memorial like this offers an anchor for our grief.

Anne Marie had a tree planted in a public garden. Her brother, who died at sea and whose body was never recovered, loved the outdoors. With the park's permission, she had a plaque placed at the foot of the tree. She visits the tree when she needs some comfort. It also makes her feel good that others can enjoy the beauty of the tree, as well as read the plaque associated with her brother.

I actually saw my loved one die. I was there! Now I feel anxious all the time . . . what's happening?

If you witnessed the tragic death and find yourself running the "movie" of the tragedy over and over in your mind, you may be storing "fight-or-flight" responses in your body resulting in major or minor anxiety. Dr. Christiane Northrup explains it this way, "The Fight-or-Flight Response is your body's way of handling acute stress by using stored glucose and fat so your muscles have the energy they need to get you out of harm's way. But you cannot function in this mode forever . . . As your anxiety builds, all of your immune cells start running around in circles, preparing your body to fight . . . but, because there is nothing to actually fight against, the cortisol stays in your system. This is when your emotions become 'toxic.' If this Fight-or-Flight Response continues for a long time, you will deplete your adrenal glands, your hormones will become imbalanced and you can set yourself up for a number of illnesses . . ."

You may need professional help and guidance to work through this anxiety. If you want to try a few ideas on your own, begin with the calming exercise in the Exercises chapter. You may find several of the herbal remedies in the next chapter helpful as well.

I inadvertently caused the death—how do I forgive myself and go on?

Perhaps you were driving the car, flying the airplane, or steering the boat. Perhaps you bought the cruise tickets, chose the restaurant, or suggested the trip. What do you do then? How can you go on with the knowledge that you may have, in some way (big or small) been inadvertently to blame? How do you go on? The answer is by putting the emphasis on the word, "inadvertently." Inadvertently means unintended, unintentional. Say these words to yourself or write them down a hundred times,

"I DID NOT INTENTIONALLY KILL OR CAUSE THE DEATH OF
_____" (fill in the person's name).

If you are having trouble forgiving yourself, try helping someone in need. There is no better cure for regaining your self-esteem. You are valuable. Your life has meaning. Turn the energy you are using in self-condemnation outward to help someone, or some organization that needs your valuable gifts.

Non-Traditional Relationships

You may be the ex-wife, "other woman" or stepchild of the deceased. You may not fit into a traditional category. "Real" wives, "real" mothers, "real" children; they all seem to be paid more attention by relatives and friends. They are seen as more authentic members of the family. And yet you have your needs as well. Pam's experience is an example of one of these non-traditional relationships,

"George was my ex-husband at the time of his death. We had developed a close friendship and co-parenting relationship since the divorce. When he died, I felt I had no legitimacy in my grief. Some uncaring individuals even voiced their disbelief at my strong reaction to his death. I found no support group category into which I fit. So, I grieved on my own—in isolation."

If you cannot find support because your relationship to the deceased was out of the ordinary, you may need to find ways to grieve on your own. The self-help exercises in this book may be especially useful to you.

If there is a non-traditional relationship within your grief circle (and it doesn't compromise your values), do what you can to be considerate of this person's feelings and experiences.

"It comes to all. We know not when,
or how, or why. It's always been
a mystery, a frightening thing,
enshrouded in the silencing.
When suddenly a loved one dies
we seem to sort of *paralyze,*
to just stop still within our track.
And oh, how much we want them back."
excerpted from "When A Loved One Dies,"
by Dolores Dahl, *Suddenly Alone*

Gun Violence in Schools

On average, the United States will witness ten school shootings each year. According to a yearlong *Washington Post* analysis released in 2018, beginning with Columbine in 1999, more than 187,000 students attending at least 193 primary or secondary schools have experienced a shooting on campus during school hours.

In the wake of these tragedies remain grieving families, students, peers, educators, and staff. Most of us hold on to a belief that school and work environments are places where we are safe. Shootings of this nature shatter that reality, often leading to a complicated mourning as we process our own grief and feelings of vulnerability in settings outside the home. We may look to blame the institution where the violence took place or ourselves for our role in choosing that setting. The National Center for Victims of Crime maintains a list of resources and support that can help grieving individuals connect with resources and support. Access their website at victimsofcrime.org.

Grief is Cumulative

This one death can be the one that is just too much. A typical case of "overload" happened to Mary. Mary's mother died of a heart attack, her grandmother died in a nursing home, her best friend died of cancer and her husband died suddenly of a stroke all in the same year. When one loss follows the other, there is no time in between to recover. For this reason, it is important to grieve each death separately or you will feel too overwhelmed to grieve at all. If you are faced with too many circumstances to handle effectively, consider seeing a counselor who can help you work through the maze of emotions. Seeing a counselor is never a sign of weakness, it's a sign that you are committed to moving on, moving through, and getting your life on track.

Consider whether you may be trying to avoid difficult emotions. You must make time even in the midst of other life events. Prioritizing and grief sessions can also be helpful. Try scheduling at least twenty minutes twice each day to experience and work with your grief. Many grievers also find it useful to take a day from time to time, without interruptions, to work through grief. Whatever method works for you is fine; all that matters is that *you make* the time. Without it, you cannot move on.

When Our Darkest Hour Becomes Front-Page News

> *"Death leaves a heartache no one can heal,*
> *love leaves a memory no one can steal."*
> —*Anonymous*

When people experience a high-visibility loss, the grieving process as well as the loss can become "public news."

Twenty-four hour news reporting magnifies each minute of the tragedy with timelines, professional commentary, and victim's stories—some useful and accurate, others hurtful and inaccurate. Concerns such as those regarding the dead, the injured (physically and/or emotionally), future vulnerability, the need to strike back, speculation, business losses, costs of restoration, and protection fill the airwaves. Sensationalism, TV, the media . . . they don't know what's really going on in *your home.* While they can speculate and offer insight and opinions, they are rarely firsthand survivors, but instead they are reporters covering a story very personal to you. Suddenly, you may be confronted by phone calls from the media and from people you haven't heard from in a thousand years.

It feels like a neverending bombardment and your personal life becomes public. The media interest in the death of your 'loved one,' as well as interest in the person's family and friends, can sometimes be difficult—or even impossible—to avoid, and such publicity may add to your distress and suffering. However, it is important to remember that the media can play an important role in investigation and in conveying the truth. Choose a friend or family member to be a spokesperson for your family and receive media inquiries. If you find yourself troubled by media coverage, tell reporters so. Use the attention to bring awareness about how painful grief is and how media and others can support those who are grieving.

Suggestions for Dealing with Media

- Broadcasters clearly have an obligation to deal sensitively with these matters. If they become overly intrusive and if you have a more serious concern, you should contact the Federal Communications Commission, www.fcc.gov. Their Consumer & Mediation Specialists are available Monday through Friday, 8 a.m. to 5:30 p.m. ET to answer your questions and to assist you in filing a complaint. Call toll-free 888–225–5322.

- Newspapers and reporters often want pictures of those who died or of their families, and they will sometimes go to great lengths to get them. You may want to give them a photograph of the person who has died in a way you would like them to be remembered.

- Choose a friend or family member to be a spokesperson for your family and to receive media inquiries. Give them a copy of the photograph to supply and basic information.

The press will usually be sensitive to the situation, however, you may feel that you do not wish to cooperate with the media. It may be that their interest in you or your 'loved one' who has died is intrusive or too distressing. If this is the case, and although you may not be able to prevent the intrusion totally, you can take steps to reduce the level of impact.

- Designate a spokesperson to handle media calls, questions, and contacts with the media on your behalf. You may choose to have your delegated person read a prepared statement written by you. Media and the public seek information. While our grief is private, if our loss is public, the relaying of selected information can help to satiate the media. You may also want to consider using the media to relay a message that speaks to others who are grieving, supports an organization, or explains how the public can help support you.

- At some point you may want to see the media as a way to facilitate your grief. They can provide a platform for expressing your anger, for letting the world know how much you need their support. It might be helpful if they show a photo accompanied by words of admiration for your loved one. You may want to set up a memorial or scholarship fund by using the media. Make sure to have someone keep track of your media contact's names, phone numbers, and email addresses.

PART FOUR
Pathways through Grief

In this final section, our goal is to offer ideas and practices that have helped in the healing process. We explore support options, glance at the grief journey ahead, explore the role of faith, and practice grief recovery exercises. Our wish is not to talk to you or at you, but to be with you . . . as people who have made the journey—from loss to self discovery—from acute grief to managed grief—from one end of the maze to another.

We conclude with sharing where we are on the pathway. We have left our original notes from 1999 and then also how grief looks and feels like to us today in 2008.

Chapter Nineteen
The Road Ahead: Understanding
the Grief Journey

"We don't 'get over' the deepest pains of life, nor should we. 'Are you over it?' is a question that cannot be asked by someone who has been through 'it,' whatever 'it' is. It's an anxious question, an asking for reassurance that cannot be given. During an average lifetime there are many pains, many grieves to be borne. We don't 'get over' them; we learn to live with them, to go on growing and deepening, and understanding ..."
—*Madeleine L'Engle,* Sold Into Egypt

The grief process is different for each person who travels the pathway, but in our years of grief work since the first edition, we have found common themes among those moving through the maze after facing the sudden loss of a loved one. Many grievers who found this book tell us they wish they would have found it sooner. The validation of feelings, the reassurance, and the insight into the journey would have eased their worry and fear.

Often by knowing what is around the corner we can better prepare for it—or at least not feel the wind has been knocked out of us because we had no idea what was coming. In any area of life, it tends to be "the unknown" that fills us with anxiety, fear, and worry. In this chapter, we aim to provide a non-overwhelming glimpse at the journey ahead.

Themes of Grief by Year

First Year . . . a First Time for Everything

In addition to the stages of grief, each year has its own challenges. The following entries offer guidelines of what these years may involve. Keep in mind that like many areas of grief, these experiences are not always linear.

The first year is characterized by disorientation, numbness, denial, sometimes a burst of happiness followed by deadening guilt, acute periods of pain, and then a return to numbness. The roller coaster ride of grief in the early stages can also include periods of euphoria (i.e. "how nice to be alone") followed by deep lows (i.e. "I can't believe she's really gone.") During the first year, some people describe themselves as robots going about the business of living without real joy.

It is easy to remember the hallmarks of the newborn's first year—the first step, the first smile, the first coo, the first word, the first tooth. When we lose someone, it is common to experience an overwhelming number of "firsts." We experience a first trip to the beach without our loved one, an Easter dinner where he isn't present, a trip planned without him, a Christmas morning where he won't open presents. Each of these experiences can be emotionally challenging and physically draining. Please find a way to share these experiences. By joining or creating a support group, you will be with others who have gone through these "firsts." You can share your hardships and heartbreaks and seek solace from others who have walked your path.

There are healing processes that can begin as early as the first year. Seeking information and finding answers to your questions is a solid starting point. However, if you don't feel ready, don't push yourself. Other grievers find comfort from getting their affairs in order. There is something about this process that can help you feel a bit more in control in a situation that is out of control. A lawyer can help you with some of the details. There are now many commercial resources also available. Reading and learning more about grief can also be helpful in the first year.

The more you are able to read, the more you will recognize yourself in others. This will help you normalize the experience.

Ideas for Remembrance from the American Association of Retired Persons

From photo collages at a memorial service to planting a tree, there are many ways we can say, "I remember and loved this person." As you consider how you might want to remember a loved one, here are some ideas to start with. Consider:

- Lighting a candle in her memory
- Creating a memory book of photos of your loved one
- Donating a gift of money or time to those less fortunate
- Wearing a photo pin of your loved one
- Starting a memorial scholarship fund in his name
- Writing a poem or story about him
- Visiting a place you both liked to visit
- Hanging a special ornament on the tree in her memory
- Playing her favorite music
- Making a quilt from his favorite clothes
- Sharing memories of her with friends and family
- Providing memorial flowers for her at your church or synagogue
- Creating a memory box of items that were special
- Honoring his favorite tradition
- Creating a new tradition in your memory
- Hanging a stocking filled with loving memories of him
- Gathering your family and friends together in celebration of him
- Reading aloud your favorite story

The AARP provides a discussion area to share ideas and suggestions for the honoring of a loved one at community.aarp.org/rp-griefnloss/start

Second Year . . . reorganizing

Reorganizing and reexamining one's life characterize the second year. Where do I want to live? How will I support myself? Which car will I sell? How will the children be cared for while I go back to work? What do I do with my son's clothes? What do I do with my mother's empty room? It's a time of readjustment which affords little opportunity for sitting still in one's grief. However, it is essential that you set aside some time to feel your grief and sadness as this is the most necessary part of the healing process.

The reality hits hard during this second year. We can no longer pretend or deny that our loved one is gone and life does continue. The expectancy for "life to continue" is all around us. Society, colleagues, even well-intentioned close friends may hold expectations for you to "return to normal." When we find our grief recovery doesn't match a societal timeline, it makes for a more difficult readjustment.

At this stage, some people are ready to begin making new plans. They are ready to identify their individual goals, hopes, fears, and dreams. People are often ready to move forward and long for a pathway out of the darkness. It's unrealistic, however, to expect complete recovery in year two. Days will be brighter—but the night still comes. You will be stronger. If you haven't already completed the exercises and reading in Part Three, this is a good time to set goals and to begin to work through some thoughts, memories, and emotions.

Third Year . . . Regaining Equilibrium

In the third year, there may be longer periods of relief and longer periods of time in between emotional ambushes, but they still come at unexpected moments. You may cry or feel sad once a week instead of once a day—followed by once a month. You will have mostly reorganized your life. You know you will make it through the grief and that you will live. You may have overcome your reluctance to trust the world again.

In the third year you will hopefully be well into your grief work. You will be confidently moving down the path of redefining and rediscovering yourself and your world. You may have found, or are working on, a way to transform your tragedy into a meaningful memorial. If you have yet to begin recovery work, it's important to start now or to examine why you haven't started. The longer the work is delayed, the longer it will take to feel confident and comfortable with life. You will need at least three years to regain your equilibrium, for others it may take longer.

Grief Steps

In Brook's Grief Step Support Programs, she developed a model of ten commonalities among those who mourned and emerged from grief's grip into a complete, although different, life. Not everyone works through each Step in the exact order listed, nor should the Steps be set against a calendar—*"By year two I should be ____."*

Brook found that those who achieved the step of "Accepting Life" had some similarities:

- They did not use a clock, calendar, or other people's expectations to measure their "progress." Instead, they let their mind and bodies guide them through the process and encourage them to take the next step when they were ready.
- They worked through each Step, applying it to their unique loss. Some worked in order, others did not, but those who reached the Step of "Accepting Life," had worked through each of the preceding Steps in one way or another.
- They continued to work through the process of grief more days than not. While detours might have sidetracked them from the journey for a day, a week, or a month, they returned.
- If they became stuck at a part of the process they may have paused for a time, but in the end, they would choose reaching out versus shutting down.

The first two Steps have been covered in detail within this book. They are the foundation from where we begin again, but they are not the end—they are the beginning of the process. Several of the other Steps are mentioned in brief in this book as they relate to the initial grief process, which is by far the most emotionally and physically challenging.

The Steps that have gone unmentioned cannot be addressed or completed thoroughly in the year following our loss. We need time to regain the energy and knowledge required to move through them. We include them, however, for three primary reasons:

When you close this book and find complex emotions and challenges confront you in the months or years ahead, we feel it is our obligation to share with you where these challenges stem from. It is not that you "grieved wrong" or "didn't grieve enough." The journey is too long to cover in a single book and is comprised of processes. This book is meant to offer a hand to hold in the first challenges of grief.

I Wasn't Ready to Say Goodbye has made it into the hands of tens of thousands of readers who are grieving a loss that occurred two or more years ago. If you are one of these readers, we want you to know that this Grief Steps model can help you. If you read this book and find yourself saying, "I wish I would have known that," or "I didn't do that," please know you can still move through your grief in a healthy way.

Many readers have told us *I Wasn't Ready to Say Goodbye* traveled with them everywhere during the first year or two. It became a security blanket of validation and safety. In time, we began receiving many letters asking, "Where do I go now?" In 2000, Brook had not yet developed this model, as she herself was still in the immediate aftermath of grief. We want to share this information with you so that when you have moved past the information within this book, you are not alone. Brook has developed tools to guide you in the same style and voice you have become accustomed to in this book.

The Ten-Step Pathway

Step One: Shock and Survival

Purpose: To survive the shock of our loss while tending to the basics of reality.

Step Two: The Feelings Rollercoaster

Purpose: To decompress from the shock and experience the full range of feelings that accompany loss.

Step Three: Understanding Our Story

Purpose: To find a beginning, middle, and end so that we may cease obsessive thinking.

Step Four: Acknowledgement & Active Grieving

Purpose: To acknowledge the reality of our loss and fully grieve our loss.

Step Five: Forgiveness

Purpose: To release ourselves from unnecessary pain through the act of forgiveness.

Step Six: Faith

Purpose: To explore, define, rebuild, and repair our faith in life and/or in God.

Step Seven: Finding Meaning

Purpose: To understand that even the deepest tragedy can bring meaning, and to uncover that meaning.

Step Eight: Redefining Ourselves

Purpose: To understand the void that has been created by our loss and how that void will change our personal belief system.

Step Nine: Living with Our Loss

Purpose: To integrate the discovered meaning into our day-to-day lives.

Step Ten: Accepting Life

Purpose: To take responsibility that life is ours to be lived to its fullest.

To learn more about Brook's upcoming ebook encompassing her ten-step pathway through grief, visit brooknoel.com.

Chapter Twenty
Faith

"Whatever religion we choose to accept, we have to recognize that it has led others through their 'dark valley of the shadow of death' in the past, and it will do so again. We are not the first to tread that bleak path, even as we know we will not be the last."
—*Robert J. Marx, Susan Wengerhoff Davidson*, Facing the Ultimate Loss

Faith is a complex and difficult concept to grapple with on any given day, let alone during a time when it has been pushed to the edge. As Robert J. Marx and Susan Wengerhoff Davidson write in *Facing the Ultimate Loss: Coping with the Death of a Child*, "All we know is that we are in pain, and quick fixes are the things we reject most quickly. In a time of suffering, we all recognize that faith is not an easy thing to grasp. There are so many moments when we are too depressed to even listen to what our faith has to offer."

In the early months of our grieving, complex questions about faith are often pushed to the side and our focus is more basic: *Why him? Why me? How could this happen?* It can take months to seek out or reunite with our faith after loss. Many people can, and do, find solace in the grace of God throughout their journey. But many others question the foundation of their spirituality.

Suddenly we are living in a foggy world with a new question at every turn—questions that do not have easy answers. The fact that there aren't easy answers make the process of restoring, or finding, or renewing faith similar to the grief process itself. We do not have a book filled with easy answers. Instead, we move forward, step by step, until we emerge on our own pathway, toward understanding.

A Fork in the Road

In Brook's work with those who are grieving, she has noticed an interesting phenomenon. For some people, loss serves as a catalyst to faith growing stronger—for others, loss becomes a reason to turn away from their faith.

Moving away . . .

Bethany considered her Catholic faith to be a guidepost in her life. Attending church each Sunday, being involved in Sunday school, praying daily, and sending her children to Catholic school were just a few of the ways she lived her faith. When her daughter was hit by a car while walking home from school, Bethany's faith crumbled. She turned to her church for support but found their advice to be shallow and inadequate for the intensity of her grief. It has been three years since her daughter's death, and Bethany has yet to return to a religious community. "It's not that I doubt God exists—I know He does. I just don't want to have anything to do with Him anymore."

Moving closer . . .

Just after 9/11, I received a phone call from a woman whose husband was a New York City firefighter and died in the rescue operations. Cathy was calling to find out if she could receive a quantity discount on hundreds of copies of this book to be distributed to families in New York City. Of course the answer way yes and we began talking. Cathy was a mother of three, a six-year-old and one-year-old twins. She mentioned that her husband had always been the "religious one," and she could "take-it-or-leave-it." However, after his death, Cathy had found a strong faith in God.

We have heard many stories like Cathy's, people who never had God in their life who turn to God for the strength to survive. Many people find comfort, knowing God is there to receive their loved one.

> *"It just occurred to me this past week, that if my love is able to transcend this mortal life, that his [my deceased son's] love for me is also able to do the same."*
> —*Janice, a Grief Steps member*

In working with hundreds of families, Brook has discovered two factors that may account for moving away or moving toward faith, (1) The ability to express anger and emotions (2) Receptiveness of our faith community.

Anger at God

It's common to question God in these dark times. We may question a faith we thought would never change or waver. This is okay. The Psalms are filled with passages of questioning God in dark and difficult times.

"My God, my God, why have you deserted me?

. . . Why are you so far away?

Won't you listen to my groans and come to my rescue?

. . . I cry out day and night, but you don't answer,

. . . and I can never rest."

—Psalm 22: 1,2 (Contemporary English Version)

In *The Grief Recovery Handbook,* John W. James and Russell Freidman write, "We have to be allowed to tell someone that we're angry at God and not be judged for it, or told that we're bad because of it. If not, this anger may persist forever and block spiritual growth. We've known people who never returned to their religion because they weren't allowed to express their true feelings. If this happens, the griever is cut off from one of the most powerful sources of support he or she might have."

> *"Don't be afraid if you get angry. Any Power that can create a universe can handle your anger."*
> —*Adelle Jameson Tilton*

It is common for grievers to yell, be angry, or scream at God. One should not feel guilty for such emotions. Like many other aspects of grief, this internal reckoning is part of the process. Pam, an Interfaith Minister, recalls:

"I remember walking up and down the halls of the hospital where George lay on life support, shaking my fist at Heaven, yelling at God. Someone who overheard suggested that I not be angry with God and that I control how I speak to Him. I replied, 'My God can handle this anger. And I know if I get angry at God, God won't desert me.'"

In its basic sense, our anger is an affirmation of our faith. Authors Marx and Davidson summarize this well when they write, "When we lose a child [or someone or something], we so often become the victims of our anger—anger at a husband or wife, anger at a doctor, even occasionally at the child who has been taken from us. Of all the rage we experience, none may be more bitter than our anger toward God. 'How could a loving and kind God do this to me?' Even the rage of a betrayed husband or wife could not be more bitter. After a lifetime of trust, how could that God of justice and loving-kindness allow this terrible injustice? The angry question can be seen as an affirmation and accusation. After all, the very anger we feel is based upon the fact that we believe. We cannot be angry with someone who does not exist."

Faith Communities and Grief

Interestingly, in Brook's work to train professionals to lead grief support groups, religious leaders accounted for the majority of enrollees. One priest shared the following:

"We are noticing that many people who experience loss stop attending the church. The number became large enough that we reached out and asked these believers if there was anything we could do to help. It became very apparent that we were ill-equipped to help in the time of need. We could organize food drives and prayer circles, but beyond that we struggled. The church is especially attuned to ceremonies and passages. We have ceremonies for birth and for death. But after the ceremony we didn't have a full understanding of how to walk through grief with our members. Our attention was focused on getting back to the Gospel, to worship, to encouraging these members to pray and be prayed for. What we didn't understand was many of our members had lost the basic vocabulary to communicate with God."

In *Transcending Loss: Understanding the Lifelong Impact of Grief and How to Make it Meaningful,* author Ashley Davis Prend offers a wonderful view on the purpose of faith and religion. "The purpose of religion is to be a vehicle, an avenue of facilitating spiritual connections with the Divine. And yet, as we've seen, many people find that religion isn't so much a helpful bridge to spirituality as a gated tollbooth with padlock and chains. In rethinking how to unlock the gate and restore free transportation, some people find that they choose to abandon their childhood religion. They choose to go on a search for a new faith community that can support rather than condemn, that can nourish rather than diminish, that can sustain rather than victimize."

If you find yourself in a faith community that cannot handle your grief, consider reevaluating your needs in time. Seek out a support group or community that can walk with you through this dark time. If your faith is important to you, do not shut yourself off from it for fear that no one will understand or accept you. After you have moved through your journey, you may want to consider going back to the faith community where you could not find initial support and begin a support group.

Can I expect my religion to offer me the answers and support I need right now?

Rev. Stephen Goldstein, a clergyperson of the United Methodist Church, shared his thoughts with us. "All too often religious professionals rely on the glib or trite religious language in the face of death or human pain, with a pat sensibility that does little to show a genuine concern for the grieving person. Our simple human availability is initially demanded in such pastoral encounters, not coded objective 'answers.' When with someone, I try to voice the questions I sense they are asking. I ask why?, etc. *with them* and communicate my own question. It is not the time for solutions or problem solving. The key is *being* with someone and expressing my own human limitations, that I have the same questions. I am certain that this is how to be available to the 'presence of God,' or the 'spirit,' or whatever your tradition 'calls' the transcendent. God is available at such times, especially when we are vulnerable enough in our care and genuine concern for the other for that presence to 'breathe' through us, perhaps even with a physical touch during prayer when we seek the love of the transcendent other.

'When looking carefully and examining through the questions with someone grieving after a sudden death or any death, it is important to hear and listen and not assume what is being expressed by the other. Sometimes it's guilt, fear, anger, or even relief, and usually a combination of these normal emotions, but to be the 'church,' 'the gospel' or the presence of God in such situations, it is of primary importance to pay attention beyond our own expectations. If we can be vulnerable enough to feel the other's experience by revisiting our own experience, we may create the opportunity for the presence of healing. Or as Henri Nouwen gave expression to this role—becoming a "wounded healer." It's not so much naming the other's feeling, but being one—open to, and in, the spirit. It is not naming the other how they feel, but being one with the person through the spirit. Offering one's own personal experience in an intuitive way may most adequately define that presence. The closure ceremonies such as funerals and memorials is the time to verbalize the 'historic language' of the faith. This brings the person into community with loved ones and the greater community of which we may be a committed part.

Of course this can only be really effectual when such community is part of the person's life. To expect religion or a religious leader to come to the rescue, is both unrealistic and unfaithful.

If a pastor only offers written prayers or pat scriptural expressions such as 'there are many mansions in my father's house,' to avoid sharing honest experience, without listening to the person's raw grief, this will surely avoid and block any significant "spiritual" expression. Religion then becomes a barrier to the presence of God and grace.

If the pastor or religious professional is only disingenuously available you will of course know it and will have to go elsewhere in your community for care and a real presence. It is of course important to already be in community, specifically religious or not, to have such availability in a time of crises. That is part of being a spiritually mature person to begin with. That a particular clergy or professional are uncomfortable dealing with someone's pain and loss is a different issue. If one is a mature follower of a religion, then either the teachings themselves have been translated to be available to you in your life so that they can be a means of grace to you as a genuine expression of your experience."

What Do I Believe?

As we stand at our own crossroad, we must look at our life and evaluate our faith. Is our faith a part of us, or is it simply something we have inherited and accepted blindly? Have we really believed prior to our loss—or have we just gone through the motions? What does faith mean to us? What do we seek to find? Once we identify our basic need and belief system, we can begin to move toward the communities and materials that will be the most helpful. Faith, by definition, should be something that encourages and supports us in our day-to-day living.

Time and time again, faith has proven to be an important tool for healing. However, that is only true if our faith supports us. If you are struggling with your faith, take some time to reflect and think about what you need from your faith community. Just because one community is not supportive does not mean that all communities will not be.

Beliefnet™ offers a tool to help people find faiths that match their beliefs—whatever those beliefs are. The free guidance tool asks non-judgmental questions about your spiritual beliefs and then displays faiths that most closely match your beliefs. www.beliefnet.com/story/76/story_7665_1.html

Amazing Grace

Amazing grace! How sweet the sound
That saved a wretch like me!
I once was lost, but now am found;
Was blind, but now I see.
'Twas grace that taught my heart to fear,
And grace my fears relieved;
How precious did that grace appear
The hour I first believed.
Through many dangers, toils and snares,
I have already come;
'Tis grace hath brought me safe thus far,
And grace will lead me home.
The Lord has promised good to me,
His Word my hope secures;
He will my Shield and Portion be,
As long as life endures.

Yea, when this flesh and heart shall fail,
And mortal life shall cease,
I shall possess, within the veil,
A life of joy and peace.

Reconnecting with God

Micki McWade, author of *Daily Meditations for Surviving a Breakup, Separation or Divorce* writes, "Staying in touch with God on a regular basis brings us serenity. This is true regardless of the circumstances. Some will ask, 'How can God let this happen to me?' but this is a trap that only brings despair. God doesn't make things happen to us, but will comfort us and give us strength. He will provide us with the tools to go on, if we ask. He comes to us at our invitation."

Praying can help us reach out toward God and does not require anything except your own willingness. In a time of suffering, do not be concerned about a "right" way to pray or a "wrong" way to pray. Take a walk and talk to God. Let Him know how you feel. Let Him know what you need. Think about this communication as you would any other relationship. If you were angry with someone, what would happen if you retreated into yourself instead of ever voicing your feelings? A wall would form between the two of you. When we communicate our innermost thoughts to God, as with any other relationship, we keep the walls at bay.

If you have built a wall between yourself and God, then consider praying for the wall to come down. Ask God how to reach Him and how to break the wall down. God is not forceful, He comes by invitation—He comes the moment you open your heart and ask Him to be present.

Some Things You Can Do

Recognize that the process of restoring faith does not happen overnight. Give yourself time and space to explore and rebuild your faith. Consider starting a prayer journal or setting a time for daily reflection.

Use a few pages in your journal to explore your feelings about faith and its role both past and present in your life. What do you need from a faith community?

Consider joining a prayer circle or prayer group online. BeliefNet (www.beliefnet.com) offers a variety of prayer circle and groups for many religions.

If you are feeling anger toward God, express it in a letter or find a private place to vent—don't hold it in.

Prayer of Faith
We trust that beyond absence
There is a presence.
That beyond the pain
there can be healing.
That beyond the brokenness
there can be wholeness.
That beyond the anger
there may be peace.
That beyond the hurting
there may be forgiveness.
That beyond the silence
there may be the Word.
That beyond the Word
there may be understanding.
That through understanding
there is love.
—author unknown

Chapter Twenty-One
Self-Help and Therapy

"What is needed is an impossible situation where one has to
renounce one's own will and one's own wit and do nothing but
wait and trust the impersonal power of growth and
development. When you are up against a wall, be still and
put down roots like a tree, until clarity comes
from deeper sources to see over the wall."
—Dr. Carl Jung

Survivors can feel isolated and may experience a loss of identity. Some may experience not only the clearly defined stages in counselors' handbooks, but also a lingering sadness. You may be aching for the deceased. Many people consult a pastoral counselor or grief therapist, but there are other sources—poetry, music, volunteer work, support groups, group therapy, self-help books and a variety of useful professional therapies which can frequently provide solace in unexpected ways. We have explored some of these in this chapter. One therapy or self-help avenue may work better for you than another. We all have unique needs, and what will work best for you depends on your background and your belief system.

What are Grief Therapy and Grief Counseling?

Most of the support that people receive after a loss comes from friends and family. Doctors and nurses may also be a source of support. For people who experience difficulty in coping with their loss, grief counseling or grief therapy may be necessary.

Grief Counseling

Grief Counseling is less structured and less formal than grief therapy. Counseling can be one-on-one or in a group setting. Sessions may be hosted by mental health professionals without grief-specific credentials. Counseling also occurs in self-formed groups where people new to the grief process are helped by those further along in the journey.

The National Institute of Health and Human Services summarizes the goals of grief counseling as:

- Helping the bereaved to accept the loss by helping him or her to talk about the loss.
- Helping the bereaved to identify and express feelings related to the loss (for example, anger, guilt, anxiety, helplessness, and sadness).
- Helping the bereaved to live without the person who died and to make decisions alone.
- Helping the bereaved to separate emotionally from the person who died and to begin new relationships.
- Providing support and time to focus on grieving at important times such as birthdays and anniversaries.
- Describing normal grieving and the differences in grieving among individuals.
- Providing continuous support.
- Helping the bereaved to understand his or her methods of coping.
- Identifying coping problems the bereaved may have and making recommendations for professional grief therapy.

Grief Therapy

Grief therapy usually occurs one-on-one to cater to the specific needs of the bereaved. Grief therapy also works in a group setting if the challenges of the bereaved are similar. The therapy is led by a mental health professional who is trained in grief and bereavement. Together client and therapist identify the unique challenges in the grief journey and apply a model or process to work through the challenges. Therapy arrangements often include an agreement between client and therapist, a fee structure, and a commitment to a number of sessions.

The National Institute of Health and Human Services offers six tasks that are often worked through in grief therapy to help those who are mourning.

1. Develop the ability to experience, express, and adjust to painful grief-related changes.
2. Find effective ways to cope with painful changes.
3. Establish a continuing relationship with the person who died.
4. Stay healthy and keep functioning.
5. Re-establish relationships and understand that others may have difficulty empathizing with the grief they experience.
6. Develop a healthy image of oneself and the world.

Does Anything Good Ever Come of All This?

In the very beginning, you will find it extremely difficult to accept that any good could eventually emerge from your tremendous loss. However, as difficult as it is to move through the stages of grief, trust that it is possible to shift from feeling grief as "something that happens to you" to "grieving is something you do to heal." You are the one person who can change the pain to possibility, the loss to some creative expression. After a while you may want to start a charity, scholarship, or foundation to honor the deceased. You may be inspired to write a book (as we have done), create a painting or sculpture, or write a song.

The wrenching and ripping apart that the sudden death of a loved one creates can leave one with an open wound subject to infection. The "infection" can then manifest itself as self-abuse (liquor, promiscuity, pills, etc.) or it can manifest itself, by choice, as growth.

For some, the bereavement process can bring a new appreciation for life, for their relationships, and for the world around them. Many report a feeling of being more strongly in tune and connected to the rest of humanity.

By choosing growth and creativity as a result of this major life transition, you may even find new friends. This is especially true if you seek out support groups consisting of people who have a mutual need. You can share your struggles at trying to create a meaningful new life, and at the same time facilitate some useful understanding of the recovery process. By choosing growth, you may begin to see your relationship with the Universe in a different way. You may begin to see God (or however you choose to name that energy in your life) in the small acts of love from those we least expect, in our communities and families, and maybe even from a stranger, as Maggie saw . . .

Maggie's Story

"My husband died suddenly while playing baseball—a heart attack. He was young. We were young. When I found myself feeling dysfunctional during the early stages of grief, I barely had the energy to cook meals for my two young children. So, off we went to McDonald's. As we were eating our hamburgers and French fries, I noticed a woman sitting at a table with her own two young children. I also noticed she wasn't wearing a wedding ring. I was new in the community and most of my friends had abandoned me because they were "our" friends. After announcing to my children that I would be right back, I approached the woman, introduced myself, told her I was recovering from the death of my husband and asked her if she knew of any support groups or therapists I might turn to for help. I simply took the chance she might know what I could do. In a few minutes of conversation she told me that she was also widowed and invited us to sit at her table. She then asked if I would come back to her house for a glass of wine where she gave me the name of her therapist. This total stranger became one of my best friends, offering me love and support over many months of pain and readjustment."

Andrea LaSonde Melrose describes this unexpected movement of human spirit in the book, *Nine Visions:* "We stumble blindly on our way, often running from a responsibility we are afraid to take on, from a burden we don't think we can carry. We thrash and flail, certain that we are drowning, panicked, as if unreasoning activity were going to help us. Somehow, into that darkness, comes a moment of peace when a friend gives us a hug, a stranger reaches out a hand . . . and we realize that we have been standing on a rock all along; supported, stable, safe. However we see that gesture, as God working through the human beings around us or simply as the generosity of the human spirit coming through the day-to-day masks we all wear, the gift is infinitely precious."

You can chose to allow the spirit (creative force, God, higher power) to move into your life, providing an opportunity to look at previously challenging and fearful situations in a new way, with the ultimate outcome of a new sense of self awareness. By choosing growth you are saying to yourself, and those in your life, that as painful as this transitional experience is, "I am going to survive and be better for it."

Is It Really Possible to Transform My Grief and Pain into Creative Energy?

Yes, as a matter of fact, it is recommended that you find a way to transform your grief and pain into creative energy. The book you are holding is an example of that transformation of energy. Olympic medalist, Ekaterina Gordeeva, used this energy the first time she went back on the ice after her husband and skating partner's sudden death. Her choreography on ice was an extremely moving and powerful example of grief turned into creative expression.

In the Prologue to *My Sergei,* Ekaterina Gordeeva wrote, "For me, a new life is coming, a different life from that which I knew. I felt it for the first time when I was back in Moscow, two weeks after my beloved Sergei's funeral. In my grief, I feared I had lost myself. To find myself again I did the only thing I could think of, the thing I knew best, the thing I'd been trained to do since I was four years old. I skated. I went onto the ice, which was always so dear to Sergei and me, and there, in the faces of young skaters training with their coaches, I recognized their bright dreams and hopes for the future. The new life is coming, I thought."

The book also reveals that, "As Ekaterina and her coach, Marina worked on the choreography for the 'Tribute to Sergei,' Marina helped her visualize the ice dance by saying, "Imagine that you're skating with Sergei for the last time . . . Now you've lost him, you're missing him, you're looking for him and can't find him. You get on your knees and ask God why it happened. Your legs feel broken, as if they have no strength. You cannot move. Everything inside you feels broken, too. You must ask God for some help. You must tell God you understand that life goes on, now you have to skate. You must thank Him for giving you Sergei for half your life, the most beautiful time in your life. This is about how all people can get up from their knees in the face of adversity, can go forward, and can have the strength to persevere. You can find someone to live for. You can have a life of your own now."

You don't need to be an Olympic ice dancer to express yourself creatively. It may be writing a small collection of poetry. You may want to write or compose a song. Creating a simple photo collage may be helpful. You may choose to write a book or start an organization. Allow yourself to discover a creative outlet that suits you.

Grief has an absolutely transformative power. When we lose someone, we lose what they gave us, whether it's economic security, love, guidance, or all of these. Taking these functions upon ourselves, or finding new ways to achieve what we have lost, can be an enriching experience. Think of one special way that person had of *being*. What we most appreciated is what we yearn and grieve for—and by making that quality stronger in ourselves, we keep the spirit of our loved one alive.

Journaling and Letter Writing

One of the most powerful tools for recovery is writing down your real thoughts and feelings in a journal—no editing or judgment. Writing a letter to the deceased can also be comforting. Some of your initial feelings will be quite strong or angry. Don't let this deter your efforts. You need to get those feelings out. After a while, your writing will turn softer as the emotional charge lessens. You have a unique and meaningful story to tell—the story of the beginning, middle, and ending of a relationship. Telling your story, writing it in a journal, creating poems, hearing others' stories . . . these are some ways we heal. No one has to read what you wrote for this exercise to work, although you may want to read portions of your journal to your support group members. One woman I spoke with said, "What worked best for me was to keep a daily gratitude journal so I could see that my life was full of more than just grief and loss. It helped me feel more balance and gave me a perspective that was empowering."

Don't put any expectations or limitations on your writing—simply write. If you find it hard to get started, set a timer for five minutes and write anything that comes to mind. Don't stop. The writing may not make sense or be coherent, but it will help you get used to placing words on paper. Don't worry about spelling, grammar, or style—just get the words out. Try doing a five-minute writing exercise each morning when you awake or at night before going to bed.

Take the time to find a way to tell your story. Listen to your story. Listen to the stories of others.

Maybe I'm spending too much time alone. Is this bad for me?

Solitude is as important as a group experience. Balance is important. In solitude comes the opportunity (if we are not afraid) to slow down, to reflect, to gain a deeper inner vision of our responsibilities, our needs, and ourselves. However, if we spend too much time alone, we risk believing the inner voices that beat up on us, so you may do better if you attend a weekly support group in conjunction with your alone time. A group offers the opportunity to check out what we "learned" in solitude and to find out if what we've been telling ourselves is true.

I feel like my life is over, that everything has been put on hold—forever.

The first step toward positive change is to recognize that the life of the person you cared about is over and that *yours is not.* To do this, recondition your thoughts and your words. Many people who are grieving hold onto the thought that the deceased is coming back. Survivors find themselves waiting or putting life on hold. This kind of waiting, or holding back, uses a lot of energy that could be funneled into other pursuits. You must consciously be aware of pulling your thoughts back from the past to the present moment so you can maximize your energy to create a positive, forward-looking present.

I don't like to take prescription medicine and my sister is encouraging me to try herbal and natural options. Do you have any recommendations?

Some people report great success and relief with the use of herbal remedies, others report mild improvement, and others report little difference. Always consult your doctor before taking any herbal medication or starting any alternative therapy.

Everyone is saying I should find group support, but I can't seem to find anything in my area.

Some of the ways these groups are listed or advertised are:

> bereavement group
> bereavement support
> newly widowed
> young and widowed
> parents of murdered children
> suicide support

If you can't find a group in your area, you may want to start one. Talk to your local library. Many libraries have a community room they will let you use. Talk to a minister, priest, or rabbi in your community—find out if they would be willing to organize a group and have you be the contact person. You don't have to go the course of loss alone! Many existing groups offer starter materials for forming a group. Contact national headquarters in the Resources chapter for these offerings. Also keep in mind that the Internet has opened up worlds of support. The great thing about the Internet is that you can "sign on" whenever you need support.

I'm considering attending a support group once a week. Will going to a group help me cope even when I'm not there?

When you commit to a bereavement support or therapy group, you "take the members with you" when you go into difficult situations. You are never really alone. Sometimes if you ask, members will go with you not just in spirit, but also in the flesh. For example, Maureen had to go to city hall to pick up her son's death certificate, and she expressed her anxiety and fear to the group. After she admitted she was scared that she might break down in a public place, Shelly, another group member, volunteered to accompany her and even drive her there if she wanted.

My friends and family all say I need the support of others who have gone through this, but I don't feel ready to talk about this face-to-face. Are there any alternatives?

Fortunately, there are. The Internet has opened up many avenues to exchange and share information. One of the most popular features of the Internet is chat rooms. While many chat rooms have no designated topic or are unmoderated, there are many specifically created to support those who are grieving. You can listen or read other's stories and share as you choose. You can also remain anonymous. Another advantage is that you can seek help when you need it. If you are feeling low in the middle of the night, you can simply "sign on" to your computer and find someone to comfort you.

Not every exercise will be right for you. Read them through and see how you feel toward the exercise. If it sparks your interest or feels like an exercise appropriate to your stage of grief, try to work it through. If you read through an exercise and it makes you uncomfortable, don't discard it immediately. Identify what makes you uncomfortable. Often uncomfortable feelings arise from our sensitivities and fears—it could be one of these exercises that would be the most valuable to you.

Lastly, these exercises are tools for your grief work; they are not a substitute for support groups or other help.

Anger Exercise

You may find it useful to turn your anger into a loud prayer or shouting match with God. For example:

Dear God! The pain is horrible. I am angry with myself. I am angry with my spouse. I am angry with you! I know you can handle my anger because I see you as loving me no matter what. But why can't you make it stop! Make the pain go away! How much do you expect me to take?

Pounding your fists on a bed or sofa while shouting this "prayer" is one way of moving painful, stuck energy through your body. You might notice a sense of relief when you're done. You may even feel like you've been blessed in some way. You may want to do this exercise with your therapist or trusted friend if you don't feel safe doing this alone.

If the sound of your own screaming and yelling is too scary for you, you might begin by writing a short note to the deceased. Each of the following was at a point in the process where all the survivor could feel was anger and where they were temporarily unable to feel *anything* at all *but* their anger:

Dear Allison: I am hurt and angered by your abandonment of the kids and me. Regards, Rob

Chris: All I want to do is rage at you and cry. Brenda

Dear Tom: If I could get my hands on you right now, I'd kill you for leaving me. Love, Annie

Dear Artie: Friends don't desert friends, man. You really messed me up.

Of course, you can write more if you want to. What's important is to find an outlet or exercise that helps you release your anger. Refer to Chapter 3 for more detail about other outlets for anger and emotion.

Thank You Exercise

As you continue to grow and heal, you will eventually discover at least something (no matter how seemingly insignificant) for which you can express gratitude. If the expression is not available to you now, it is probably a temporary condition.

After you have honored your anger, and when you are ready, you might want to try this Thank You Exercise. Compared to all other acts, personal and spiritual growth is greatest through the expression of gratitude. No matter how difficult at first, expressing appreciation for the life that is gone can help make some meaning in the face of tragedy. Acknowledging, in writing, what was empowering and uplifting about your relationship to the deceased will help you keep sacred what you had together—to retain what was valuable and to let go of the false belief that they are incapable of inspiring you (now that they are dead.)

Why pick up a pen and write a note—why not just think about it? The act of writing, choosing the type of pen and paper, the color of the ink, moving the pen across the paper, seeing the words—all make what you are saying more real—more concrete. You will notice your energy shift—from confusion about what to write, anger at having to sort through your life for the first time (or the thousandth time), tears as you recognize what you have lost, and ultimately a sense of relief at having given yourself the chance to express the unsaid.

Date and save your notes in a special place or put them in your journal. You may want to destroy the note. Remember, this is about expressing feelings that need to be expressed. Rereading it again, however, after several months or years, is sometimes useful, so you may want to save it for future reference. It is also useful to write another note after some time has passed. Each time you write, you will gain new insights. If you have young children, you may even want to read it to them when they are older.

Here is an example:

Dear Jim, Thanks for the holding. You were good at holding when I needed to be held—when I was having trouble learning to trust—you helped me to know that I was capable of loving.

You held me when I was sad. I had so much sadness then. Thank you for the many times you were able to say, "Everything will be all right." Thank you for coming into this lifetime. This time I received the lesson I was so long denying that I needed to learn. What did I learn? I learned that it is unwise to marry someone to give you what you didn't get from your parents as a child. It is important to nurture and love yourself.

Thank you for being a good father to our son—you were the kind of father I would have wanted for myself. Thank you for the ten years of our marriage—for ten years I felt loved. Thanks for being with me at the birth of our son and for supporting us so I could stay home with him when he was a baby—yes, MOST OF ALL, thank you for our son for without you, he would not have been born. Love, Joan

Although she sobbed on and off for the better part of an hour after writing this, Joan admitted to experiencing a sense of relief and to feeling better about herself than she had in some time through expressing her appreciation for her husband in her letter to him.

Learning through Loss

Patricia lost her fourteen-year-old son, Doug, to a self-inflicted gunshot wound. She offers ten affirmations of life that she learned from her grieving process:

1. "I let my feelings flow; they are my life's blood; they will not kill me; they will heal me. (By the way, a punching bag is a good way to move from rage to tears.)
2. I follow my lead. I only need to know and then honor the next step.
3. I can trust the Universe to support me and it will in ways seen and unseen.
4. Help is there—I need only let it in at times, to ask others and to trust that people want to help in these ways:
   Physically—mow my lawn, scrub my deck (where my son died)
   Metaphysically—pray for me, hold me in the light
   Psychologically—send me your memories of Doug, poems that mean something to you
5. I will confront my demons. Anxieties are not stoppers or signs to give up, they are just a new place to step slowly and to be creative.
6. Gratitude—every situation has a gift and a limit. I won't deny the limits and the pain and I will let myself see the gifts and the goodness as well.
7. Be there as a friend—the greatest gift I can give to someone is to accept him or her fully as they are.
8. Life is a journey, not a destination. I will live each day fully for its gifts of grief and gladness.
9. Grief comes in waves. Each carries me forward to the next step. An ocean never becomes stagnant water.

10. I will pray, meditate, and stay in touch with the spirit in whatever way works for me."

Patricia's final note: "Upon completion of this . . . a fresh wave of grief hit as spring and Easter arrived. I found myself needing to read what I had written over and over to remember the lessons I had so painfully learned. Which brings me to an old affirmation of mine . . . *I will tell a friend what I see as my truth so that someday when I forget, my friend can tell it back to me.* So dear reader, help me remember when times get tough."

Patricia chose to use the power of lessons learned in facing her grief. This practice is both healing and empowering. Try it for yourself. Purchase a small and beautiful bound book at a stationary store. In this book, record the lessons you learn moving through the grief process. It can be a great reminder of the steps you are taking and a wonderful way to become more aware of purpose and meaning.
—Contributed by Patricia Ellen

What My Loved One Has Left Me

When someone dies suddenly, it is not unusual to have a sense that one was rejected or abandoned in some way. When you are feeling the searing pain and anger of abandonment, it is even more difficult to consider that your pain may be transformed into something meaningful or that the end of the relationship through death can be in any way beneficial to your growth. It can be, especially if you were dependent on the other person for good feelings about yourself. Now is the time to look within and to affirm yourself as a person of value. It is also the time to remember and replay the positive messages you heard from your significant other before they died. Everyone has heard at least one life-affirming, positive message from their deceased loved one worth repeating to oneself. List those messages in your journal or write them in letter form (i.e. Dear ___, these are the life affirming messages I bequeath to you. Love _____).

Allow these positive messages to lift and inspire you.

Screaming Exercise

Sometimes the only thing left to do is SCREAM! Emotions may well up inside you and they need a place to go. It can be a release and a relief to scream as loud as you can and to say whatever comes to mind. It will be a challenge to find an appropriate place to do this exercise. You may have to travel some distance to find a wide open space where no one can hear you. Here is an example of how Pam and her sister Marilyn solved the problem:

"A few months after my sister's husband died suddenly and I was still reeling from George's death, we decided to go to Canada to attend a workshop. In our free time we drove across vast empty spaces with miles of road and no one around. We found ourselves in the car one afternoon in the middle of a Canadian "no man's land" highway screaming 'Why did you die!,' 'I hate you for dying,' 'This death stuff really sucks!' and a host of other expletives. We laughed at how ridiculous we sounded and we cried because we needed to. We decided it was safest if the one who wasn't crying drove the car because it's hard to see the road with tears in your eyes!"

Our intense emotions need to have an outlet, otherwise they can make us sick. A very potent outlet for our grief is to go to a private location (your parked car can serve this purpose very well) and SCREAM and RANT as loudly as you can. By giving ourselves permission to do this, we validate ourselves and our healing process. Do not stifle this need to give voice to your pain. It is your right as a human being to express your deepest feelings in this way if you choose to do so.

Defining Priorities

After losing a loved one, the world often seems to have spun out of control and we are left trying to make sense of our place within it. Thinking about what is important to you and exploring ways you can make a difference can be very helpful. The following exercise asks you to identify your priorities. Keep in mind that there are no right or wrong answers.

What three things matter most to you?

What do you value most spiritually?

What do you value most emotionally?

What possessions do you value most?

What people are most important to you? (List them by name.)

What do you feel you need to accomplish to make your life worthwhile?

When you die, how would you like to be remembered?

What are two things you could do *each and every day,* to make every day special?

What in your life are you most grateful for?

After answering these questions in a journal, write a page on what you discovered about yourself. Answer these questions in your entry:

What are the most important elements of life for me? (Often you'll discover a common thread in your answers.)

Based on what I've learned, how would I describe a fulfilling life for me?

What steps can I take now to move toward that fulfilling life? What steps can I take later?

Coping with Guilt

If you are suffering from the "if onlys" or the "I should haves," and you are left with a deep feeling of regret that you couldn't do more to help your loved one or prevent the death, try the following exercise:

Write at least a one-page letter to the individual who died. Tell them whatever you want, but remember to include the following:

the facts of what happened

how you feel about what happened

how their death has affected your life

Now, turn the page over and imagine the deceased responding to your letter. Asking questions of the deceased will make this exercise extremely valuable. So write down such questions as, "How do you feel about what happened?" and "Will you please forgive me for _____?" "Have I been punished enough for my part (real or imagined) in all this and is there anything else I can do to show you how sorry I am?" "How can I show you how much I have suffered?" Then close your eyes and answer each question as if they were speaking through you.

If you find this is a difficult exercise to do on your own, you may want to ask a therapist or trusted friend to sit quietly with you. If you are being "told" by your inner voice to hurt yourself in any way, seek professional help immediately.

Benefits of Music

Music decreases levels of the stress hormone cortisol just as well as massage therapy does. Listening to slow music before bed can help you fall asleep faster and feel more rested in the morning, according to the National Sleep Foundation. And, listening to music that brings you joy causes blood vessels to expand, increasing blood flow and improving cardiovascular health.

Poetry

Poetry creates a bridge of feelings between the material world and the world of creativity and spirit. Visiting and/or joining a poetry group can have an extraordinary effect on the way we heal our grief. Poets, by definition, get to the raw feelings behind the masks we all wear. When we are wearing the mask of grief, we may feel that others cannot possibly know the pain we are experiencing, yet we must still continue living day to day in spite of our tremendous loss. As a result, we may feel out of touch with friends who have not experienced such a loss. We may feel that the strength of our feelings is unacceptable to others. Yet feelings are the dynamic force behind poetry groups. Within these groups, you will find a welcome and sensitive home for the expression of your grief through the written and spoken word.

Search the Internet for "Artists Salons" and/or "Poetry" in your state; also check your local paper for poetry readings. Attend the readings and ask participants about other local events in your area.

You can also write poetry on your own. Many books exist that can fuel creativity and offer guidance. Check the writing/reference section at your local bookstore. It can be extremely cleansing to spend a morning, once a week, at a café or park writing poetry in a beautiful journal. Don't worry about form—just creatively put down words to express yourself. Write poetry.

In the book, *The Poet's Companion: a guide to the pleasures of writing poetry*, author's Kim Addonizio and Dorianne Laux have a specific section on death and grief. They offer ten suggestions for working with this subject. "Write a poem about a ritual that accompanies a death. It might be about a traditional funeral, a wake, or some more private or individual observance. If you find an occasion for joy of beauty in the midst of mourning, include it." Another suggestion is, "If you own some object that used to belong to someone who is no longer alive, describe it in detail, along with your memories or images about how that person used it. You might also talk about how it is used in the present."

The Gratitude Journal

In her best-selling book, *Simple Abundance: A Daybook of Comfort and Joy,* Sarah Ban Breathnach advocates the use of a gratitude journal. She cites this as "a tool that could change the quality of your life beyond belief." We completely agree. This is how Sarah explains the gratitude journal:

"I have a beautiful blank book and each night before I go to bed, I write down five things that I can be grateful about that day. Some days my list will be filled with amazing things, most days just simple joys. 'Mikey got lost in a fierce storm but I found him shivering, wet but unharmed. I listened to Puccini while cleaning and remembered how much I love opera.'

Other days—rough ones—I might think that I don't have five things to be grateful for, so I'll write down my basics: my health, my husband and daughter, their health, my animals, my home, my friends and the comfortable bed that I'm about to get into, as well as the fact that the day's over. That's okay. Real life isn't always going to be perfect or go our way, but the recurring acknowledgment of what is *working* in our lives can help us not only survive but surmount our difficulties."

Recognizing the positives in our lives is especially important when we are engulfed in dark times. We often focus so heavily on our loss and what isn't going right, we can't see any of the good things. For the first few months, it will be extremely difficult to find the positives, but after that time period, we need to begin looking again—no matter how simple these positives might be. Your list might include something as basic as "I was able to get out of bed today." What's important is that we be open to the fact that there are positives. By recognizing them, we attract more positives to our life.

Purchase your own special notebook to use as a gratitude journal and keep it by your bed. Each night, before turning out the light, search your day for five positive happenings.

Calming

Stress, anxiety, sadness, depression—these emotions can leave us knotted inside. Practicing breathing exercises can help us to relax and to unwind our wound emotions. The following exercises will help calm you during trying times.

Place one hand on your abdomen. As you inhale, you want to feel the movement in your abdomen, not in your chest. Inhale for the count of ten, then exhale for the count of ten. Repeat this ten to fifteen times for deeper relaxation.

To relax your whole body, lie down in a quiet place. Breathe deeply, slowly inhaling and exhaling. Beginning with your left leg, clench your muscles as tightly as you can for the count of three. Then relax them. Do the same to the right leg, left arm, and right arm. Then move up your body, tightening your pelvis, then stomach, then chest, then shoulders, then neck, and lastly facial muscles. When you have completed this exercise, you should feel extremely calm and peaceful. Visualize an ocean beach or other calming scene to deepen the relaxed feelings.

Visualization

Creative visualization can be a wonderful way to calm our mind and body. When our body is relaxed, we can play calming, healing, and encouraging "movies" on the screen of our mind. These movies or imaginings can promote healing, forgiveness, and peace.

Visualization may take a while to get used to. The first time you try it, you may feel you aren't "getting anywhere." Give yourself some time. Like any exercise, visualization takes practice. Also, you may want to do your visualizations while lying on the floor or sitting in a chair. If you do them in bed, you could very likely fall asleep, since the process is extremely relaxing.

To begin, follow the whole body relaxation from the calming exercise. When your body is relaxed and you do not feel any excess tension, begin your visualization.

As you do the exercises, thoughts and images may come to you that would be valuable to record. For this reason, it's a good idea to keep a visualization journal nearby.

Following are some visualization ideas. Choose one that feels comfortable to you or create one of your own. Feeding these positive messages into your mind will help reduce anxiety and depression—and help you to feel more joy and peace in life.

- Visualize yourself using your grief in a creative way. Notice what you are doing, who is around you, how you feel, and what you see.

- If you feel guilt for the death, imagine blowing all the guilt within you into a balloon. See the guilt move out of your body, up through your lungs, and into the balloon. See the balloon getting larger and larger until it contains all of your guilt. Hold on to the string of the balloon tightly, feeling all your guilt one last time. Then let it go. Watch the balloon carry the guilt away from you. You can use this same visualization with any other emotion that you want to get rid of—hatred, anger, jealousy, or revenge, to name a few.

- If you want to communicate with the deceased or want to feel their presence, visualize them sitting in familiar surroundings. Go to them with your question or concern and let an exchange take place.

- Visualize yourself one or two years from now. Visualize the person you will have become and the positive changes you will have made. What comes to mind? Who is around you? What is your day-to-day life like? What do you believe in?

See the suggested reading section for an audiotape that may be useful for relaxation and visualization guidance.

Memory Books

Creating a memory book is a wonderful keepsake of our loved one. When Brook's brother died, she collected articles, photos, and other memorabilia to put in a keepsake album. Using different papers, stencils, markers, and stickers she created special pages to "frame" her memories.

Album making has become popular in recent years. Many scrapbooking stores now exist that offer classes on how to archive our memories creatively. Through collage, rubber stamping, paper decorations, and other means, we can make a beautiful book to serve as a remembrance.

In addition to stores that can serve as creative outlets, many magazines and books offer guidance. Even if you don't consider yourself creative, there are tools to help you get started. Check the craft section of your local bookstore for books on scrapbooking. A large newsstand or craft store may carry magazines such as *Memory Makers* and *Somerset Studio,* which offer ideas.

There are also consultants for companies like D.O.T.S. and Creative Memories that sell supplies and can help you choose supplies and offer creative guidance. Check your yellow pages for these companies. Current is another great source of materials. They can be accessed on the Internet at www.current.com. Many scrapbook hobbyists host online shares to exchange ideas and tips. Visit our online resources guide for additional links.

Here are a few basic tips for building your memory book.

1. Choose a good album to hold your memories. Creative Memories and D.O.T.S. both offer wonderful albums. Also make sure to use acid-free papers and supplies whenever possible. When papers are acid-free, they will not damage your photographs over time.

2. Collect all the materials that you think you would like to include. The possibilities are endless—postcards, words clipped from magazines, photos, special poems—anything that you like can be included.

3. Sort the items you have gathered until you see a natural progression take form. You may want to move through the book chronologically, or another theme may occur to you.

4. Gather stencils, stickers, stamps, and papers to use as decorations. Craft and scrapbooking stores are obvious suppliers. Additionally, office supply stores and stores like K-Mart, Wal-Mart, and Target often have good selection at reasonable prices.

5. Choose the materials you would like to use for a given page. Lay them out and move them around until you are comfortable with the design. If you have problems coming up with ideas for layout, consult one of the aforementioned magazines.

6. Take your time. There is no need to try and rush through the process of creating a memory book. Many people find joy in the "putzing" and creating. It may be a book that you continually add to throughout your lifetime.

Online Memorials

The Internet has created new ways to share, cherish, and remember our loved ones through online memorials. Videos, text entries, recordings, music, and photographs can be combined into a permanent web page to memorialize and remember the deceased.

This also helps for younger members of a family when they are growing up and may want to know about a deceased relative who died when the child was very young, etc. For more information visit www.legacy.com or www.muchloved.com

Rituals

Rituals are an important part of life. Through rituals we are able to observe, remember, and structure our beliefs and feelings. In her book, *Surviving Grief*, Dr. Catherine M. Sanders writes, "In the past, rites of passage for every shift point in life were marked by rituals, which commanded a respected place in our culture. Large extended families came together to honor the person being celebrated. During chaotic times of change and transition, these rituals provided important direction and spiritual strength."

Funeral services are an example of a ritual. They give us guidance and direction that allows us to come together and celebrate life with those who share our loss.

Creating your own ritual may seem like a difficult task, but it doesn't have to be. To begin, ask yourself what you are trying to remember or celebrate. For many, a ritual on the anniversary date of the death is valuable. Others find they'd like to create a ritual for the birthday of the deceased. If the deceased was a spouse, the wedding anniversary may be a good time for a ritual. There are no limits on rituals. You can have one each season of the year, or one annually or every other year. Think about the purpose of your ritual as you decide on frequency. For most who are grieving, the ritual period becomes a time of breaking away from the day-to-day demands so we can experience our grief fully and focus on the memories we hold of our loved one.

Next, decide if you want the ritual to be just for yourself or if you want to share it with others. You may find that having a group of friends engage in the ritual is helpful. Others like this time to explore their emotions by themselves.

Where you should conduct your ritual is the next question to answer. There may be a special place that you associate with the deceased. You may want to stay close to home or you may wish to travel overseas. Again, keep your purpose in mind as you choose your location.

Here are a few rituals that those who we've known have conducted and found comforting. Feel free to conform these to rituals that suit your needs or to use them as a springboard for other ideas.

Karen was living in France when her mother died suddenly at the age of fifty, leaving her father alone in the United States. Each year, Karen returns home for a week over the anniversary of her mother's death. She and her father use this time to recall their memories and visit the grave site.

Jessica, Monica, Laura, and Allie were close college friends, all living together. When Laura was killed suddenly in a car accident, the other three young women were torn apart. Each year, on the anniversary of the death, the three women get together and take a cruise. They recall their fun college days together. It has been five years since these women graduated, and they still continue with this ritual.

David wanted to be alone on his deceased son's birthday. He rented a small cabin in the mountains and took nothing with him but spare clothes. He walked in the mountains, absorbed the beautiful scenery, and "talked" to his son.

Cassandra, a single mother, was lost after the sudden death of her daughter. On the anniversary of her death, she asked her ex-husband to watch their other children. She took the weekend to write, cry, watch movies, and look through old photos.

Take some quiet time to sit and think about what might help you to heal. Then commit to a ritual. Mark off the dates on your calendar.

Chapter Twenty-Three
The Journey Continued . . .
Parting Notes from the Authors

When it came time to release the second edition of this book, Pam and I wondered if we should leave our original entries in this section, replace them, or delete them. Laughingly, I told Pam I wanted to delete mine as my writing has improved ten-fold. In all seriousness, I did want to change or edit my original entry. Years later, I know what I believed to be "emerging from grief" was actually my entrance into grief. In the end, we decided to leave these original stories unchanged and to add notes about where we are today. One thing is for certain, the quote we chose to open this book in the 1999 edition holds true:

"What we call the beginning is often the end.
To make an end is to make a beginning.
The end is where we start from."
—*T.S. Eliot*

Brook Noel . . . October 4, 1999

Pam and I have been working like crazy to finish this draft of the book. This was my one section left to write, and believe it or not, the day it came up in my to-do pile was on the second anniversary of Caleb's death (October 4, 1999). It's interesting—last year I couldn't function at all. I went away by myself. This year I find I can still function during this anniversary, though I feel more like a robot than a human.

I am proud of the strides I have made. My mother, myself, and a few close friends have started a water-ski tournament in my brother's honor. We held the first tournament this past summer. It feels good to keep his interests and passions as part of our lives.

As for me, specifically, I'm doing all right. In many ways, I haven't fully felt the loss yet. I still tend to run from my pain instead of feel it—but writing this book has helped me to quit doing that. It's taught me to explore the full range of my feelings—though I still have a way to go.

I'm not afraid of death, or of life, anymore. I've developed a trust in the processes and cycles of nature and the Universe. I don't understand much of the Universe on most days, but I've learned to trust that I will understand as I am able.

I've emerged from the dark cocoon of acute grief and come to a place where the grief now "lives with me," smaller in size, but molded into my being. Grief has taught me to laugh, enjoy, and be present for every moment.

Where am I now? I'm surviving and rebuilding. At one point you could have tried to convince me that something good would come from my loss and I would have laughed at you! But now, I see it. This loss has given me life—through the death of my brother, I have learned how to live.

Brook Noel . . . July 29, 2007

It is two months shy of the ten-year-anniversary of my brother's death, the catalyst for the book in your hands. In the aftermath of tragedy, I longed to find context in the chaos; meaning in a heart that had lost it; purpose and bearings in a world that knew not East, West, North or South, but only spun—fast and blurry while I stood in the middle helplessly uttering, *Why me? Why him?* and *What now?*

I never anticipated writing a second entry for the "Where am I now?" section. But then I never expected to write a first entry either. In high school, when contemplating my life path, and in college while paging through the course catalog, I hadn't envisioned a day where my phone would ring with a reporter seeking my comment on tragedy.

"I am contacting you because I need the opinion of a grief expert," were the words of these unfamiliar voices. With every call, I blinked hard, even though they could not see me. I was living a life I hadn't and couldn't imagine, filling the shoes of a role I had not signed up for.

My intentions in 1997 were simplistic and pure. I needed to transform my journey for others. If one person could see further down grief's path than I could, then maybe I could find some small speck of sense in the senseless. Yet, I can't deny I also longed to wrap my grief neatly and tightly between this book's covers. I hoped I could contain it, tucking its rough edges inside something that could be pulled from a shelf—and then put back.

I have learned that grief doesn't work that way—even when you become a "grief expert." Life doesn't work that way either. No matter how I steer and plan and dream and hope, life has its own turns, sometimes unwanted turns—terrifying, dark turns.

In a split-second in 1997 I was delivered to an unwelcome road. I immediately knew I was now "different" than those who had not walked here—although I couldn't tell you exactly how so.

On October 4, 1997, I acquired a pair of grief-colored glasses without a choice of whether to accept them or not. In the years to follow I would learn owning a pair is life's greatest responsibility, heaviest weight, and potentially a gift—if one can adjust them and learn how to focus in spite of them.

I have worn glasses all my life; glasses that helped me see what I *wanted* to see more clearly and *corrected* my vision to that of the average person. My grief-colored glasses have no resemblance to the glasses I had known before. At first they were a massive blur from my tears. I could see only the inch in front of me, and I struggled to find something to steady myself. I ached to remove them, break them, send them back, but that was impossible then—and still is today. I own them for life.

Eventually, a small opening appeared in the blur—I saw *something*. As the years passed I discovered my vision hadn't been corrected, nor had it been ruined—it had been *changed*. I saw a new depth in everything—the front, the back, the middle, the space around, the space between.

Tonight, as I write this, I wear my grief-colored glasses and they are no longer blurry or heavy. In fact, the longer I wear them the more I can see. While I have seen many things as I adjust their focus, there are few in particular I need to share with you.

Originally, when we wrote this book, we added this section because the book did not feel "complete." I didn't know then, like I know now, there is not an end, just a series of beginnings. These years have been a journey. It is not over, of that I am sure, yet I do know which part I am on or at. Is this a beginning, a turn, a turning point, a turning back, a turning inside out? I no longer need to know. I can live richly without a compass.

That wasn't always the case. In the days I was first immersed into the unruly, unwelcome world of grief, I needed to know: *What comes next? Is there something else?* Grief made me ask the unanswerable questions. The types of questions I hadn't asked since I was five-years-old. *Who made the world? What came first? Why are we here?* Puzzled authority figures and mentors had grappled with different replies. As I grew into a young adult, I began to understand some questions do not have easy answers—or answers at all.

I don't believe I ever learned to live comfortably with unanswered questions; for the most part I just quit asking them. Slowly, birthday after birthday, they faded into the "unknowable"—a vast holding tank for the unanswerable that couldn't be sorted and placed somewhere in the logic and busyness of daily life. Yet grief dumped this holding tank into my lap without warning. Like that five-year-old I was asking those questions and many more. *What happens next? Can he hear me? What am I supposed to do? Is he proud of me? Did he know? I am now older than he was at the time of his death—is he still my older brother? Do people ever get over this? Am I crazy? Is it supposed to hurt this bad?*

Ten years ago, because of the depth of my pain, I felt I *deserved* answers. *I would find answers.* I have since learned grief is not about answers; but learning to live with the questions. Questions too big to be tucked away, too important be ignored, too complicated to be answered neatly and tidily. These are the questions that ultimately have transformed me from a settler to a seeker, from a bystander to an adventurer, from someone who exists to someone who truly lives each moment.

It is July 29, 2007 and I am sitting on the dock of my childhood home with my feet dangling in the water of the lake that inspired this book's cover. This is the childhood home my mother created and raised me and Caleb safely within. It is here Caleb taught me to skip a rock across calm water, to climb a Northern pine, to ride my bike, to barefoot waterski, to swim, to snorkel, to draw, to identify every football team in the NFL by helmet, to build a ski boat out of Legos, to throw a football, to hold my breath under water, to dream. It is here that my mother, myself, and a few of Caleb's closest friends spread his ashes last summer. The name of this lake is Rest Lake.

It seemed a good place to write, because I would likely see an eagle. I almost always do. When Caleb and I were kids, still in the single digits, we asked so many innocent, hypothetical questions in the hours we spent at this lake. We had once asked each other: *If you could be any creature other than human, what would you be?* Caleb didn't need more than a second to reply, *I would be an eagle.*

It is a bit late for an eagle sighting tonight. I have been sitting here two hours, part of me longing to see an eagle swoop down; making a marked line so deliberate I would feel that glowing peace within. I look to the sky, but I cannot see a cloud, or a sun, or a moon. It is in the in-between time over this lake. It is the in-between time in my journey.

Where am I now? Every year since Caleb's death, I have stood at this lake waiting, straining, yearning, to see an eagle. I *needed* to see an eagle. And every year, I did.

As for the questions *Is he still here? Can I remember? Can I survive?* . . . A year ago, I would have looked to the sky for an answer. Tonight on his thirty-seventh birthday, the tenth he has celebrated in heaven, I need only look within. Sure, I would like to see an eagle—but I no longer *need* to. *Is he still here? Can I remember? Can I survive?* I have answered these formerly unanswerable questions. The answer for all three is undeniably: "Yes."

Brook Noel . . . June 30, 2018

It has now been twenty-one years since my twenty-seven-year-old brother died on that October morning that changed my life and the course of my life. My life has been enriched by holding the hands of many kindred souls that walk a similar path, some in person and others in spirit. Undoubtedly, one thing that unites us is an understanding of the true value of a smile, a touch, a moment—and that we do not take a single moment for granted. In many ways I believe I live more richly and yet emptier; the depth of every experience has been heightened because I have felt the saddest of pains, and in doing so, have carved a space for the intensity of joy. It is an oxymoron that I think only fellow travelers can understand. It is a journey I would never choose, but a journey I now choose to embrace.

Pamela D. Blair . . . 1999

It's been nine years since George's death. I'm married to a great guy. I'm a therapist specializing in loss and transition—death and divorce specifically. My son, Ian, is in college. He is a musician and works part-time as a shift manager for Starbucks Coffee. My daughter Aimee gave birth to a beautiful son, Derek, who is now eight years old. He will never know George except through his mother's eyes. She remembers the unconditional love, the trust, the playfulness of the man. I'm not sure what Ian remembers. My guess is he remembers catching the ball with his dad at Yankee Stadium, and visiting his dad at work in the camera store and the family trip to Disneyland. Me? I remember the bitter sweetness of our too short marriage, the hugs he gave, the miracle of the child we made together, the day the life sustaining machines were shut down—the day the new memories stopped forever.

I still feel the loss. I also feel the new life it gave me. In every loss there lies a hidden possibility. It stays hidden until one shakes it loose—like the lost sock that ends up in the corner of the newly washed fitted sheet. It's there—you just need to ruffle up that sheet a bit and out it comes.

Where does sudden loss take us? It takes us to places we never asked to visit. It take us on uncharted, mysterious, unfamiliar journeys to the depths of our souls, where we clatter and crash about, slog through the molasses of grief and come out the other side. That's all. I am here to tell you that one can survive that mess and come out the other side and that although death surely ends a life, it never ends a relationship.

Pamela D. Blair . . . July 29, 2007

When it came time to write this update, I wondered how my husband would feel if he read that I still think of George a little bit each day. Would he feel that I was betraying our love if I admitted to thoughts and feelings associated with the loss of George? Many of you who read this will wonder the same thing. But those of you who have lost a spouse and remarried will certainly relate to what I am saying. George will forever be a part of my history and the histories of my children. My husband, Steve, understands that history cannot be erased—that we learn from it, grow from it, and like a textbook we open it from time to time to check a fact, to immerse once again in the strength of the story.

Fifteen years have passed since George's sudden death. Our son, Ian, has grown and left the nest. He's managing a restaurant in Burlington, Vermont. I can't help but think how proud of him his dad would be if he could just visit Ian's life for a day. I can still feel strong emotion when I consider what George is missing of his son's life—or is he? Is he "there" watching over him, beaming with pride? Yes, I believe so.

My daughter, Aimee (George's stepdaughter) lives close by with her son, Derek. She still remembers George as the wonderful guy who came into her life to give her what she was missing from her own dad—warm hugs and kind words. I like to think that George's energy surrounds her, protecting her. She and I reminisce about George from time to time and Ian, when prodded, talks about his memories of him. A large photo of his dad hangs in his bedroom along with a framed essay he wrote about his dad on Father's Day shortly before he died. He doesn't want to forget.

I'm very grateful to my husband, Steve for filling the father role the best he could. I'm still happily married to him these twenty-four years and we're looking toward retirement. I'm at an age now where death will become more and more evident in the lives of my friends and family. I know I will get through those times and come out stronger. I know that the help and support of people like you, dear reader will be there to lift me up when I fall, to inspire me as I walk forward into an unknown future.

I Wasn't Ready to Say Goodbye was my first book and I owe my co-author many thanks for seeing the project through to the end with me. It hasn't been "an end" however. I have written another book, *The Next Fifty Years,* and will continue to write others. But, no matter how many more I write, this book will always have a special place in my heart—and so will George.

Pamela D. Blair . . . June 3, 2018

At seventy years old, it's been almost twenty-seven years since George's sudden death. There are times when I feel sad still, but mostly around events in our son's life, where I know he's missing his father. In 2014, our son Ian starred in *Les Miserables* and placed a photo of his father just behind the curtain, so he could see if when he made an entrance onstage. Ian will be getting married in 2019, and both he and I will be wishing his father were there to witness the amazing day. Grief changes in subtle ways over time, and life, indeed, goes on. To this day, my forty-seven-year-old daughter Aimee says she is reminded of George and their shared love of the Beatles every time a song comes on the radio or in a store.

May you see light where there was only darkness, hope where there seemed nothing but despair, may your fear be replaced with faith and insight, may you feel some victory in the defeat and a sense of the sacred web into which we are all woven. Most of all may you stay in tune with your capacity to love life even as you are engulfed by death.

Appendix I

Here we have provided several worksheets and guides
to help you in various parts of the grief process.
Use these as templates or springboards for ideas of your own.

The Memorial Service

When the person in charge of the memorial service does not know the deceased, consider filling out this form and giving it to them. Keep a copy for yourself. The information included on the form will be an aid in creating a meaningful service. The form will also be useful if the person in charge knew your loved one.

If at all possible, do not fill out this form alone. Ask friends and family to contribute information. If your loved one had a career, chances are they have a resume in a file somewhere. Their resume may help fill in some of the blanks.

INFORMATION TO PROVIDE TO
THE PERSON (OR CLERGY) IN CHARGE

Name of deceased: Age:

Cause of death: Date of birth:

Religious background (if any):   Date of death:

Type of service the deceased would have liked (i.e. quiet, casual, formal, offbeat):

Those who would like to participate:

Family background:

Education:

Career (or career aspirations):

Club memberships or affiliations:

Activities or hobbies:

Relationships:

What kind of books did they read:

What kind of music did they enjoy:

Favorite bible verse or inspirational verse:

Favorite poet or poems:

Favorite charity/charities:

NOTES:

The Eulogy

You've been asked to deliver a eulogy. What now? According to Terence B. Foley and Amanda Bennett (*In Memoriam,* Simon & Schuster, 1997), "The most important thing to remember when delivering a eulogy is that it is a gift. A gift for you to be able to speak about a family member or friend before those who also loved and respected him . . . It is not a performance, nor will it be judged as such. Your job is to be thoughtful and genuine . . ."

This form should get you thinking about those things that were most important about the deceased. As you deliver the eulogy, do not rush, take your time. If you decide to use humor, make sure it is done with affection. Avoid jokes and stories that would embarrass those present. If you lose your composure, give yourself a moment of quiet, take a deep breath or a drink of water, and go on.

FORM FOR DELIVERING A EULOGY

My relationship with the deceased:

I've known him/her for how long:

How we met:

What I remember most. . .

What was best about them:

What was eccentric about them (presented with affection):

Kindnesses I received from the deceased:

What would the deceased say about the events today:

Integrating what we learned from this person into our own lives is a constant memorial and source of comfort for the family. Therefore, consider the following three questions:

What did I learn from this person (through example or teaching):

How do I plan to implement what I learned from them:

What words of wisdom would the deceased want us to remember:

NOTES:

A Checklist of Calls to Make

The following list can be a useful reference for calls that need to made. Give this form to your support person to help you complete the calls.

- ❑ Call a support person to help you. Give the support person this list and let them work through it and ask questions as necessary.

- ❑ Choose a funeral home to assist in arrangements. Set date and time for funeral and memorial services.

- ❑ Contact a clergyperson to officiate services. If a mediator is needed, contact them as well.

- ❑ Select pallbearers for the funeral if you will be having a burial.

- ❑ Make a list of people who need to be notified. Obtain the deceased's address book for phone numbers and other people to notify.

- ❑ Contact the newspaper for the obituary. An obituary typically includes: age, cause of death, place of birth, vocation, college degrees, military service, outstanding work or achievements, list of survivors in immediate family, time and place of services.

- ❑ Choose a memorial or charity for any gifts or donations.

- ❑ Notify all insurance companies—social security, credit union, trade union, fraternal, military, standard life, credit card, etc. Check for income from any of these sources as well.

- ❑ Call all debts in a timely manner. Insurance may cancel out some debts. For other debts ask for a payment plan.

- ❑ If the deceased lived alone, contact the landlord and utilities. Select a group of people to help move the deceased's belongings from the apartment/home.

- ❑ Contact a lawyer and the executor of the will, if a will is in place. If there is no will, contact a lawyer for guidance.

Friends Support Group Invitation

The letter that follows is an example of a creative response to the need for support. The following invitational letter was written to family and friends by the deceased's sister, Karen. Kathleen's death was a suicide which occurred after a long struggle with cancer and mental illness. The letter was written on stationary with this quote imprinted in the corner: "What we call the beginning is often the end. To make an end is to make a beginning. The end is where we start from."—T. S. Eliot

Dear Family and Friends,

During the past few weeks I have had the opportunity to speak with some of you regarding the impact of Kathleen's death on your life. These discussions have served to assist me in dealing with my grief.

Some of you mentioned that you've been so busy that you've hardly had time to feel, much less deal with the loss. Many societies throughout the world have rituals built into their communities to facilitate the difficult walk through grief. Our "progressive" society has only begun to realize its shortcomings, and in efforts to counter the emotional isolation, society has assigned the task of assisting us with our grief work to counselors and mental health care (bereavement groups). These are valuable, however, I'd like to propose that another helpful way might be for the members of Kathleen's community come together to talk, sit, just be together, in an effort to promote healing.

The nature of Kathleen's death has left us all with many questions. In discussing these issues with some of you privately, it has come up that talking about the issues together may assist us all in finding peace.

I have enclosed information our family received from the Albany Medical Center the night Kathleen died. We have found it helpful to review this information regularly in an attempt to monitor our healing.

If Kathleen had been a participant in a hospice program, they would be offering a program for bereavement for the family and friends to have a framework to evaluate progress along the grief walk. Her mental illness was indeed terminal. In an effort to create a structure for us to walk in our grief I'd like to host the following afternoon gatherings.

Also, my family is trying to piece together a historical outline of Kathleen's life, birth to death. We would find it helpful to hear your experiences with Kathleen so we can add them to the tapestry we hope to create.

Thank you all for taking the time to call and talk. I look forward to further discussions and insights.

Schedule of Bereavement Gatherings:
3:00–5:00pm at 134 Ridge Avenue
(for those of you who wish to stay after,
soup and sandwiches will be served)
Saturday, January 27—3 month anniversary of Kathleen's death
Saturday, April 27—6 month anniversary of Kathleen's death
Saturday, July 27—9 month anniversary of Kathleen's death
Saturday, October 26—1 year

The first year of feeling the void and figuring out ways to compensate is the most difficult. If you cannot attend these gatherings, I would request that you make time to remember the memories.

I'd appreciate an RSVP call.

For those of you who experienced Kathleen's association with the Native American culture, you may recall her referring to their custom of communication to "all my relations." This demonstrates the understanding that we are all part of a network, a web, a community. When the fabric of the web is broken, loose ends flap around until the members can come together and mend the space. How we choose to repair the hole will depend on who we are and what we will bring to offer each other. Thank you all for your willingness to offer and obtain comfort. The hope is that the memories which cause pain in the initial blow can, in time, serve as great comforts and a means for our own growth.

Blessings to all.
In light and love,
Karen

Appendix II: Grief Resources and Support

In the first edition, we provided over fifty pages of supportive resources. We have now created an online library of grief support links and articles in order to keep our ever-expanding information base current while providing easy access by topic.

In this section, we provide information on some general resources and support available to the bereaved.

Support for Loss of a Partner
American Association of Retired Persons (AARP)
601 E St., NW, Washington, D.C. 20049. 1–800–424–3410 (1–888-OUR-AARP).
AARP Grief and Loss Programs offer a wide variety of resources and information
on bereavement issues for adults of all ages and their families. Services include: one-
to-one peer outreach, a grief course, bereavement support groups, informational
booklets and brochures, and online support. www.aarp.org/griefandloss.

WidowNet (Internet Resource)
This is the most comprehensive site we've found for those who are widowed.
WidowNet is an information and self-help resource created for, and by, widows
and widowers. "Topics covered include grief, bereavement, recovery, and other
information helpful to people, of all ages, religious backgrounds, and sexual orien-
tations, who have suffered the death of a spouse or life partner." You can access the
site at www.widownet.org. They also have a chat room and message board.

Books
How to Go On Living When Someone You Love Dies by Therese A. Rando, PhD,
1988, New York, Lexington Books—Includes suggestions for ways to deal with
sudden or anticipated death. Offers self-help techniques to work on unfinished
business, take care of the self, and when to get help from others. Leads you through
the painful but necessary process of grieving and helps you find the best way for
yourself. Offers guidance to help you move into your new life without forgetting
your treasured past.

    Living with Loss: Meditations for Grieving Widows by Ellen Sue Stern, 1995,
Dell Publishing, NY—This book, small enough to fit in a purse, is full of supportive and empowering reflections. This daily companion is designed to help you cope
today, cherish yesterday, and thrive tomorrow.

Support for Grieving Children
Camp "Good Grief"
Camp "Good Grief" is a summer camp program which offers grief education work-
shops and provides support and understanding for youth ages six through thirteen

who have experienced the death of a sibling, parent, grandparent, or close friend. The camp is held in Lake Worth, FL. For more information, visit the website at www.campgoodgrief.org or call (561) 416–5059.

KIDSAID (Internet Resource)

KIDSAID is an extension of GriefNet, a comprehensive Internet community that has provided support to over three million people in the last year. The KIDSAID area provides a safe environment for kids and their parents to find information and ask questions. To learn more about KIDSAID, visit GriefNet at www.griefnet.org or kidsaid.com/about.html.

Books for Children and Teens and Their Caregivers

Bereaved Children and Teens: A Support Guide for Parents and Professionals by Earl A. Grollman, Beacon Press, 1996—Explores the ways that parents and professionals can help young people cope with grief. Topics covered include what children can understand about death at different ages, the special problems of grieving teenagers, how to explain Protestant, Catholic, or Jewish beliefs about death in ways that children can understand, and more.

Don't Despair on Thursdays! (ages four through twelve) by Adolph Moser, EdD, Western Psychological Services, Los Angeles, CA—This gentle book lets children know that it's normal to grieve in response to loss and that grief may last more than a few days or weeks. Offers practical suggestions that children can use, day by day, to cope with the emotional pain they feel. Young readers will be comforted by the reassuring text and colorful illustrations.

Part of Me Died, Too: Stories of Creative Survival Among Bereaved Children and Teenagers by Virginia Lynn Fry, 1995, Dutton Children's Books, NY—Eleven true stories about young people who experienced the loss of family members or friends in a variety of ways including murder, suicide, and accident. Includes writings, drawings, farewell projects, rituals, and other creative activities to help younger children and teens bring their feelings out into the open.

The Grieving Child: a Parents Guide by Helen Fitzgerald. Fireside, 1992—Compassionate advice for helping a child cope with the death of a loved one. Also addresses visiting the seriously ill, using age-appropriate language, funerals, and more.

Support for the Loss of a Child

Bereaved Parents of the USA

This national organization was founded in 1995 to aid and support bereaved parents and their families who are struggling to survive their grief after the death of a child. Information and referrals, a newsletter, phone support, conferences, and meetings are available. They also offer assistance in starting a support group. You may contact them at P.O. Box 95, Park Forest, IL 60466 or by calling (708) 748–7866 or visiting www.bereavedparentsusa.org.

Mothers in Sympathy and Support (MISS)

From their website: "The mission of Mothers in Sympathy & Support is to allow a safe haven for parents to share their grief after the death of a child. It is our hope that within these pages you discover courage, faith, friendship, and love. Grief education for parents and professionals is our main focus. Our child has changed our lives forever. Come with us and get lost in our pages . . . find healing, honesty, hope, and a rediscovery of yourself." Visit www.misschildren.org

SHARE: Pregnancy & Infant Loss Support, Inc.

This group offers support to those who have lost a child during pregnancy or infancy. Their extensive website offers a chat room and many valuable reading areas. Additionally, they offer a free newsletter. You can visit their website at www.nationalshareoffice.com/ or you may contact them at: National SHARE Office, St. Joseph Health Center, 300 First Capitol Drive, St. Charles, MO 63301–2893, Phone: (800) 821–6819 or (636) 947–6164. All of SHARE's information packets, correspondence, and support is free of charge for bereaved parents. They also publish a bi-monthly newsletter that is available to bereaved parents.

Books

A Broken Heart Still Beats: When Your Child Dies edited by Anne McCracken and Mary Semel, Hazelden, 1998—Edited by two mothers who have lost a child, this book combines articles and excerpts—some fiction, some nonfiction—that featured the death of a child. A brief introduction to each chapter describes a different stage of the grieving process and how it affected their lives.

The Worst Loss: How Families Heal from the Death of a Child by Barbara D. Rosof, Henry Holt & Co., Inc., 1994—The death of a child overwhelms many people. This book describes the losses that the death of a child brings to parents and siblings, as well as potential PTSD reactions and work of grief. A very thorough and wise book. One of our favorite books on the topic.

Support for Loss through Suicide

American Suicide Foundation

This national organization offers state-by-state directories of survivor support groups for families and friends of suicide. Contact them by email at inquiry@afsp.org or write to **120 Wall Street, 22nd Floor,** New York, NY 10005; or call 1 (888) 333-AFSP.

Friends for Survival, Inc.

Organized by and for survivors, this non-profit group offers its services at no cost to those who have lost a loved one to suicide. Resources include a newsletter, referrals to local support groups, a list of suggested resources, and more. You may contact them at Friends for Survival, Inc., P.O. Box 214463, Sacramento, California 95821. Or call (916) 392–0664 or visiting www.friendsforsurvival.org.

Books

Healing After the Suicide of a Loved One by Ann Smolin, John Guinan, Fireside, 1993—The authors address the special needs and emotions of the survivors and those affected by the suicide of a loved one. It explores the natural grief, and the added guilt, rage, and shame that dealing with a suicide often engenders. Includes a directory of worldwide support groups.

No Time to Say Goodbye: Surviving the Suicide of a Loved One by Carla Fine, Doubleday, 1997—Suicide is something most people are unable to talk about, which makes the pain all the more unbearable. Written by a suicide survivor, this book explores the overwhelming feelings of guilt, shame, anger, and loneliness that are shared by survivors. Offers guidance to those who were left behind and are struggling to pick up the pieces of their shattered lives.

Why Suicide? Answers to 200 of the Most Frequently Asked Questions About Suicide, Attempted Suicide and Assisted Suicide by Eric Marcus, Harper San Francisco,

1996—No matter what the circumstances surrounding suicide, those of us who are affected are left with difficult and disturbing questions. This book provides thoughtful, comprehensive answers to two hundred of the most frequently asked questions about suicide, attempted suicide, and assisted suicide.

Internet Support for Siblings

Adult Sibling Grief (Internet Resource)

This website reaches out to grieving adults who have lost a sibling. They offer resources, a special remembrance area, message boards, and support groups. Access the site at www.adultsiblinggrief.com.

SOLOS-Sibs Suicide (Internet Resource)

An email support group for adults who have lost a brother or sister to suicide at any age. Discussion revolves around mutual grief support and sibling survivor issues. health.groups.yahoo.com/group/SOLOS-sibs/

Mourning Our Brothers and Sisters (Internet Resource)

Offers message board support and the opportunity to connect with others who may understand what it's like to be a surviving sibling. health.groups.yahoo.com/ group/ M_O_B_S_/.

General Bereavement Support

Beyond Indigo (Internet Resource)

This site offers comprehensive support to individuals who are grieving and those who want to help them. They have a monthly newsletter that is delivered via email and online memorials. They also have message boards, polls, grief tools, advice columns, and articles. Check out their offerings at www.beyondindigo.com

Concerns of Police Survivors, Inc. (COPS)

This national association provides services to surviving friends and families of law enforcement officers killed in the line of duty. COPS can be contacted at P.O. Box 3199, Camdenton, MO 65020; or by calling (573) 346–4911 or by email at cops@ nationalcops.org.

GriefNet (Internet Resource)

GriefNet is an internet community consisting of almost fifty email support groups and two websites. Over three million people have visited the website in the last year. A very supportive site. Visit it at www.griefnet.org.

Grief Share (Internet Resource)

This Internet resource provides a comprehensive support group directory, special resources, and a bookstore. Additionally, they have a wonderful area about journaling and a six-week-guide with a Christian focus that includes scriptures, ideas for writing, and journal pages you can print. Visit their site at www.griefshare.org

Tom Golden's Grief and Healing Discussions Page (Internet Resource)

This site uses a web message board where you can post and respond to issues of grief and loss. Access the message board at www.webhealing.com/forums/.

Transformations (Internet Resource)

This well-designed site offers support in many areas, including grief. They offer a chat area and a schedule of events, as well as a place to share your thoughts, stories, poetry, and more. You can access the site at www.transformations.com/contents.html.

Other Recommended Books by Topic:

General Books for Adults

A Time to Grieve: Meditations for Healing After the Death of a Loved One by Carol Staudacher, Harper San Francisco, 1994—365 daily readings offer comfort, insight, and hope. This book is written specifically for people after the death of a loved one, however it is appropriate for anyone who still copes with the effects of a loss of any kind. A great gift for yourself or a grieving friend.

Beyond Grief by Carol Staudacher, New Harbinger Publications, 1987—This book is about understanding and then coping with loss, with clearly stated suggestions for each part of the grieving process. Written both for the bereaved and the helping professional, it combines supportive personal stories with a step-by-step approach to recovery. *Beyond Grief* acknowledges the path, reassures, and counsels. Includes guidelines to create support groups and guidelines for helping others. It says to the grieving person: you are not alone, you can get through the pain, and there is a path back to feeling alive again.

Companion Through Darkness: Inner Dialogues on Grief by Stephanie Ericsson, Harperperennial Library, 1993—As a result of her own experience with many kinds of loss, the author offers an intimate, touching guide for those in grief. The book combines excerpts from her own diary writings with brief essays.

The Courage to Grieve by Judy Tatelbaum—This book covers many aspects of grief and resolution. Divided into five sections, it explores the grief experience and creative recovery.

What to Do When a Loved One Dies: A Practical and Compassionate Guide to Dealing with Death on Life's Terms, by Eva Shaw, Dickens Press, 1994—Presents excellent guidelines describing what to do when a death occurs. It has an extensive listing of support groups, resources, and other sources of help. The approach is extremely detailed and includes sections on dealing with catastrophic deaths.

Books about the Loss of a Friend

Grieving the Death of a Friend by Harold Ivan Smith, Augsburg Fortress Publications, 1996—The death of a friend is one of the most significant but unrecognized experiences of grief in American culture. This unique new book moves with, rather than against, the natural grief process by exploring its many aspects—the friending, the passing, the burying, the mourning, the remembering, and the reconciling.

When a Friend Dies: A Book for Teens about Grieving and Healing by Marilyn E. Gootman, Ed.D., 1994, Free Spirit Publishing, Minneapolis, MN—A small, powerful book whose author has seen her own children suffer from the death of a friend. She knows firsthand what teenagers go through when another teen dies. Very easy to read, some of the questions dealt with include: How long will this last? Is it wrong to go to parties and have fun? How can I find a counselor or therapist? What is normal?

Books about Losing a Parent

How to Survive the Loss of a Parent: A Guide for Adults by Lois F. Akner, Catherine Whitney, 1994, William Morrow & Co.—Therapist and author, Lois Akner, explains why the loss of a parent is different from other losses and using examples from her experience, shows how it is possible to work through the grief.

Losing a Parent: Passage to a New Way of Living by Alexandra Kennedy, Harper San Francisco, 1991—Based on the author's personal experience, she writes on topics such as keeping a journal, saying goodbye, tending to your wounds, and the "living parent within you."

Mid-Life Orphan: Facing Life's Changes Now That Your Parents Are Gone by Jane Brooks. Berkely Books, 1999—Many mid-life orphans feel isolated, even abandoned, when their parents dies, but they also learn how to cope and extract life lessons from their experience. This book focuses on a loss that has been a fact of life for centuries, but has moved to the forefront as baby boomers, who represent one-third of the U.S. population, are forced to deal with this age of loss.

Bibliography

Adrienne, Carol. *The Purpose of Your Life Experiential Guide.* William Morrow, 1999.

Akner, Lois F. Whitney, Catherine (contributor). *How to Survive The Loss of a Parent: A Guide for Adults.* Quill, 1994.

Albertson, Sandy. *Endings and Beginnings.* Random House, 1980.

American Association of Retired Persons Brochure, *Frequently asked Questions by the Widowed.*

American Association of Retired Persons Brochure, *On Being Alone.*

American Association of Retired Persons website article, "Common Reactions to Loss."

Arent Ruth. *Helping Children Grieve.* Sourcebooks, 2007.

Balch M.D. James F. and Phyllis A. Balch C.N.C. *Prescription for Nutritional Healing.* Avery Publishing Group, 1997.

Bowlby, John. *Loss: Sadness and Depression.* HarperCollins, 1980.

Bowlby, J: "Processes of mourning." *Int J Psychoanal 42:* 1961.

Bowlby, J: "Attachment and Loss." Vols. 1–3, New York: Basic Books, Inc., 1969–1980.

Bozarth, Alla Renee. *A Journey Through Grief: Specific Help to Get You Through the Most Difficult Stages of Grief.* Hazelden, 1994.

Bramblett, John. *When Goodbye Is Forever: Learning to Live Again After the Loss of a Child.* Ballantine, 1997.

Breathnach, Sarah Ban. *Simple Abundance: A Daybook of Comfort and Joy.* New York: Warner, 1995.

Challem, Jack. "Relief for Chronic Fatigue: How NADH Can Help." *Let's Live,* October 1999. pp. 48–50.

Chevallier, Andrew. *The Encyclopedia of Medicinal Plants.* Dorling Kindersley, 1996.

Childs-Gowell, Elaine. *Good Grief Rituals: Tools for Healing.* Station Hill, 1992.

Clarke, Jack. *Life After Grief.* Personal Pathways. First edition, 1989.

Coffin, Margaret M. *Death in Early America.* Thomas Nelson, 1976.

Collins, Judy. *Singing Lessons: A Memoir of Love, Loss, Hope, and Healing.* Pocket Books, 1998.

Conway, Jim. *Men in Midlife Crisis.* Chariot Victor, 1997.

Cunningham, Linda. *Grief and the Adolescent.* TAG: Teen Age Grief.

Curry, Cathleen L. *When Your Spouse Dies: A Concise and Practical Source of Help and Advice.* Ave Maria Press, 1990.

Deits, Bob. *Life After Loss: A Personal Guide Dealing With Death, Divorce, Job Change and Relocation.* Fisher, 1992.

Doka, Kenneth J (editor). Kenneth, Kola J. (editor). Hospice Foundation of America. *Living With Grief After Sudden Loss: Suicide Homicide Accident Heart Attack Stroke.* Taylor and Francis, 1996.

Edelman, Hope. *Motherless Daughters: The Legacy of Loss.* Delta, 1995.

Editors of Prevention Health Books. *Prevention's Healing with Vitamins.* Rodale Press, 1996.

Ericsson, Stephanie. *Companion Through the Darkness: Inner Dialogues on Grief.* Harperperennial Library, 1993.

Felber, Marta. *Grief Expressed: When a Mate Dies.* Lifeword, 1997.

Fine, Carla. *No Time to Say Goodbye: Surviving the Suicide of a Loved One.* Main Street Books, 1999.

"Final Details." Brochure by The American Association of Retired Persons.

Fitzgerald, Helen. *The Mourning Handbook: The Most Comprehensive Resource Offering Practical and Compassionate Advice on Coping With All Aspects of Death and Dying.* Fireside, 1995.

"Forgotten Mourners: after the death of a brother or sister, family members often don't realize the extent of the siblings' grief." *The Journal News,* July 29, 1999.

Freud, Sigmund. From a letter to Ludwig Binswanger who had lost a son.

Friedman, Russell and John W. James. *The Grief Recovery Handbook: The Action Program for Moving Beyond Death Divorce, and Other Losses.* HarperCollins, 1998.

Fumia, Molly. *Safe Passage: Words to Help the Grieving Hold Fast and Let Go.* Conaris Press, 1992.

Ginsburg, Genevieve Davis. *Widow to Widow: Thoughtful Practical Ideas for Rebuilding Your Life.* Fisher Books, 1995.

Grey, John. *Men Are from Mars, Women Are from Venus: A Practical Guide for Improving Communication and Getting What You Want in Your Relationships.* Harpercollins, 1992.

Golden, Tom LCSW. "A Family Ritual for the Year Anniversary." Tom Golden Grief Column.

Goldman, Linda. *Breaking the Silence: A Guide to Help Children with Complicated Grief.* Western Psychological Services.

Gootman, Marilyn. *When a Friend Dies: A Book for Teens about Grieving and Healing.* Free Spirit Publishing, 1994.

Goulston, Mark MD and Philip Goldberg. *Get Out of Your Own Way.* Perigee, 1996.

Grollman, Earl A. *Living When A Loved One Has Died.* Beacon Press, 1995.

Halifax, Joan. *The Fruitfull Darkness: Reconnecting With the Body of the Earth.* Harper San Francisco, 1994.

Harris, Maxine. *The Loss That is Forever: The Lifelong Impact of the Early Death of a Mother or Father.* Plume, 1996.

Hays, Edward M. *Prayers for a Planetary Pilgrim: A Personal Manual for Prayer and Ritual.* Forest of Peace Books, 1998.

Heegaard, Marge Eaton. *Coping with Death and Grief.* Lerner Publications, 1990.

Hendricks, Lois Lindsey. *Dreams that Help You Mourn.* Resource Publications, 1997.

Henricks, Gay. *The Learning to Love Yourself Workbook.* Prentice Hall, 1992.

Hewett, John H. *After Suicide.* Westminster John Knox, 1980.

Johnson, Elizabeth A. *As Someone Dies: A Handbook for the Living.* Hay House, 1995.

Kennedy, Alexandra. *Losing a Parent: Passage to a New Way of Living.* Harper San Francisco, 1991.

King, Marlene. "The Surrogate Dreamers." *Intuition.* January/February 1998.

Klass, Dennis, Phyllis R. Silverman, and Steven L. Nickman, eds. *Continuing Bonds: A New Understanding of Grief.* Washington, DC: Taylor & Francis, 1996.

Kolf, June Cezra. *How Can I Help?: How to Support Someone Who Is Grieving.* Fisher Books, 1999.

Kubler-Ross, MD, Elisabeth. *On Children and Death: How Children and Their Parents Can and Do Cope with Death.* Simon and Schuster, 1997.

Kushner, Harold S. *When Bad Things Happen to Good People.* Avon, 1994.

L'Engle, Madeleine. *Sold into Egypt: Joseph's Journey into Human Being*. Harold Shaw, 1989.

Lerner, Harriet. *The Dance of Anger: A Woman's Guide to Changing the Patterns of Intimate Relationships*. HarperCollins, 1997.

Livingston MD, Gordon. *Only Spring: On Mourning the Death of My Son*. Marlowe & Company, 1999.

Mabe, Juliet. *Words to Comfort, Words to Heal: Poems and Mediations for Those Who Grieve*.

Marshall, Fiona. *Losing A Parent: A Personal Guide to Coping With That Special Grief That Comes With Losing a Parent*. Fisher Books, 1993.

Marx, Robert J. and Susan Davidson. *Facing the Ultimate Loss: Coping with the Death of a Child*. Sourcebooks, 2007.

Matsakis, Aphrodite. *Trust After Trauma: A Guide to Relationships for Survivors and Those Who Love Them*. New Harbinger Publications, 1998.

Matsakis, Aphrodite. *I Can't Get Over It: A Handbook for Trauma Survivors*. New Harbinger Publications, 1996.

Mechner, Vicki. *Healing Journeys: The Power of Rubenfield Synergy*. Omniquest, 1998.

Melrose, Andrea LaSonder (editor). *Nine Visions: a Book of Fantasies*. Seabury Press, 1983.

Mental Health Association in Waukesha County. "Grief After Suicide." Pewaukee, Wisconsin.

Miller PhD, Jack. *Healing our Losses: A Journal for Working Through your Grief*. Resource Publications.

Mitchard, Jacquelyn. *The Deep End of the Ocean*. Penguin, 1999.

Noel, Brook. *Shadows of a Vagabond*. Champion Press, 1998.

Noel, Brook. *Grief Steps*. Champion Press, Ltd., 2003.

Noel, Brook with Art Klein. *The Single Parent Resource*. Champion Press, 1998.

Nouwen, Henri J. *Reaching Out: The Three Movements of the Spiritual Life*. Image Books, 1986.

O'Neil, Anne-Marie, Karen S. Schneider, and Alex Tresnowski. "Starting Over." *People* magazine, October 4, 1999. p 125.

Overbeck, Buz and Joanie Overbeck. "Where Life Surrounds Death." Adapted from Helping Children Cope with Loss.

Parkes CM: Bereavement: *Studies of Grief in Adult Life. 2nd ed.,* Madison: International Universities Press Inc., 1987.

Parkes CM: Bereavement as a psychosocial transition: processes of adaptation to change. *J Soc Issues 44,* 1988.

Prend, Ashley Davis. *Transcending Loss: Understanding the Lifelong Impact of Grief and How to Make It Meaningful.* Berkely, 1997.

Rando, PhD, Therese A. Treatment of *Complicated Mourning.* Research Press, 1993.

Rando, PhD, Therese A. *How to Go on Living When Someone You Love Dies.* Bantam, 1991.

Rilke, Rainer Maria. *Letters to a Young Poet.* WW Norton, 1994.

Rosof, Barbara D. *The Worst Loss: How Families Heal from the Death of a Child.* Henry Holt, 1995.

Sachs, Judith with Lendon H. Smith. *Nature's Prozac: Natural Therapies and Techniques to Rid Yourself of Anxiety, Depression, Panic Attacks & Stress.* Prentice Hall, 1998.

Sanders, Dr. Catherine M. *Surviving Grief.* John Wiley, 1992.

Schiff, Harriet Sarnoff. *The Bereaved Parent.* Viking, 1978.

Shaw, Eva. *What to Do When A Loved One Dies: A Practical and Compassionate Guide to Dealing With Death on Life's Terms.* Dickens Press, 1994.

Silverman, Phyllis R. *Never Too Young to Know: Death in Children's Lives.* New York: Oxford University Press, 2000.

Singer, Lilly, Margaret Sirot, Susan Rodd. *Beyond Loss: A Practical Guide through Grief to a Meaningful Life.* Blue Point Books, 2002.

Staudacher, Carol. A *Time to Grieve: Meditations for Healing After the Death of a Loved One.* Harper San Francisco, 1994.

Staudacher, Carol. *Beyond Grief: A Guide for Recovering from the Death of a Loved One.* New Harbinger Publications, 1987.

Staudacher, Carol. *Men and Grief: A Guide for Men Surviving the Death of a Loved One: A Resource for Caregivers and Mental Health Professionals.* New Harbinger Publications, 1991.

Stearn, Ellen Sue. *Living With Loss: Meditations for Grieving Widows (Days of Healing, Days of Change).* Bantam, 1995.

Stoltz PhD, Paul G. *Adversity Quotient: Turning Obstacles into Opportunities.* John Wiley & Sons, 1999.

Tatelbaum, Judy. *The Courage to Grieve.* HarperCollins, 1984.

Temes, Dr. Roberta. *Living With an Empty Chair: A Guide Through Grief.* New Horizon, 1992.

Viorst, Judith. *Necessary Losses: The Loves, Illusions, Dependencies, and Impossible Expectations That All of Us Have to Give Up in Order to Grow.* Fireside, 1998.

Webb, Denise, PhD "Supplement News." *Prevention,* October 1999. p 61.

Westberg, Granger E. *Good Grief.* Fortress Press, 1971.

Woodson, Meg. *Making It Through the Toughest Days of Grief.* New York: Harper Collins, 1995.

Worwood, Valerie Ann. *The Fragrant Mind.* New World Library, 1996.

Zarda, Dan and Marcia Woodaard. *Forever Remembered.* Compendium, 1997.

Zunin MD, Leornard M. and Hilary Stanton Zunin. *The Art of Condolence.* Harper Perennial Library, 1992.

Index

About the Authors

Pamela D. Blair, PhD

Pamela D. Blair, PhD, is a psychotherapist, life coach, and motivational speaker with a PhD from the American Institute of Holistic Theology. She has appeared on national TV and radio programs and was filed for a television special titled *Widowsville*. She is also the author of two books for women; *The Next Fifty Years: A Guide for Women at Midlife and Beyond* and *Getting Older, Better*. She is currently retired, facilitating a group for women writers, mentoring in the school system, working on a novel, and living in Shelburne, Vermont, with her husband and two cats.

Brook Noel

Brook Noel is the author of more than twenty books, specializing in life management, balance, and life transitions. Known for going "beyond the book," Noel uses many means to interact with and support her readers, from motivational podcasts to free newsletters and an online community. "While some of my work deals with life's hardest blows, other work deals with the day-to-day stressors and challenges. My life experiences have taught me that today is what matters. . . right here and right now. I am committed to helping others reap the gift of today."

Noel has appeared on hundreds of media outlets, including *CNN Headline News*, *ABC World News*, *FOX Friends*, *Woman's World*, *Parent's Journal*, *Town & Country*, *New York Post*, "Ask Heloise," and Bloomberg Radio. Her work has been recognized by the Midwest Independent Publisher Awards, the Best Book Awards, and the IPPY Awards.

Noel was recognized in 2003 as one of the 40 Top Most Influential Business People Under the Age of 40 by the *Business Journal*. She is a spokesperson for the Home Business Association and was chosen as one of ten entrepreneurs of the year.

Brook lives in Wisconsin with her husband, twelve-year-old daughter, one golden retriever, a black lab named "Kitty," and one very large cat named Tom. Visit her website at brooknoel.com.